Studies in Higher Education

Dissertation Series

Edited by
PHILIP G. ALTBACH
Monan Professor of Higher Education
Lynch School of Education, Boston College

A RoutledgeFalmer Series

A Dream Deferred?

Examining the Degree Aspirations of African American and White College Students

Deborah Faye Carter

RoutledgeFalmer
New York & London/2001

Published in 2001 by
RoutlegdgeFalmer
A member of the Taylor & Francis Group
29 West 35th Street
New York, NY 10001

10 9 8 7 6 5 4 3 2 1

Library of Congress Cataloging-in-Publication Data is available from the Library of Congress.

ISBN 0-8153-3955-0

Printed on acid-free, 250 year-life paper
Manufactured in the United States of America

To my parents, Clyde and Margaret.
In memory of my grandparents.

Acknowledgments

I would like to express my gratitude to Sylvia Hurtado and Eric Dey for their assistance and guidance during the completion of this study. Their involvement made this book possible. Also, I appreciate the assistance I received from Ada Simmons with the editing of the chapters.

I would also like to acknowledge the National Center for Educational Statistics (NCES) and the Cooperative Institutional Research Program (CIRP) for collecting information nationally on college students and making the data available to researchers. I would also like to thank the respondents to the CIRP and the Beginning Postsecondary Students Longitudinal Study (BPS) for providing the data. This study could not have been done without the assistance of the thousands of students and the researchers at NCES and CIRP.

Contents

I

Introduction: The Realization or Abandonment of Dreams

A dream deferred or a dream sustained? Various scholars have debated whether African Americans view their life chances and educational goals with optimism or pessimism. The degree to which African Americans' dreams are kept alive or dashed is reflected in the writing of Langston Hughes and Richard Wright. Hopeful, Hughes (1932) writes, "hold fast to dreams" or else "life is a barren field." Several years later and more pessimistic, Hughes (1958) asks, "What happens to a dream deferred...does it dry up like a raisin in the sun?" Similarly, Richard Wright (1941) stated that his impulse to dream was slowly beaten out of him by experience.

Educational researchers also have contrasting visions of African Americans' hopes and expectations for the future. Ogbu (1988) comes to the conclusion that some African American high school students, frustrated by the unlikelihood they will succeed in U.S. society, do not aspire to earn college degrees and reject school culture. Allen (1991), on the other hand, concludes that African American educational aspirations are quite high, even though many do not later attain the degrees to which they aspire. Is there a more accurate vision? Do African Americans tend to hope or despair concerning their educational opportunities?

EDUCATIONAL HISTORY OF AFRICAN AMERICANS IN THE U.S.

The educational history of African Americans in the United States is one marked by inequality. Since the seventeenth century, African Americans have struggled for the right to be educated. African Americans emerged from the institution of slavery with the singular purpose of becoming educated: "'There is one sin that slavery committed against me,' professed one ex-slave, 'which I will never forgive. It robbed me of my education.'" (Anderson, 1988, p. 5). Nearly every account of the activities of former slaves in the late nineteenth century highlights African Americans' insistence on public education (Anderson, 1988). African Americans "rushed to build schools and to obtain education, which they believed would enable them to secure their lives and the future of their children" (Peeks, 1971, p. 108).

This hope of a more secure future began to materialize during the years of World War II. During the war, White male workers went overseas to fight leaving thousands of employment openings. African Americans filled this employment need and saw their economic situations improve dramatically (Knight & Wing, 1995). The belief that African Americans could achieve equality through educational opportunities was further strengthened at this time, and a decade after the war, the Supreme Court specifically recognized the need for equal educational opportunities with the *Brown v. Board of Education* decision (Knight & Wing, 1995). However, the Supreme Court's decision did not lead to immediate desegregation or equality of opportunities. When schools finally did begin the process of integration, African American children were the ones who bore the burden of adapting to the existing educational system. For instance, African American children endured long commutes to schools, while White children were not bused to predominantly African American schools (Feagin, Vera, & Imani, 1996). In addition, "desegregated schools and colleges have taught, and still teach, [African Americans] to be 'Europeanized Whites' culturally, but without the privileges of that status" (Feagin et al., 1996, p. 13). In spite of (or in resistance to) experiences of oppression in the United States, African Americans on the whole have high educational goals for themselves and their offspring:

> African Americans place a heavy emphasis on education.... Education is about a liberated future that must be better than the oppressive past. . . . [F]or Black parents the education of their children gives meaning to their struggle against racism . . . (Feagin et al., 1996, p. 22)

It is in this context of hope for a liberated future, despite a history of oppression, that the current educational aspirations and attainments of African Americans need to be understood.

THE GAP IN ATTAINMENT

Despite increased educational opportunities in the latter part of the 20th century, there remains a great deal of racial/ethnic stratification with respect to educational achievement and attainment. Underrepresented minority students (African American, Latino, & American Indian specifically) and students from low-income families are much less likely to complete baccalaureate degrees (Carter & Wilson, 1993; Levine & Nidiffer, 1996). Many minority students experience delays in their postsecondary education compared with White students, and are less likely to attain a post-baccalaureate education (Astin, Tsui, & Avalos, 1996; U.S. Department of Education, 1996).

According to the 1990 census (Hoffman, 1991), African Americans composed 12.4% of the United States population, and yet received 7.9% of the Associate degrees, 5.8% of the Bachelor's degrees, 4.8% of the Master's and First Professional degrees, and 3.8% of the Doctoral degrees conferred to United States citizens. In contrast, 84% of the U.S. population is White, and White students received 82.1% of Associate degrees, 84.3% of Bachelor's degrees, 85.2% of Master's degrees, and 88.4% of Doctoral degrees (Carter & Wilson, 1993). Despite the gaps between the two racial/ethnic groups in postsecondary degree attainments, the current high school graduation rate of African Americans is within a percentage point of the White students' graduation rate (Carnoy & Rothstein, 1997).

One of the most important reasons for postsecondary degree attainment is that educational attainment has dramatic effects on earnings. In 1995, African American high school graduates had a median income of $13,678, while White high school graduates earned a median income of $23,937. African Americans who earned Bachelor's degrees improved the high school graduates' median income by nearly 200% to $30,453—less than $500 lower than the White median income for Bachelor's degree attainers. Finally, African American doctoral degree earners had median incomes of $53,181 in comparison to the White doctoral degree median income of $52,308 (data from the U.S. Census Bureau cited in "Vital Signs," 1996, p. 67). The income data clearly show how important postsecondary degrees are for African Americans economic security. The gap between African American and White individuals lessens as degree attainment increases. Although the overall gap between White and African American educational attainment rates has narrowed over the last two decades, income disparities between the groups are still large, and a lack of postsecondary education can mean poverty. Therefore, the lower degree attainment for African Americans, in comparison to their representation in United States population, is a disparity that still needs our collective attention.

EXPLANATIONS FOR THE ATTAINMENT GAP

The lower degree attainments of African Americans most often have been explained from the perspective of individual deficiencies. In research and in the popular media, African Americans have been shown as suffering from (or constrained by) physical, psychological, cultural, familial, or sociological "problems." Recent books such as *The Bell Curve* have purported that African Americans as a group do not have the mental capacity and skills to achieve the same success as White students—while ignoring environmental attributes that may contribute to African American student achievement (Gardner, 1995). Ogbu (1988; 1990) and others describe that culturally, some African American parents and students reject school culture and think negatively of the students who achieve in school. Thus, "perservance at academic tasks . . . becomes difficult for Black children" (Ogbu, 1990, p. 127). Rather than dismissing low achievement as something that is the "fault" of a particular racial/ethnic group, as educators and researchers we should view low achievement as an outcome that can be improved.

There are other explanations for the gap between African American and White students' attainments in the United States. Rather than placing all the onus of lower attainments on African Americans' individual situations, perhaps an analysis of the processes by which society and institutional environments constrain or enhance outcomes is warranted. In higher education, historically Black colleges and universities (HBCUs) graduate more Black students than predominantly White institutions (PWIs), even though more Black students attend PWIs (Carter & Wilson, 1993). HBCUs have environments that are more welcoming and supportive of African American students than those at PWIs (Allen, 1992). A great deal of evidence suggests that educational environments can make a difference in students' later achievements (Allen, 1992; Astin, 1990).

These findings run counter to some of the published articles and books appearing in the popular press during the 1980s and 1990s concerning race relations on college campuses. Bloom (1987) feels that White students attending universities in the 1980s "just do not have prejudices anymore" (p. 89), and White students and faculty members are "egalitarian meritocrats who believe each individual should be allowed to develop his [sic] special—and unequal—talents without reference to race . . . " (Bloom, p. 90). Bloom further "blames Black students for being unwilling to melt into the melting pot, 'as have all other groups'" (Bloom cited in Feagin, et al., 1996, p. 2). Steele also charges African American students with having "an unconscious need to exaggerate the level of racism on campus—to make it a matter of the system, not just a handful of students" (cited in Feagin, et al., 1996, p. 2).

If indeed the issue of racism and differential treatment on college campuses is only a "problem" for a select group of African American students, why is it that African American graduation rates from the top universities in the country trail White graduation rates by up to 20% ("Overall Graduation Rates," 1996, p. 68)? The disparity between graduation rates is even more severe at flagship state universities ("Black Graduation," 1996, p. 69). In addition, African Americans consistently report feeling isolated and alienated, and turn to other African American students and people in the community outside the campus for support (Darden, Bagaka's, & Kamel, 1996; Feagin, et al., 1996; Institute for the Study of Social Change, 1991). The problem of racism and lower African American degree attainment is not negligible and only pertinent to a small group of African American students.

The current struggle to improve the achievement of African Americans comes at a time of increased fiscal pressures in higher education institutions. State and federal appropriations for higher education have stayed at the same levels for the last several years despite inflation and increasing costs (Breneman, 1995). Frequently, institutions have compensated for the lack of increased government support by increasing tuition, which also has the effect of limiting access to those students who cannot afford to pay for college. However, financial aid assistance can lessen the negative impact of tuition increases by increasing access to college (Somers & St. John, 1993). Given the fact that African American families tend to have lower incomes than White families (Deskins, 1994), institutions that strive to make their programs affordable are providing opportunities for increased access.

IMPORTANCE OF STUDYING ASPIRATIONS

Increasing access to higher education is an important national goal, particularly considering that approximately one-third of the students in the United States are racial/ethnic minorities. Additionally, women and non-Asian minority group members tend to be concentrated in careers that offer "low long-term earning capacity [and] remote opportunities for upward mobility" (McJamerson, 1992, p. 35). Since specific populations in society (people of color, particularly) tend to earn fewer advanced degrees, they are continually disadvantaged in employment pools. Besides the concern of the employability of millions of people in this country, there are even broader issues at stake. Some researchers have suggested that increased minority participation in graduate programs should become a national priority:

> Increased minority participation in graduate education is an important national goal to be realized for the social, economic, intellectual, and cultural well-being of all persons. It is for the collective benefit of society that the representation of minority group persons among those earning advanced degrees be increased (National Board on Graduate Education cited in Deskins, 1994, p. 144).

For example, a recent study found that the racial/ethnic representation of physicians affects the health care of poor and minority communities. In California, African American physicians cared for 42.9% more African American patients than did physicians of other races/ethnicities (Komaromy, Grumbach, Drake, Vranizan, Lurie, Keane, & Bindman, 1996). Fifty-two percent of the patients seen in African American practices are African American, whereas 9% of the patients are African American in non–African American medical practices (Shuit, 1996). The study also found that African American doctors tend to practice in predominantly African American areas of California—areas that tend to have a shortage of physicians. Therefore, the aspirations and subsequent graduate degree attainments of African Americans not only impact individual factors such as income, but can impact the welfare of entire communities.

Educational aspirations are important because people cannot attain what they do not dream (or think possible). If a student does not have a goal at some point in their educational career to earn a medical degree, for example, he or she will not be a physician. Therefore, educational aspirations are a fundamental part of the attainment process and yet are among the least understood concepts in higher education. With the exception of a few researchers, higher education scholars have not engaged in a comprehensive study of how colleges and universities affect students' dreams, aspirations and eventual occupational attainments.

A few higher education researchers have studied the factors that influence educational aspirations (for example: Astin, 1977, 1993b; Hearn, 1984, 1992; Pascarella, 1984). Currently, the research community has cursory knowledge about why African Americans and White students differ significantly in their aspirations. As will be shown in the next chapters, models of educational aspirations typically work quite well with samples of White men. However, with White women and minority student samples of both genders, the explanatory power of models of educational aspirations decreases significantly.

The importance of measuring educational aspirations in research on students has been highlighted in quite a few comprehensive studies on undergraduate experiences and in general models of degree attainment and attrition. Educational aspirations have very strong relationships with a variety of outcomes, especially degree attainment and graduate school enrollment (Astin, 1977). Degree attainment and attrition have been studied extensively for several decades, but several years of focusing on these final outcomes seems not to have improved the percentage of underrepresented ethnic minority students who are completing college. The first step in working toward increased equality must be in affecting students' aspirations. Higher education researchers have only scratched the surface in increasing our knowledge of students' educational aspirations—the development of which has been shown to significantly impact degree completion.

SIGNIFICANCE AND PURPOSE OF THE BOOK

The study of aspirations in general, and specifically the study of African American and White educational aspirations, can be characterized as having a lack of clarity—particularly in the findings of research studies and in the definitions of outcomes. There is little agreement in the literature with regard to how (or whether) African Americans' levels of aspirations differ from those of White students. Some studies find that African Americans have higher levels of aspirations (Astin, 1990; Weiler, 1993), even after controlling for socioeconomic status (Solorzano, 1992). The current study examines aspirations levels for two national populations of postsecondary students in an attempt to resolve this issue. In addition, studies have not been uniform in their measurement of educational aspirations. This study attempts to bring clarity to previous research on aspirations by comparing two different databases with different operational definitions of student aspirations.

Because African American students complete Bachelor's and graduate degrees at lower rates than White students, it is imperative that we, as researchers, administrators, and members of communities, understand how pre-college and in-college experiences affect aspirations, which will later affect degree completion and occupational attainment. For instance, having high aspirations for African American high school students seems to (at least partially) mitigate the negative effect of low academic achievement on college attendance (St. John, 1991). Understanding educational aspirations can assist us in structuring environments and interactions that can help students aspire to higher degrees. Students may begin college from a variety of different measured abilities and financial circumstances, but universities can actively contribute toward increasing students' interest and commitment to completing their Bachelor's and graduate degrees.

This study was based on two main assumptions:

1. Given that attainments differ for White and African American students, the factors contributing to the aspirations for each group will also differ.
2. Ascriptive (e.g. gender, socioeconomic status) and financial circumstances, student behaviors, as well as aspects of the college environment in which students find themselves, shape students' degree aspirations.

These assumptions led to the main objective of this study—to gain insight into the educational experiences of White and African American students that affect their educational aspirations. I sought to investigate the factors that cause students to "hold fast to their dreams" or alternatively see their dreams "dry up like a raisin in the sun." The investigation of this issue was based on longitudinal data, enabling an examination of the types of educational experiences that thwart or enhance dreams of educational attainment.

SCOPE OF THE STUDY

The study used two longitudinal databases of college student data. The first database, Beginning Postsecondary Students Longitudinal Study (BPS) included 4,727 students who entered higher education for the first time in the 1989–90 school year. The second database, Cooperative Institutional Research Program (CIRP), contained records for 4,170 students who entered higher education in the 1988–89 school year. The samples for both databases were restricted to students attending non-profit, two- or four-year institutions.

A comparison by institutional type allowed for determinations of the role of community colleges in comparison to four-year institutions in constraining or raising aspirations—an important distinction given that community colleges are points of access for millions of students. The data included several pre-college measures, as well as measures from a follow-up survey in the 1991–92 academic year for BPS and 1990–91 for CIRP.

The samples in both databases were national and covered several institutions of varying sizes and types. Therefore, the effects of a wide range of institutional, structural environments were examined. In addition, since the study covered two time points, it was possible to examine changes in students' aspirations over time. Each database had strengths and weaknesses with respect to the measures used in the study. BPS has more varied and complete measures of socioeconomic status, while CIRP contained several more measures of students' experiences in the campus community. The use of both databases allowed more complete understanding of the process by which students develop and change their educational aspirations.

This investigation of educational aspirations utilizes theoretical frameworks primarily from the field of sociology. Although psychological concepts like motivation and self-efficacy may be important to examine with regard to students' degree goals, it is outside the scope of this study.

The focus of this study was on educational aspirations during the first few years of college. Although measures of final educational and occupational attainments were not available in these data sets given that many students had not yet finished their degrees by the second survey interview, the attainment literature was pertinent to the study of aspirations and provides a theoretical base for the research questions and analyses. Educational aspirations have been tied closely to educational attainment and retention in college. In many articles examining retention, educational aspirations have been key predictors of whether students remain in college or leave before they complete a degree. One of the main theoretical frameworks for examining aspirations in this study is the status attainment literature, which uses aspirations as a key variable in predicting the future educational and occupational attainment of students.

CONTENTS OF BOOK

Chapters 2 and 3 describe the literature review and theoretical framework for the study. Chapter 2 begins with a description of the ways in which previous studies have measured aspirations and then turns to a discussion of the theoretical foundations for studies of high school students' aspirations, including status attainment, contest vs. sponsored mobility, cultural explanations for low attainments and critiques of these theories. The final part of the chapter discusses theories relating to college students' aspirations.

Chapter 3 synthesizes the empirical research of aspirations and related studies and summarizes the theoretical framework used in the study.

The methodology for the study is detailed in Chapter 4, including the hypotheses, data sources and variable descriptions. Some detail about the datasets is included in this chapter, but Chapter 4 describes the measures in significantly more detail and explains the analytic techniques used in the study.

The results of the study are split into two chapters: Chapters 5 and 6. Chapter 5 describes the results of the bivariate analyses while Chapter 6 describes the results of the multiple regression analyses. Simply put, the purpose of Chapter 5 is to discuss generally how African American and White students within and across both datasets differ. The means and frequencies of African American and White students are compared within data samples and across data samples. Chapter 5 also contains the discussion of a reduced regression model tested across both racial groups in both samples.

After establishing how African American and White students compare, within and between the data sets, I next completed analyses to determine how variables, specific to each dataset, may affect aspirations. In Chapter 6, I discuss the results of extended regression models that take advantage of the unique differences of each dataset.

The final chapter in this book, Chapter 7, discusses the conclusions of the study and the degree to which the study's hypotheses were supported. The chapter concludes with theoretical, research, and practical implications of the study.

2
What Are Aspirations? Definitions and Theoretical Foundations

Research perspectives in the area of educational aspirations have been limited—especially with respect to the educational aspirations of college students. Educational aspirations have mostly been studied as a predictor of a variety of outcomes, most notably in relation to educational attainment and/or attrition. While the research reviewed in this book explores the varied roles of educational aspirations in educational research, it is important to state that this study seeks to examine educational aspirations as an outcome of both individual and institutional influences. In addition, there has been some debate in the educational research community about whether researchers have measured aspirations or expectations in studies of aspirations and educational attainment. In detailing the controversy and surveying prior published research, I strive to bring clarity to the issue.

In this chapter, I review previous studies of aspirations and related outcomes to examine how researchers have defined aspirations. In addition, I detail the theoretical controversies with respect to the study of aspirations and describe previous theoretical approaches to the study of educational aspirations.

OPERATIONAL DEFINITIONS OF ASPIRATIONS

There is controversy and confusion with respect to the measurement of educational aspirations and expectations. The terms are often used interchangeably and many researchers have measured aspirations in different and competing ways. To bring some order to this confusion, this section explains the terms used to operationally define both concepts in the published research and analyzes previous research to determine the actual concepts most often measured. As will be discussed in greater detail later in this chapter, the study of educational aspirations first became popular when Sewell, Haller, and Portes (1969) justified its use in status attainment research. Sewell et al. (1969) used aspirations as a measure of the contribution that social psychological factors have in students' later attainments, and thought that students' interactions with peers, parents, and teachers influence their aspirations as much as (or more than) ascriptive characteristics like socioeconomic status. For Sewell et al. (1969), the term "aspirations" is synonymous with "educational plans." Since the late 1960s, dozens of researchers have acknowledged the importance of studying aspirations—both as a predictor for outcomes and as an outcome itself.

The ways in which educational aspirations have been operationally defined seem to differ by the researcher or researchers involved. Even the same items on a particular survey often are not referred to in the same terms by different researchers. For instance, Peng and Fetters (1978) refer to an item in the National Longitudinal Survey (NLS) as "aspirations", while Vélez (1985) refers to the same item as "plans" and Agnew and Jones (1988) call the item "expectations."

Appendix A contains two tables that list fifty-two aspirations and related studies—published over the past thirty years. Table A-1 lists the studies, alphabetically by author, that use measures of educational aspirations. The operational definitions of aspirations (the actual survey items) and related measures used in the studies are in Table A-2. These tables are the result of extensive literature searches and represent all of the published studies using aspirations and expectations that were listed in social science indices and/or studies referenced in other published research.

These two tables organize the studies according to the operational definitions of the aspirations measures. The following is a list of the eight categories of studies, based on the operational definitions of the measures of educational aspirations:

1. Educational plans;
2. Educational "expectations" for degree attainment;
3. Factors and scales of aspirations items where aspirations are measured with multiple variables instead of one;
4. Educational preferences ("what is the highest amount of education you would like to have?" (Berman & Haug, 1975)
5. Educational intentions ("what is the highest degree that you intend to obtain?" Drew & Astin, 1972);
6. Educational predictions ("how far in school do you think you will get?" Solorzano, 1992);
7. Other—a category that includes other measurement of aspirations; and
8. No detail (studies providing no detail about the actual measures of aspirations used).

After examining the studies of students' educational aspirations, I conclude there is little uniformity with which the terms "aspirations" or "expectations" are used. Berman and Haug (1975) define aspirations as "a goal that a person would like to achieve" while an expectation "refers to a goal that one intends or expects to attain" (p. 166). Hearn (1992) describes aspirations as being more abstract than expectations or plans, but Hauser and Anderson (1991) state that researchers have no reason to find close agreement between aspirations and plans either at the individual level or in the aggregate" (p. 272). Indeed, the observed relationship between aspirations and expectations seems quite dependent on the methods employed in the studies and on the samples used: Hearn (1987) found a .45 correlation between aspirations and plans (defined by application to graduate or professional school), Hanson (1994) found that 83 percent of college aspirers expected to attend college, and Hauser and Anderson (1991) found that aspirations and plans are closely linked among White, high school students from two-parent families but not as closely linked among other families.

Therefore, though a few researchers like to make a distinction between aspirations and expectations, these distinctions clearly are not universally made. In fact, several researchers use aspirations interchangeably with "attainment" or "expectations" (Lee, Mackie-Lewis, & Marks, 1993; Pascarella, 1984; St. John, 1991). Sewell and Hauser (1980) assert that educational plans and expectations are synonymous and that the inclusion of students' wishes (as opposed to expectations) into educational attainment models added little to the explanatory power of the models. Because aspirations has most often been measured as "plans"—a term Hearn (1992) considers less abstract than "aspirations"—it is difficult to assert with strong empirical evidence that there is a difference between the measurements of students' aspirations and expectations for degree attainment.

At least six different concepts have been measured as aspirations and expectations in the above studies: aspirations, educational plans, intentions, wishes, satisfaction, and expectations. One study referred to "expectations" as "ambition", though these two concepts seem rather different from each other, and some researchers have found "ambition" difficult to measure (Porter, 1974). The non-uniform measurement of expectations and aspirations in the research community strengthens the need for future researchers to define constructs carefully when developing survey items. Researchers seem to be interested in the following: the highest degree students want to attain; the highest degree students realistically expect to attain; the degree to which students intend or are determined to attain their degree goals; and finally, the obstacles that may interfere with students realizing their goals. No single survey item can capture all of these concepts. Studies that incorporate several of the above questions can be used to determine the relationship between educational goal-setting (wishes), the extent to which students are committed to attaining their goals (goal-commitment, intentions, and plans), and goal-reassessment (raising and/or lowering aspirations).

Thus, researchers have empirically blurred the distinctions between aspirations, expectations, and other related concepts. This study examines the effect of different measurements of aspirations on the prediction of aspirations. To simplify the discussion in this and the next chapter, I use: aspirations as a general term to refer to the studies covering the concepts reviewed in this section. However, when distinctions between the differing measurements of aspirations are important for understanding the findings of previous studies, the specific concepts (e.g. aspirations, expectations, plans) are used. The next section of the chapter details the theoretical foundations of past research on educational aspirations.

THEORETICAL FOUNDATIONS FOR ASPIRATIONS STUDIES

Status Attainment

The study of the educational aspirations of high school and college students has its main foundation in the status attainment literature in the field of sociology of education. Blau and Duncan (1967) developed the first status attainment model, using data which focused on the occupational attainments of males from a variety of social classes and minority populations. Blau and Duncan's model assumes that ascriptive characteristics (e.g. father's education and income) determine the son's occupational attainment. The model is quite parsimonious—consisting of five variables. Father's educational attainment and occupational status predict the respondent's educational attainment and first-job status; all four variables predict the respondents' occupational attainment. Educational aspirations were not included in Blau and Duncan's original model, but subsequent status attainment research have extended the model to take aspirations into account.

Many researchers have noted one main weakness in Blau and Duncan's model: The relationships between the variables could not be sufficiently explained (Kerckhoff, 1984; Sewell et al., 1969; Sewell, Haller, & Ohlendorf, 1970). There seems to be little theoretical support for the concept that fathers' education determines sons' occupational attainments besides a strict notion of social reproduction: That is, socioeconomic status is determined by parents' status, and there is little mobility between generations. In attempting to further enhance Blau and Duncan's model by explaining the processes by which a parent's socioeconomic status can affect the status of the adult child, Sewell et al. (1969) and others expanded the model to include social psychological variables. They reasoned that social psychological variables, previously shown to be important to educational attainment, were important as intervening variables with respect to educational and occupational attainment. Research completed in the late 1950s and early 1960s identified several elements of the education process that are related to the degree attainment process: significant others, reference groups, self-concept, aspirations, and experience of school success (Sewell et al., 1969). Measures of ability were highlighted as particularly important for researchers to take into account because mental ability (as measured by IQ and other standardized tests) was assumed to affect the student's "academic performance and the influence significant others have on him [sic]" (Sewell et al., 1970, p. 1015).

The social psychological model of status attainment (also referred to as the "Wisconsin model" and as a socialization model) assumes that the socioeconomic status and ability of the student affect the encouragement and support the student receives from significant others, which in turn, affect the student's goals and aspirations (Kerckhoff, 1976). The Wisconsin model posits causal arguments "linking social origins and ability with educational and early occupational status attainments by means of intervening behavioral mechanisms" (Sewell et al., 1970, p. 1015). In developing this theory, Sewell et al. (1969) applied the work of previous psychological researchers who, as early as 1935, concluded that individuals obtain their "social behavior tendencies largely through the influence of others" (p. 85) and that "one's conception of the educational behavior others think appropriate to him [or her] is highly correlated with [the] level of educational aspiration" (p. 85).

Sewell et al.'s (1969) model presents four sets of causal relationships in a 1957 study of a homogenous sample (all White, farm youth) of Wisconsin high school male seniors: 1) social structural (SES) and psychological factors (mental ability) affect significant others' influences; 2) significant others' influences affect educational and occupational aspirations; 3) aspirations affect attainment; and 4) educational attainment affects occupational attainment. Significant others in this study refer to parents, peers, and instructors. "Predetermined social structural and psychological factors . . . affect the youth's academic performance and the influence significant others have on him; the influence of significant others and possibly his own ability affect his levels of educational and occupational aspiration; and levels of aspiration affect educational and occupational status attainment" (Sewell et al., 1970, p. 1015).

The socialization model views aspirations as a central element in the status attainment process and conceives of aspirations as being formed in students' social interactions (Knotterus, 1987). Social interactions are structured by socioeconomic status groups, and "aspirations develop in response to the evaluations one receives from significant others and the self-assessment of one's potential based upon academic performance" (Knotterus, p. 116). Therefore, in the late 1960s, two competing theories of the process of status attainment (and by implication the development of educational aspirations and degree plans) emerged: One perspective is that educational aspirations and attainment are the direct result of socioeconomic/ascriptive factors (the Blau & Duncan model); the competing perspective is that of socialization: a student's socioeconomic status affects the way he or she interacts with others (and in turn how others interact with the student) which affect aspirations and ultimately attainment (Sewell et al., 1969). Both theories of the status attainment process were supported by the research completed through the early 1970s, with the findings that the social psychological models explain more of the variance in attainments than the ascriptive, Blau and Duncan model (Sewell et al., 1970).

Another perspective of status attainment was developed in response to what some researchers felt were the theoretical shortcomings of the social psychological model. This perspective, first advanced by Kerckhoff (1976), is called social allocation. Kerckhoff's view is that the process of status attainment is not so much a process of socialization as it is a process of social allocation. Kerckhoff's criticism of the Wisconsin model is that it views an individual as relatively free to move through society; attainment is determined by what the individual chooses to do and how well the individual does it. The social allocation perspective views the individual as constrained by social structure—an individual's attainments are determined by what he or she is allowed to do. Researchers have found strong associations between "ambition" and attainment; therefore, the socialization model assumes that a student's goals direct and motivate the student's efforts which lead to attainment (Kerckhoff, 1976). On the other hand, the measures of ambition in past research do not measure motivation as much as they measure knowledge of "the real world." Most questions measuring motivation and ambition ask for students' plans or expectations, not their wishes or aspirations (Kerckhoff, 1976). Kerckhoff feels that the difference between wishes and plans are the most important distinctions between the socialization and social allocation perspectives. The social allocation perspective purports that:

> Expectations are strongly associated with attainments because [students] become sufficiently knowledgeable to be able to estimate the probabilities of various outcomes. . . . People's observations of the attainments of others like themselves undoubtedly do have a feedback effect on their expectations. (Kerckhoff, 1976, p. 371)

It is assumed that individuals may want the same outcomes, but that they may expect different outcomes based on their assessments of their life chances. Therefore, while the social psychological model of status attainment views the individual as unconstrained by society and success as determined by the individual's abilities, the social allocation model views the individual as constrained by society. The social psychological model views aspirations as resulting from an individual's social interactions and abilities. An assumption of the model is that one reason certain students are not upwardly mobile is because they are of low ability and/or that they do not have the goals and motivation to succeed. The social allocation interpretation views individuals as constrained by their life circumstances.

Individuals only have degree expectations that they believe they can achieve given the system constraints in which they live. Kerckhoff (1976, 1984) admitted that it may be difficult to empirically distinguish between the socialization and the social allocation interpretations of the status attainment model. However, Kerckhoff considers the social allocation perspective a different explanation for the same phenomenon.

A related conception of aspirations is cost-benefit analysis. Essentially, the academic outcomes of students are directly affected by the students' material circumstances. In this way, students' aspirations represent a "realistic evaluation of likely outcomes" as opposed to a cognitive state (e.g. motivation) (Jencks, Crouse, and Mueser cited in Kao & Tienda, 1998, p. 352).

One limitation of Kerckhoff's (1976) perspective is that few researchers have demonstrated clear empirical differences between what students' want to happen versus what they expect to happen. As was discussed in the previous section, "aspirations" have been measured as intentions, expectations, plans, and wants. There has not been uniform measurement of aspirations, and although there are many studies that use measures of aspirations as independent measures, there are only a few studies that examine the predictors of aspirations. It is difficult to determine if the differences in research findings are attributable to the measurement of educational aspirations or to the differences in samples.

A second limitation of Kerchkoff's (1976) perspective is the role that the concept of "opportunity" plays in the national culture of the people in the United States. "From the earliest days of the Republic, Americans have possessed an abiding faith that theirs is a land of opportunity" (Brint & Karabel, 1989, p. 3). The United States, unlike European societies, was founded on the belief that people have limitless opportunities and can succeed through hard work and ability (a notion referred to as "contest mobility" and described in the next section). Compared with other industrial nations, the United States sends more individuals to postsecondary educational institutions resulting in millions more individuals in this country aspiring to high levels of education and prestigious occupations than the educational and occupational systems can support (Brint & Karabel, 1989). "For example, over half of high school seniors [in the early 1980s] 'planned' careers in professional/technical jobs . . . but in that same year, only 13 percent of the labor force was employed in such jobs" (Brint & Karabel, p. 8). Thus, drawing a distinction between what a student wants and expects may be a particularly difficult and unique problem, especially for a population of students who have already reached postsecondary education and are faced with a changing job market.

Contest and Sponsored Mobility

In addition to status attainment, another theoretical perspective applicable to understanding educational aspirations is contest and sponsored mobility. Turner (1960) proposed a framework for understanding the differences in the educational systems of the United States and England. Turner's view is that the U.S. educational system resembles a "contest" system of mobility where access to elite status is an open contest. An established elite does not have control over the final outcome of who may attain upward mobility and therefore education is a field in which open competition is the means by which people can improve their statuses. On the other hand, sponsored mobility is a system in which the elite controls the process. "Elite status is given on the basis of some criterion of supposed merit and cannot be taken by any amount of effort or strategy" (emphasis in original, Turner, 1960, p. 856). Upward mobility in a sponsored system can be compared to gaining entrance into a private club—

> Each candidate must be 'sponsored' by one or more of the members. . . . The governing objective of contest mobility is to give elite status to those who earn it, while the goal of sponsored mobility is to make the best use of the talents in society by sorting persons into their proper niches (Turner, 1960, pp. 856–857)

Turner also discusses how the societies ensure and maintain loyalty to the social system. In a contest mobility system, individuals think of themselves as competing for positions in the elite. When individuals think of themselves as future members of the elite, they begin to identify with the members of the upper classes, view high status society members as "ordinary" people, and begin to form the conviction that they may become members of the elite in the future. A contest mobility system influences the internalization of high achievement values in most members of society—especially those in the lower socioeconomic strata. Those members of society who are not ambitious are "individual deviants" and not a threat to the cohesiveness of society. In a contest mobility system, education is considered an "opportunity" whereby an individual who has strong initiative and drive may make the best use of it. The finding that the "general level of occupational aspiration reported by high school students was quite unrealistic in relation to the actual distribution of job opportunities" was interpreted by Turner as evidence that the United States educational system is primarily a contest mobility system. The aspirations of low-income students are not lowered (or kept low) early in the educational process, as would be predicted in a sponsored mobility system.

In a sponsored mobility system, social control is maintained by guiding the members of the lower socioeconomic classes to feel inferior to the elite. The future members of the elite are selected very early in their schooling so that the others can be "taught to accept their inferiority and to make 'realistic' rather than [f]antasy plans" (Turner, 1960, p. 859). Early selection of future members of the elite prevents the "masses" from raising their hopes and thereby becoming powerful members of a discontented force.

The assumptions of contest mobility systems are similar to the assumptions of a meritocracy and of the social psychological models of status attainment: individuals' achievement affects their educational aspirations, expectations, and attainments. Sponsored mobility and the social allocation perspective of mobility view the individual as constrained by what the members of the elite will allow the individual to do; individuals' achievement is largely dependent upon their statuses at birth.

Critiques of Theories of Mobility

The status attainment model is the primary way in which aspirations have been studied over the past thirty years. This section discusses critiques of status attainment research (and therefore much of the research on aspirations that use the status attainment model). Status attainment research—using Blau and Duncan's model (1967) and socialization models—have been found to work well for samples of White males. When the models have been tested on White females and on students of color, the models explain little of the variance. This section posits some reasons for lack of success of the status attainment research in explaining the outcomes of minority students and White women.

The limited explanatory power of status attainment models for gender and ethnic differences is one of the main criticisms of the status attainment model, and probably is a reason why the social psychological status attainment model has been cited sporadically in research articles in the last ten years. The socialization model explained very little of the variance in aspirations and attainment for women and minority men (Berman & Haug, 1975), and often the pattern of relationships between the White samples and the minority samples was completely different (Portes & Wilson, 1976). In critiquing status attainment models, Campbell (1983) concluded that an important and necessary direction for status attainment research is in the area of "minority group differences in achievement processes" (p. 59). Campbell believes it would be "possible to determine if there might be a 'minority group status attainment process' which applies to racial minorities . . . " (p. 59). In addition to the criticism that the status attainment model has limited application to minority populations and women, there are several other critiques of the model and studies of aspirations in general (Kerckhoff, 1984).

Kao and Tienda (1998) take this critique further by suggesting that future studies of students' educational aspirations need to "clarify the historical processes by which school performance became coupled with racial and ethnic identities" (p. 380). Researchers need to go further in "theorizing about the race and ethnic differences in cognitive underpinnings of aspirations, expectations, and plans" (p. 380). One of the main issues in examining gender and race differences in students' aspirations is the "aspirations-achievement paradox" (Kao & Tienda, 1998). This paradox refers to the fact that many underrepresented minority students (African American and Mexican American) have high aspirations despite low educational attainments.

A second criticism of status attainment research, which may be related to the limited explanatory power of the model for White female students and minority students, is that one of the core assumptions of the status attainment model is that the United States society functions as a meritocracy. In other words, the researchers who study students using the attainment model view educational systems as functioning mostly on merit—the students who are the most able will have the highest aspirations and attain the highest degrees. In response to the claim that socioeconomic status affects who attends college but has little relationship to who graduates from college, Eckland (1964) asserts:

> Social-class differences will increasingly determine who graduates among the college entrants of the [future]. . . . To the extent that higher education develops the same mass conditions as our system of secondary education in which dropout has been so closely associated with social status, a similar process will occur in our college (p. 50)

Other researchers purport that the unequal opportunities for students from lower socioeconomic backgrounds are created by an educational system that purports to reward students based solely on merit. Educational institutions transmit inequality by legitimating ascriptive statuses through academic achievement (Morrow & Torres, 1995). Therefore, a student's life chances can be determined by the student's circumstances at birth. This is counter to the assumptions of a meritocracy.

Contest mobility may describe the educational opportunities of certain members of the United States population, but at the time Turner published his article, the *Brown v. Board of Education* decision concerning the unequal and biased nature of African American elementary education was barely six years old. "The American system of stratification and mobility has caused Black mobility to approximate Turner's sponsored mobility" (Porter, 1974, p. 313). African Americans had and continue to have legal battles to gain entrance to the doors of the educational institutions where the "meritocratic contests" were supposedly taking place. All members of United States society could not participate in an "equal contest" for upward mobility, and status attainment models assume that the United States is an open opportunity structure (Wilson-Sadberry, Winfield, & Royster, 1991). This can be an incorrect assumption especially when occupational outcomes are considered. Women earn lower salaries than men, and the situation is particularly acute for African Americans: In 1980, Black women and Black men tended to earn salaries that were 46% and 68% respectively of those earned by White men (Grubb & Wilson, 1989). It seems that the system of mobility in the United States cannot be broadly categorized as a "contest" for all groups; the patterns of mobility may vary greatly by ethnicity, SES, and gender. Therefore, it is reasonable to conclude that the assumption of meritocracy may be one problem with the applicability of the status attainment model to different populations.

A third criticism of the early status attainment literature, although this is less true of recent educational aspirations studies by higher education researchers, is the focus on individuals' characteristics and the lack of or limited use of institutional variables. Researchers have suggested that status attainment studies should take into account the characteristics and effects of the educational institution in addition to individual characteristics (Kerckhoff, 1976). Educational institutions are not equal in terms of resources and affect the outcomes of students differently.

A fourth criticism of the status attainment literature is more pertinent for the social allocation analysis than the socialization perspective. Social allocation tends to view the process of status attainment and aspirations development as deterministic. Structural constraints in society limit the aspirations and attainments of individuals such that those whose parents are from the lower socioeconomic statuses will, more likely than not, remain at the same status through adulthood.

However, there are individuals in society who resist the mechanisms of reproduction and succeed. Resistance theory posits that individuals in the lower socioeconomic classes of society resist the upper classes' control of resources through subtle or direct means (Giroux, 1983). Resistance has taken the form of direct confrontation in student protests and in more subtle means by way of students' rejection of messages from others that claim they cannot succeed (Feagin et al., 1996; Hurtado, 1990). A key element of resistance theory is the transformation of institutional structures. High aspirations may be a way that increased numbers of African Americans can achieve high levels of educational attainment. Perhaps one way African Americans in particular refuse to internalize "do not succeed" and "African Americans are mentally inferior" messages is by maintaining high aspirations. Indeed, in spite of economic inequality, African Americans have historically maintained high hopes of becoming upwardly mobile through the education process (Knight & Wing, 1995). This counters the caste theory explanation offered by Ogbu (1983), and may explain why African Americans maintain high aspirations despite an awareness of inequality in opportunity.

CULTURAL EXPLANATIONS FOR LOW ASPIRATIONS AND ATTAINMENTS

African Americans have low educational and occupational attainments in comparison to White individuals in this country. One explanation for the comparatively lower attainments is the cultural deficit perspective. This perspective assumes that "Black cultural values, as transmitted through the family and specifically the parents, are dysfunctional, and therefore the reason for Blacks' low educational . . . attainment" (Solorzano, 1992, p. 30). The cultural deficit perspective also assumes that some African Americans do not place as high a value on education as White individuals. Although Black parents tend to communicate to their children the need to work hard, Black children do not put a lot of effort into their schooling for three reasons:

> (a) it has not developed as a part of their cultural tradition to persevere at academic tasks; (b) the actual texture of their parents' lives of unemployment, underemployment, and discrimination convey a powerful message that counteracts parental verbal encouragement; and (c) children learn from observing older members of their community that school success does not necessarily lead to jobs and other necessary and important things in adult life (Ogbu, 1983, p. 181).

Therefore, Ogbu feels that because of the history of poor education of African American youth in this country, Black parents and children have a deep distrust for schooling. This distrust prevents Black children from internalizing the "values of the schools, accept[ing] school criteria for success, or follow[ing] school rules of behavior for achievement" (Ogbu, 1983; p. 181). Thus, because Black children do not internalize the values of schools, they tend to do much more poorly than White students.

Ogbu's (1983) research on the educational experiences of African American students has led to the development of the caste theory explanation of school failure. This theory asserts the following: (1) there is a caste system in this country based primarily on race/ethnicity; (2) there is a typology of experiences of minority group members whereby "involuntary" minorities and "voluntary" minorities have historical differences with respect to their relationships with the country, and the negative historical experiences that "involuntary" minority group members endured continue in the present; (3) in response to oppression and limited opportunities, "involuntary" minority group members develop various adaptive or survival strategies that are quite often negative adaptations (Foley, 1991; Ogbu, 1983).

Ogbu (1983) identifies Mexican Americans, Native Americans (American Indians), and African Americans as the primary involuntary minority groups in the United States. Ogbu feels that involuntary and voluntary minority group members "perceive their historical deprivation" quite differently (Foley, 1991, p. 65). Ogbu's thesis is that recent immigrant groups ("voluntary" minority group members) "do not perceive the racial barriers and the lack of opportunity in . . . American society" and therefore they view the United States as a "land of opportunity" in comparison to their country of origin. Because of this, voluntary minority group members have a sense of optimism about their future and do better in schools (Foley, p. 65). On the other hand, involuntary minority group members have negative views of society and of their chances to succeed in society. Ogbu's primary emphasis is on the negative adaptive strategies of involuntary minority group members:

> [Involuntary minority group members] are overwhelmed by the 'community forces' of a job ceiling and racial oppression, and by a variety of 'school forces.' Their typical psychological and cultural adaptation is self-defeating in several ways. They succumb to the dominant societies' myths about them as inferior. They are unable to create a folk theory of schooling that is optimistic about their future. They develop a dysfunctional oppositional culture that leads them to believe that they cannot be both academically successful and ethnically different . . . Caste theory makes a powerful case that involuntary minorities are not likely to succeed in school or in life (Foley, 1991, p. 67)

In addition, Fordham and Ogbu (1986) put forth the analysis that Black students, who are capable of doing well in school, do not do well because they do not want to be accused of "acting White." Certain behaviors are conceptualized by Black students as inappropriate because those behaviors are characteristic of White students.

There have been several critiques of Ogbu's research, but I will focus on the critique that is the most salient for this study: Ogbu's emphasis on the negative adaptive patterns of involuntary minority group members (Foley, 1991). Ogbu theorizes that oppressed minority group members develop oppositional cultures, and these oppositional cultures come "trapped in a counterproductive pattern of reacting to racial stereotypes and myths" (Foley, p. 76). In this way, Ogbu's conception of African American school behavior resembles the oft-maligned "culture of povery" concept. However, in the "culture of poverty" perspective of African Americans in inner cities, African Americans are psychologically damaged: They have low self-esteem, pessimism, and a sense of fatalism. Ogbu's view of African Americans is less that the group is psychologically damaged, but that African Americans are "discouraged and trapped in the racist myths of the dominant society. They are unable to see that they can be both successful and Black" (Foley, p. 77). Caste theory tends to ignore the ways in which oppressed groups engage in "positive" resistance. Thus, caste theorists tend to "underestimate the capacity of ethnic resistance movements to empower individuals" (Foley, p. 78).

Fordham's (1996) study of African American high school students in Washington, D.C. does not rely exclusively on analyses of African American school failure, like Fordham's previous research with Ogbu (Fordham & Ogbu, 1986). However, Fordham's study does focus on the negative adaptive patterns of African American youth—high-achievers and low-achievers: "the high-achieving students . . . believe that if they are able to demonstrate that African-American students can perform in ways that are comparable to those of their White counterparts, they will . . . obtain the same opportunities and rewards as their White cohorts" (p. 328). Fordham further describes the high-achieving students as tending to "minimize the impact of race and gender-related obstacles" and that they "often override the barriers to achieving their dreams" by conforming to school norms (p. 329). In addition, a large segment of the high-achieving students Fordham studied believe that African Americans are largely responsible "for their own current lowly status. They have come to this understanding of existing social conditions in the Black community because in their schools they have been carefully taught the integration ideology, with its built-in denigration of [African Americans], and they have uncritically accepted its central premises" (p. 336).

Ogbu and Fordham's research—completed together and separately—brings together Turner's notions of contest and sponsored mobility. The high-achieving African American students in Fordham's (1996) study seem to believe that the United States is a meritocracy and that they will not let themselves be constrained by society. According to Fordham, the high-achieving students have begun to think of themselves as future members of the elite (they are acting "White") and have the conviction that they may become members of the successful middle class in the future. Therefore, the high-achieving students in the study are behaving in ways similar to the "voluntary" minorities of Ogbu's research—the students have a sense of optimism about their future and tend to do better in school. Perhaps a reason why African American college attendees (high-achieving students in comparison to the total population of college-age adults), have high aspirations is because of this sense of optimism about the future and a strong belief that society, and the educational system in particular, will reward them for hard work. These views closely represent the notions of contest mobility.

Ogbu's research has parallels to the social allocation model of status attainment: Members of involuntary minority group members see their opportunities as constrained by society and that in turn affects their behavior in schools. Ogbu's research in the United States has primarily focused on the school failure of African American children. Given that the population of this study is postsecondary education attendees, and therefore already successful by many standards, the application of Ogbu's caste theory to this study may be limited.

Studies of Ethnic Differences in Aspirations

Researchers typically cannot explain why the patterns of relationships between variables in African American student samples differ so greatly from that of White student samples. When African American students have high aspirations, they have been referred to as "unrealistic", or that lower-income students and/or African Americans inflate their educational expectations as an adaptation to deprivation (Agnew & Jones, 1988). Students categorized as having "unrealistic expectations" do achieve their dreams (attend college or complete a college degree, for instance), though perhaps in smaller numbers than their higher-income, higher-scoring peers (Agnew & Jones, 1988). Referring to African Americans specifically as having "unrealistic" aspirations seems especially unnecessary given the high aspirations of the people of the U.S. in general and the finding that lower-income White students have had higher than "realistic" aspirations for several decades (Brint & Karabel, 1989). In fact, research indicates that high aspirations may at least partially mitigate the negative effects of low socioeconomic status on college attendance (St. John, 1991), thus assisting African American students in achieving their goals.

In the 1960s, African Americans were thought to have lower levels of aspirations than White students, but in later studies where socioeconomic class is controlled, African Americans were found to have as high or higher aspirations within socioeconomic stratification groups (Portes & Wilson, 1976). These findings have led researchers to conclude that White students' higher attainments than African American students is due to White students' advantages in background variables and characteristics (Portes & Wilson, 1976). In fact, even when minority students have "the aspirations, the ability, and the qualifications to go to a four-year college, they do not attend the college of their choice to the degree that whites do" (Labovitz, 1975, p. 248).

In addition, the cultural deficit view of attainment "has become the social scientific norm even though little empirical evidence exists to support many of its claims" (Solorzano, 1992, p. 31). As was discussed above, African American students tend to have as high or higher aspirations than White students—especially when SES characteristics are controlled (St. John, 1991). Thus, the cultural deficit model seems to have little foundation in empirical research. Many African American students have achievement goals. The assumptions of the cultural deficit model may hold true for some selected groups of African Americans (Ogbu, 1983), but has yet to be demonstrated to be a universal norm, especially through national databases (Solorzano, 1992).

What is especially lacking in discussions of the educational aspirations of African American and White students is the role that educational institutions play in the development and maintenance of aspirations. Focusing on the ways in which institutions contribute to the development of aspirations moves the discussion away from cultural and individual characteristics and toward the types of educational environments that are most conducive for student achievement. In this way, the literature on college impact and on the experiences of college students informs status attainment research.

COLLEGE STUDENTS' DEGREE ASPIRATIONS AND COLLEGE IMPACT

The literature on college students' degree aspirations, that is, the literature on college students' plans to attend graduate school is more sparse than the high-school-to-college literature. Pascarella (1984) applauds and criticizes previous studies of college students' aspirations because on the one hand, the research of Astin (1977) and his colleagues made some contributions to an understanding of the institutional characteristics that influence students' aspirations. On the other hand, these research publications "have a number of methodological problems . . . the most important of these . . . is the orientation toward an empirical rather than theoretical framework for the data analyses" (Pascarella, 1984, p. 753). Few researchers have theorized why and how the characteristics of an institution impact an individual student's degree plans.

The social psychological status attainment model is the foundation of college student aspirations studies. College students are thought of as individual actors who have access to several parts of the campus and interact with the individuals they choose. It is true that many researchers do recognize the ways in which institutional structures can constrain the behavior of individuals (Astin, 1993b). How is it that some institutions have higher proportions of student degree completion than others? Particular institutional characteristics and students' college experiences work to produce positive student educational outcomes. For example, African American students who attend HBCUs tend to go to graduate school in greater numbers than African Americans who attend PWIs. Women who attend women's colleges attend graduate school in greater numbers and have more positive affective development than women attending coeducational institutions (Smith, 1989; 1990).

The college choice literature also centers on the discussion of aspirations. College choice literature has evolved over the years into the formulation of a three-stage model: predisposition, search, and choice (Hossler & Gallagher, 1987). The predisposition stage has particular parallels to the study of aspirations. Predisposition is described as "a developmental phase in which students determine whether or not they would like to continue their education beyond high school"(Hossler & Gallagher, 1987, p. 209). The theoretical underpinnings for the predisposition stage is grounded in the status attainment literature (Hossler, Braxton, & Coopersmith, 1989). Much of the research on the predisposition stage finds significant relationships between level of aspirations and ethnicity, size of family, parents' education attainments, parents' income, student academic ability and achievement, and peer and teacher influences (Paulsen, 1990).

Person-environment fit—the degree to which an individual belongs in (is congruent with) an environment—has been a popular explanation for understanding why some students seem to succeed and some fail in an institution (Feldman & Newcomb, 1969). Person-environment fit has been used to explain the degree to which students with particular background characteristics fit with the institutions they attend.

> Students from lower status backgrounds differ from those of higher status backgrounds in ways that presumably produce greater incongruence between the lower status group and the demands and opportunities of the college environment. Thus entering students of lower socioeconomic status, in comparison to their higher status counterparts, (1) are less culturally sophisticated . . . ; (2) have had a more restricted range of experiences . . . ; and (3) are more likely to be oriented to college in terms of vocational or professional training and less likely to be oriented in terms of intellectual growth (Feldman & Newcomb, p. 277).

One limitation of the traditional person-environment fit perspective is the burden of congruence is placed on the student. Little responsibility is placed on the members of the campus community who have constructed and maintained the campus environment.

The person-environment fit explanation of college impact—especially as it relates to SES—corresponds best with the contest view of social mobility (as described in previous sections). Those persons who are most like the environment they enter will be the most successful. More recent perspectives of the campus environment come from a "talent development" perspective: "Excellence is determined by our ability to develop the talents of our students and faculty to the fullest extent possible" (Astin, 1993a, p. 6). Aspirations change, from a talent development perspective, can be viewed as the ability of an institution to enhance the degree goals of students from varying backgrounds.

Many models of higher education outcomes operate from the assumption that higher education is an open structure where students choose the environments in which they will be socialized. Weidman (1989) developed a model of undergraduate socialization that takes into account the social structural aspects of the socialization process. The model specifies the social processes in college that affect the outcomes of students. Weidman posits that students enter college with certain aspirations, values, and aptitudes. Then, they are exposed to the socializing influences of faculty and peers through the academic and social normative contexts of the postsecondary institution. After such exposure, students assess the importance of the various normative pressures for attaining their goals and then change or maintain the "values, aspirations, and personal goals that were held at college entrance" (p. 301).

Weidman's model of undergraduate socialization assumes that colleges and universities function as an open opportunity structure where students' achievement is determined by what they choose to do. Weidman (1989) mentions that students' socialization in colleges and universities can be affected by their race/ethnicity and that "it is necessary to adapt conceptual frameworks to the differing patterns of socialization that may be represented among specific ethnic and gender groups" (p. 313). Thus, student background characteristics not only impact the kinds of experiences students have in college, but also may impact the kinds of postsecondary educational institutions students are able to attend.

African Americans in Higher Education

Few models of degree aspirations have been tested on African American students specifically. Those models that have been tested on African American students are substantially different from models tested on White students (Allen, 1992). An explanation for this difference is given by researchers in African-American psychology who believe that African Americans'

> learning mode is based on the African world-view and assumes that learning is primarily an affective process or a process which involves the emotions. . . . This relates to the [African American] college student in that if learning is primarily an affective process, then encouragement toward self . . . is a critical component (Washington, 1996, p. 80).

Therefore, it is important to understand the processes by which students develop and maintain educational aspirations and expectations, if only to understand the educational experiences of African American students. In a study of High School and Beyond (HSB) participants who graduated from college, Weiler (1993) found that roughly the same percentage of minority and White students who enrolled in graduate school initially did not expect to attend. However, there were large differences between the numbers of minority and White students who expected to attend graduate school and did not. Weiler concluded that "the key reason for lower post-baccalaureate attendance of minorities is the fact that a relatively large fraction of them who planned to continue their education beyond the baccalaureate at the time they entered college changed their minds" (p. 446). It is important to study the individual and institutional attributes of the process by which some college students decide not to pursue graduate study.

Feagin et al. (1996) detail some of the negative experiences African Americans have in PWIs. A central theme in the study is that of Black invisibility. Much like the main character of *Invisible Man* by Ralph Ellison, African American students in Feagin et al.'s study are not seen by "White professors, students, staff members and administrators . . . as full human beings with distinctive talents, virtues, interests and problems" (p. 14). Black students at PWIs often feel anxiety and fear at being the only one or one of a few African Americans in a particular environment. This anxiety can mean that African Americans look for the increased company of other African Americans for their support. Feagin et al. also report that "a recent survey of Black students at mostly White universities found they were so concerned about intellectual survival that they were unable to devote as much attention to their personal, social, and cultural development as they should" (p. 75).

As with high school studies, researchers on college students have implied that African Americans have unrealistic educational aspirations. Astin (1990) stated that Black students' aspirations are inconsistent with their career choices given the fact that 15.7%, 14.3%, and 37.7% of African Americans planned to earn a doctorate, advanced professional (M.D., J.D.), or Master's degrees, respectively, while only 11%, 10.1%, or 36.9% of White students planned to earn such degrees. In addition, African Americans planned to be businesspersons or computer programmers 4%-6% more than White students. Doctorates are not necessarily required for such professions as businesspersons and computer programmers, leading Astin to his conclusion that Black students have unrealistic educational aspirations. In a study using prestige scores for occupations (instead of discrete categories), White students tended to have nearly the same short-range occupational expectations as Black students at HBCUs and PWIs, and the long-range occupational expectations of White students tended to be slightly higher or about the same as the expectations of Black students (Dawkins, 1982).

The degree to which college students' aspirations for graduate education are "unrealistic" is a topic that has been addressed in this chapter but cannot be definitively examined in this study. Students who attend postsecondary institutions have already demonstrated success. They completed secondary education and have the personal goals, initiative, and achievement to apply to college and be admitted. College students are successful and talented and probably all are capable—even likely—to earn graduate degrees. However, as research reviewed in this section found, there are significant patterns of stratification within higher education: African American students disproportionately attend less "prestigious" institutions, drop out of postsecondary institutions and tend not to go on to earn graduate degrees in similar numbers as White students (Carter & Wilson, 1993). Therefore, it is important to again assert the main point of this study: To examine longitudinally the ways in which institutions facilitate or constrain aspirations during the early years of college. The influence of institutions on student outcomes is an important point in discovering why, as Weiler (1993) found, African Americans who planned to continue their education beyond the baccalaureate changed their minds.

SUMMARY OF THEORETICAL FRAMEWORK

The main theoretical framework used in the current study of aspirations can be summarized by discussing three themes presented in this chapter: the roles of ascribed status or merit in influencing students' aspirations, the effects of institutional characteristics and experiences, and the unique experiences and characteristics of African American students in higher education.

The social psychological status attainment model (Sewell et al., 1969; 1970) and Turner's (1960) concept vs. sponsored mobility are the main lenses through which the roles of ascribed status and merit in affecting students' aspirations was examined. The status attainment model and Turner's theory of the mobility process in the United States versus the United Kingdom hold significant assumptions about the ways in which students achieve (or acquire) status, and these assumptions—focusing on student aspirations for degree attainment—were tested in this study.

In addition, the unique experiences of African American students in higher education were also examined theoretically. Some researchers conclude that African Americans' aspirations were depressed by their experiences in schools; others conclude that African Americans' aspirations are too high. There still is not a solid theoretical understanding of how African American's degree aspirations are shaped. Chapter Three extends the discussion of how previous research informed this study by focusing on empirical evidence in what affects aspirations.

3
What Affects Aspirations? Empirical Evidence

Chapter 2 detailed the theoretical foundations of studies of educational aspirations. Several theories were considered relevant to the study of college students' aspirations: status attainment, contest and sponsored mobility processes, cultural deficit perspectives, college choice, person-environment fit, and undergraduate socialization. What has been learned by investigations of students' aspirations is that individual background and institutional characteristics are important in affecting outcomes.

This study of college students' degree aspirations uses an approach to the investigation of educational aspirations that takes into account both individual characteristics and institutional characteristics. Background characteristics—race/ethnicity, gender, marital status, socioeconomic status (SES), age, and academic self-concept—have all been shown to impact educational aspirations directly. Many of the previous studies on students' aspirations—especially at the high school level—have focused on individual characteristics and did not take into account institutional environments and students' experiences in college. Students may enter college with certain levels of aspirations that may increase or decrease depending on their institutional experiences. One set of variables that represents both institutional experiences and individual characteristics is financial aid. The types and levels of financial aid are both indications of institutional financial support and individual financial status; financial aid can have important effects on a variety of educational outcomes (Mow & Nettles, 1990).

This chapter discusses the empirical studies of aspirations and related outcomes in the following order: the effect of student background characteristics and initial aspirations, the role of social psychological variables, institutional characteristics, and concludes with a discussion of financial aid variables.

STUDENT BACKGROUND CHARACTERISTICS AND DEGREE ASPIRATIONS

Higher education research has identified several background characteristics that affect student aspirations: race, gender, socioeconomic status, and ability (achievement). African American students have been found to have as high or higher aspirations as White students over several years of studies (Allen, 1991; Astin, 1977, 1993b). However, the aspirations models tend not to work as well for African American populations. Blau and Duncan (1967) were the first to point out that their hypothesized model does not work well in explaining African American attainments. Their explanation for this is that educational employment discrimination impede the life chances and opportunities of African Americans.

> Education does not produce the same career advantages for [African Americans] as for Whites. The difference in occupational status between [African Americans] and Whites is twice as great for men who have graduated from high school or gone to college as for those who have completed no more than eight years of schooling. . . . The same investment of time and resources in education does not yield [African Americans] as much return in their careers as it does Whites. (Blau & Duncan, p. 405)

Blau and Duncan's comparison of African American and White individuals, who spent the same amount of time in educational institutions, found that African Americans held more lower status occupations than White men. This fact remains true today and the differences in income are often large (Grubb & Wilson, 1989). Portes and Wilson (1976) detailed the extent to which educational attainment differs between African Americans and Whites, using data from a national sample of high school boys who were attending tenth grade in 1966. Controlling for socioeconomic status, African Americans out-perform (i.e. received higher grades and had higher aspirations) White students at each stage of the attainment process. Given this finding, the authors suggested that White students' advantage in attainment "depends directly on their initial advantages in the input variables" (Portes & Wilson, p. 423).

Epps and Jackson (1985) researched African American educational attainment and aspirations in two national samples of students—1980 High School and Beyond (HSB) and 1972 National Longitudinal Study (NLS). Their prediction of aspirations in each of their models for the HSB sample was much better than the Wisconsin models of aspirations. For females, they explained 34% of the variance, for males 35%. The models for NLS explained much less of the variance in the level of attainment: 21% of the males and 14% of the females. In the HSB model, the direct effects on males' aspirations included coursework, academic track, high school grades, standardized test scores, and significant others' influence.

For females, coursework, track, significant others' influence, and test scores also directly affected aspirations, but socioeconomic status also had a strong direct effect. Labovitz (1975) studied the effects of ethnicity, SES and fulfillment of college aspirations. Labovitz' model included measures of race, IQ, SES, college plans, GPA, school SES, and neighborhood SES as predictors of college attendance for 1966 San Diego high school seniors. Minority students were found to "have the aspirations, the ability, and the qualifications to go to a four-year college, [but] they do not attend the colleges of their choice to the degree that White [students] do" (p. 248). Again, the notion of contest mobility with respect to minority students is questioned. In Labovitz's study, attendance at a four-year college was not simply the result of an even "contest" based on ability and goals. There were other factors—unexamined in the study—that seemed to disadvantage minority students in the college attendance process. This was particularly true when you consider that the students in Labovitz' study graduated from high school thirty years ago. The current study examined the degree to which similar societal dynamics constrained the degree aspirations of high school graduates from the 1980s.

Women have lower aspirations than men, on average (McClelland, 1990), tend to be more adversely affected by delays in entry to higher education (Kempner & Kinnick, 1990), have more unexplained variance in aspirations models than men (Hearn, 1987), and tend to be less likely to pursue a postbaccalaureate degree immediately after college graduation (Isaac, Malaney, & Karras, 1992). Astin (1977) found that over a four-year period, women had almost uniformly lowered aspirations. However, women who attend women's colleges significantly raised their degree aspirations over a four-year period (Smith, 1990).

Socioeconomic status (SES) is the variable most often studied in status attainment models. Sewell and Shah (1967) completed a study to determine whether ability or socioeconomic status affects college-going and completion more. They found that socioeconomic status and intelligence had positive relationships to college attendance for both males and females. Further, for men, the effect of SES decreases over time, and SES has comparably smaller effects on college outcomes than intelligence does. However, the same is not true for females. SES had a much greater effect on the outcome measures than intelligence (measured by scores on the Henmon-Nelson Test of Mental Maturity). The main point of their study is "that along with intelligence, socioeconomic status continues to influence college graduation even after socioeconomic selection has taken place in the process of determining who will attend college" (p. 20).

McDonough's (1997) study of White, female students' college choices found that students' social class was a major determinant of students' higher education choices. The high school culture and the encouragement received from parents functioned similarly across social class. Students who were lower-middle class attended community college or less selective public institutions while upper-middle class students attended private institutions or more selective public universities.

Levine and Nidiffer (1996) describe two main barriers to poor students attending college: getting out of poor neighborhoods and getting into college (p. 153). Colleges who service poor students seem adequately equipped to assist students in getting into college. "The colleges provide warm, inviting, and educationally, well-planned environments for their poor students." However, poor students often encounter "opposition to, or lack of understanding of college" (p. 153). Therefore, socioeconomic status plays a part in determining who can participate in the contest for upward mobility. This finding again contradicts the notion of meritocracy in U.S. educational systems. We know from the literature that lower income students, and students whose parents achieved lower levels of education tend to have lower aspirations and expectations than higher SES students. SES seems to affect the aspirations and achievement of women and minority students more than it affects the aspirations and achievement of White male students (Burke & Hoelter, 1988). Other researchers have come to the conclusion that the educational attainment of the same-sex parent is what most affects the educational behaviors of the student (Isaac et al., 1992).

The research on ability reveals complicated effects on aspirations. Ancis and Sedlacek (1997) state that "SAT scores tend to underpredict women's grades" and the use of other variables "provides for a more accurate and complete understanding of women's educational development" (p. 6). When colleges and universities rely on SAT scores to make academic decisions (e.g. financial aid based on "merit", admissions decisions) they may be limiting the extent to which talented women students can obtain financial aid, participate in certain programs, and may restrict the admission of women students to certain institutions (Ancis & Sedlacek, 1997). In addition, academic advisors may have lower expectations of women students' achievement if they judge ability only by SAT scores. This has direct implications to the socialization view of social mobility—how significant others influence the goals of students. If the basis by which significant others' expectations of what women students are able to do is not a "true" measure of their ability (e.g. the SAT score), this could unnecessarily constrict students' future goals.

When ability is measured by aptitude tests and grade point average, ability seems to have mostly indirect effects on educational aspirations. Perhaps this is because aptitude (as measured by performance on standardized tests) is strongly related to socioeconomic status (Thomas, Alexander, & Eckland, 1979). However, another study found that ability (as measured by IQ and GPA) has clear direct effects on the aspirations of White students, but no direct effects on the aspirations of African American students (Burke & Hoelter, 1988). Several researchers have found significant relationships between college GPAs and aspirations (Astin, 1977; Hearn, 1987; Pascarella, 1985), though in other studies, grade point average had no significant relationship to aspirations (Burke & Hoelter, 1988). These conflicting results suggest first, that models of educational aspirations need to be tested on Black and White student populations separately to determine the within and between group differences. Second, tests of direct effects taking into account other background characteristics are important in determining the relationship of ability measures to aspirations.

THE ROLE OF SOCIAL PSYCHOLOGICAL VARIABLES IN STUDENT DEGREE ASPIRATIONS

Burke and Hoelter (1988) use identity theory to conceptualize their approach to status attainment. They assert that people choose behaviors that correspond to their self-concept or identities. Thus, they assume that people who have strong, positive academic self-concepts should have higher educational aspirations and goals. Burke and Hoelter also take the same approach to studying aspirations as the Wisconsin (or social psychological model) in that social psychological variables (e.g. academic identity/self-concept) mediate the effects of SES on educational intentions (Sewell et al., 1969). They found that academic identity (as defined by students' evaluation of schoolwork independent of grades, perceived academic ability, and perceived ability to achieve high grades) mediates the effects of the main predictor variables—IQ and grade point average for instance—on the educational plans of three of their sub-groups. Academic identity impacted the educational plans of White males and females, and African American females, but not those of African American males.

The researchers offer very little explanation for the different findings for African American males, only that the meaning of educational expectations may differ for this particular group, and that the source of academic identity differs for the groups. Teacher influence has effects for the three groups, but not for Black males, and family background impacts White students' academic identity, but not the identity of Black students. Burke and Hoelter (1988) concluded that "many of the variables of the traditional Wisconsin model are thus not relevant for [African Americans], even though, for [African American] females, academic identity is" (p. 41).

Burke and Hoelter's study provided support for the notion that different models may be needed for separate ethnic and gender populations, and for the assumption that identity theory can be used successfully to broaden the Wisconsin model. Given that the researchers could not explain why the African American male students did not fit their identity theory assumptions, the usefulness of self-concept measures with respect to predicting aspirations may be limited. Burke and Hoelter's recommendation that self-concept variables should be incorporated into the Wisconsin status attainment model—without verifying the utility of the construct for African American males—remains an insupportable conclusion of their research.

In addition, recent research has found a negative relationship between positive self-concept and college grade point average for women students from a variety of races/ethnicities (Ancis & Sedlacek, 1997). Ancis and Sedlacek explain their findings by saying that the high-achieving women in their sample may have feelings of self-doubt much like the Imposter Phenomenon noted in previous psychological studies. The extent to which self-concept affects students' degree aspirations will be tested in this study for both African American and White college students.

The explanatory power of the social psychological model (the Wisconsin model) for the African American young men in the sample is much weaker than for the young White men (Portes & Wilson, 1976). The correlation between self-esteem (measured in part by the Rosenberg Self-Esteem scale) and educational aspirations is .24 for White students, in contrast to .13 for African American students. The model explains 35% of the variance in educational aspirations for White students as opposed to 13% of the variance for African Americans. Portes and Wilson believe that African Americans are able to move through the educational and occupational systems due to self-reliance and ambition, while White students also use these attributes as well as benefiting from a social structural system that can "carry them along to higher levels of attainment" (p. 430). Portes and Wilson's findings seem to support a notion that aspirations are a function of individual attributes (contest mobility) as well as structural limitations (sponsored mobility).

As was explained before, the college choice literature intersects with the aspirations literature in many ways. There are direct implications of college choice on college student outcomes as well. As is discussed in the next section, the type of institution a student attends has significant implications for the student's future degree attainment and future occupational earnings. The process by which students choose institutions is an important element of understanding the process of educational aspirations development. Significantly smaller portions of African American students compared with White students attend their first choice institution (Hurtado, Inkelas, Briggs, & Rhee, 1997; Maxey, Lee, & McLure, 1995). Researchers have offered several interpretations for this finding. In a study conducted by the American College Testing (ACT) organization—the organization that administers one of the two most used standardized tests for college admission—African American students attending their first-choice college tended to have lower ACT scores than those attending second- or third- or other-choice colleges. Explanations offered for this finding are that "students receiving higher scores on the ACT lift their aspirations, are recruited by other colleges, or find that financial aid opportunities have increased for them" (Maxey et al., 1995, p. 101). This is not surprising given that 81%

of African American students were in twelfth grade when they took the ACT, as opposed to less than 70% of White students. Therefore, African Americans in general tend to spend a shorter amount of time preparing for college attendance than White students and may need more support in developing postsecondary education plans (Maxey et al., 1995).

There is some evidence in aspirations studies that the longer a student holds an aspiration, the more likely he or she will meet that goal. Alexander and Cook (1979) found that students who, before the 10th grade, planned to go to college were about 47% more likely to attend college as students who decided in the 12th grade to go to college. Therefore, early and sustained aspirations are important in the future attainments of students.

Astin (1977) incorporated analyses of students' degree aspirations in his study of the four-year effects of college. Astin found that "the student's degree aspirations at the time of college entrance are the most potent predictors of enrollment in graduate or professional schools." (p. 112). In terms of change in students' aspirations, several findings of Astin's (1977) are particularly interesting: Astin found that students' degree aspirations increase after college entrance—at the time of the study, 51% of first year students planned to achieve a postgraduate degree and four years later, this percentage increases to 65% of the students. What is also important about the findings of Astin's study is that students' changes in degree plans increase gradually over the four years. About 4% of students increase their aspirations each year of the study.

Astin updated his 1977 study in 1993 and found that 63 percent of students entering college in 1985 planned to earn a postbaccalaureate degree. By the fourth year of college, the numbers of students with postgraduate degree aspirations were 68 percent. In addition, there is only a .35 correlation between 1985 and 1989 aspirations, which suggests that most of the students change their aspirations over time, or that changes in aspirations are due primarily to college experiences. There continues to be a positive correlation between those who have high 1985 aspirations and graduate school attendance. The positive predictors of high aspirations are intellectual self-esteem, and indicating "'to prepare for graduate or professional school' as an important reason for attending college" (Astin, 1993, p. 265). Astin's findings seem to support the previous findings that academic identity is related to educational aspirations (Burke & Hoelter, 1988). Because Astin's research was not conducted separately by ethnic group, analyses are necessary to determine if self-esteem (or self-concept) variables are related to both White and African American students' aspirations.

THE EFFECT OF INSTITUTIONAL CHARACTERISTICS ON STUDENT OUTCOMES

Institutional experiences and characteristics and can mediate or counteract background characteristics (Alwin, 1974), and can independently affect several educational outcomes including academic achievement and aspirations. This is especially true for African American students:

> The educational goals and activities of Black students are acted out in specific social environments that influence not only their ambitions, but also the possibility that they will realize their goals. Actors or agents in a particular setting—indeed, the setting itself—can either facilitate or frustrate the academic achievement of Black students. (Allen, 1992, p. 40)

Researchers have tried to broaden the status attainment models by introducing measures of students' experiences in educational institutions. Otto (1976) wanted to expand Blau and Duncan's model by investigating the extent to which social integration (as defined by participation in school activities) affects educational attainment. According to Otto, past research on high school effects on educational attainment have found that within-school effects are far more important than between-school effects. Since Spady (1970) hypothesized that membership in extracurricular activities can provide opportunities for students to acquire, develop and rehearse attitudes and skills, Otto decided to study if extracurricular involvement impacts educational attainment. Studying a sample of 1957 Michigan high school graduates who participated in a follow-up study in 1972, Otto's hypothesis was that prior social integration (participation in extra-curricular activities) facilitates the "acquisition, development, and rehearsal of achievement-related attitudes" (p. 1379), and that the benefits of social integration should apply to outcomes other than educational attainment. Otto's hypothesis is partially supported by the research. Social integration is the only variable in the model that has a significant total effect on the three main outcomes: educational attainment, income, and occupational attainment. However, most of the effect of social integration on occupational attainment and income is mediated by educational attainment. Otto's explanation for the mixed results is that social integration may be a proxy for aspirations, and that a study of the effect of social integration, controlling for aspirations, needs to be completed. This suggests that aspirations studies should take into account college experiences where students benefit from peer socialization.

In addition to college experiences, institutional characteristics affect student outcomes. Pascarella, Smart, and Smylie (1992) found that the cost of an institution had an independent effect on occupational attainment. Students who attended high-cost institutions tended to have higher occupational attainments than students who attended lower-cost institutions.

High tuition has also been shown to influence persistence (educational attainment). The higher the tuition, the less likely students will persist (St. John, Oescher, & Andrieu, 1992).

Astin et al. (1996) found that private universities (as compared to religious colleges, private colleges, and public colleges and universities) have the highest nine-year degree attainment rates for every racial/ethnic group (72% overall). Catholic institutions have the second highest attainment rates at 54.9%. Therefore, attendance at a private university compared to attendance at other institutional types can affect whether a student earns a Bachelor's degree. Since the link between attendance at a private university and degree achievement is so strong, perhaps institutional type has an impact on the development of degree aspirations.

Attending a large college (in terms of size of student body) tends to lower educational aspirations of African American men in predominantly White institutions (PWIs) and historically Black colleges and universities (HBCUs) (Smith, 1989). Highly selective institutions tend to have a positive effect on aspirations for White (Pascarella, 1985) and African American students (Smith, 1989). In a national study of undergraduates, Astin (1977) found that students attending more highly selective institutions tend to increase their aspirations over time, while students attending selective, public institutions and large institutions tend to lower their aspirations. In a follow-up study in 1993, Astin also found that the percentage of women in the student body was also a positive predictor of increased aspirations among students. In contrast, a study of the effects of institutional type on educational aspirations found that many of the institutional effects on aspirations were modest, leading to assertions that institutional environments have primarily indirect effects on aspirations, being mediated by variables such as achievement (Pascarella, 1984). There are clearly conflicting conceptions of the ways in which institutional differences affect individual students' aspirations.

The effect community colleges have on the aspirations and attainments of students has been a point of controversy for several decades. In discussing the role of the community college in the educational and occupational attainment of students, Clark (1960) notes that lower SES students were directed to two-year colleges and were subsequently "cooled out" (lowered their aspirations) as a result of their experiences in the institutions. The process of cooling out is one in which the "socializing agents" in the two-year college—faculty and peers, the curriculum, and administrative procedures—all influence the lowering of educational plans (Pascarella & Terenzini, 1991). There is considerable evidence that merely attending a two-year college as opposed to a four-year college lowers a student's chances of attaining a Bachelor's degree by 19% (Brint & Karabel, 1989; Vélez, 1985).

> Community colleges are significantly less able than four-year colleges to facilitate the educational and economic attainment of the approximately 30 to 40 percent of community college entrants seeking bachelor's degrees. . . . [G]enerally baccalaureate aspirants entering community colleges secure significantly fewer bachelor's degrees, fewer years of education, less prestigious jobs and in the long run, poorer paying jobs than comparable students entering four-year colleges . . . (Dougherty, 1987, pp. 99–100)

In this way, community colleges function as a form of "tracking" in higher education, such that the more able, higher SES students go directly to four-year colleges and universities and the lower SES, less able students enroll in community colleges and attain two-year degrees. The function of community colleges in terms of lowering attainment (and presumably aspirations) has been described by some researchers as part of society's role in "managing ambition": The United States society generates more ambition than the opportunity structure can support; therefore, the attendance of lower SES students at community colleges is one structural way of depressing high ambitions (Brint & Karabel, 1989).

The institutional effects of historically Black colleges and universities (HBCUs) and predominantly White institutions (PWIs) on African American student achievement have been the focus of several studies over the past two decades. Given the fact that HBCUs comprise 9 percent of the nation's baccalaureate-granting institutions, but "account for more than 30 percent of the all Bachelor's degrees awarded" (Trent, 1991, p. 56) to African Americans, it appears likely that HBCUs are better able to facilitate aspirations and attainment of African American students. Unfortunately, HBCUs have been described as providing a "very mediocre educational experience" given their comparative lack of resources (Jackson & Swan, 1991, p. 127). Despite HBCUs' relative disadvantages with respect to resources, these institutions evidently have "been able to create a social-psychological campus climate that not only fosters students' satisfaction, sense of community, and adjustment to college, but also increases the likelihood of persistence and degree completion" (Bohr, Pascarella, Nora, & Terenzini, 1995, p. 82). In contrast, many of the studies find that African American students tend to experience social isolation and suffer identity problems in PWIs that may interfere with academic achievement (Jackson & Swan, 1991):

> Black students on White campuses, compared with their counterparts who graduate from [HBCUs], generally have lower grade-point averages, lower persistence rates, lower academic achievement levels, higher attrition rates, less likelihood of enrolling in advanced degree programs, poorer overall psychological adjustment, and lower post-graduate attainments and earnings. (Darden, Bagaka's, Kamel, 1996, p. 56)

According to Fleming (1984), HBCUs facilitate students' academic development in three ways: friendship among peers, faculty, and staff; participation in the life of the campus; and feelings of academic success. HBCUs encourage African American students to interact with peers, faculty and staff to a greater degree than PWIs; African American students hold more positions of leadership in HBCUs than in White colleges; and finally, the academic successes of African American students are supported by faculty in HBCUs more than in PWIs (Fleming, 1984). In addition, attendance at HBCUs has been shown to facilitate the life circumstances of students. African American students who attend HBCUs tend to have higher incomes twenty years later than students who attended other kinds of postsecondary institutions (Constantine, 1995). As far as educational aspirations, one study found that African American students attending HBCUs tend to aspire to doctoral degrees in greater numbers than African American students at PWIs. However, the students at PWIs tend to aspire to more "prestigious" professional degrees (e.g. law and medical degrees) than the students at HBCUs (Allen & Haniff, 1991).

The structural diversity of an institution (the numerical representation of various racial/ethnic groups) is an important characteristic of colleges and universities. College environments with very high percentages of White students (in comparison to students of color) tend to provide few cross-race interactions for White students, tend to treat students from minority groups as symbols rather than as individuals, and tend to convey the message that maintaining a campus multicultural environment is a low institutional priority (Hurtado, Milem, Clayton-Pederson, & Allen, 1999; Loo & Rolison, 1986). In addition, minority students have experienced significant levels of alienation and harassment based on their ethnic group membership (Loo & Rolison, 1986). One African American student reported her views of an Ivy League university after a campus visit:

> I applied to a lot of different schools . . . and I got accepted to this Ivy League school. . . . One reason I didn't go was because it reeked of [W]hiteness. I was only there for two days, and after one day I wanted to leave. . . . I talked to other Black students; I talked to all of them because there aren't a lot. I said, 'Do you like it here?' And they said, 'No, we're miserable.' (Feagin & Sikes, 1995, p. 91)

Students of color at PWIs can experience minority status stress and alienation from the campus community (Loo & Rolison, 1986; Smedley, Myers, & Harrell, 1993). Thus, the racial composition of the students in a postsecondary educational institution can affect students' outcomes independent of other characteristics.

In addition, it is important to consider how the students at particular institutions differ. Students are not randomly distributed throughout the different college levels and types; different colleges attract different types of students (Feldman & Newcomb, 1969; Astin, 1993a). A student's socioeconomic status is significantly related to the type of college he or she attends. Karabel and Astin (1975) studied the effect of SES, academic ability and college selectivity and found that a "student's social origin is significantly related to the status of the college he [sic] attends" (p. 394). The lower the SES, the more likely a student will go to a less-expensive, public, and less-selective institution (Karabel & Astin, 1975; Pascarella et al., 1992). Hearn (1991) studied the types of colleges 1980 high school graduates attended and concluded that "the most stubborn barriers to meritocracy seem to be those that are directly and indirectly based in SES, rather than those that are based in race, ethnicity, or gender" (p. 168). In other words, although more students are attending postsecondary institutions, lower SES students attend less selective institutions more often than higher SES students. African Americans may have had comparable access to educational institutions in Hearn's study, but their educational and occupational outcomes are far lower than White students.

The college choice and talent development theoretical perspectives coupled with the above research showing the relationship between SES and type of college a student attends may indicate that income plays an indirect role in the development of degree aspirations and that institutional characteristics play a direct role in developing or constraining students' aspirations. However, after finding few significant effects of institutional type on degree aspirations, Pascarella (1984) suggests that institutional characteristics play an indirect role in affecting students' aspirations. Whether the effect of institutional type is direct or indirect (indirect effects are not examined in this study), these findings from studies on the effect of institutional characteristics on student outcomes highlight the importance of controlling for background characteristics in order to assess the true effect of institutional characteristics.

THE EFFECT OF FINANCIAL AID VARIABLES

There is very little research, if any, on the effect of financial aid on educational aspirations. Financial aid can be seen as representative of both institutional financial support and of individual financial need. Traditionally, broad financial aid support for students to attend college was intended to lessen any financial difficulties students may have in paying tuition. The Higher Education Act of 1965 is the first example of broad federal support for attendance at postsecondary institutions. This act featured grants and low-interest government-insured loans (Rippa, 1997). Therefore, financial aid awards to lower SES students should mediate the financial limitations of their backgrounds and increase the probability they will attend four-year institutions and desire to continue on to post-baccalaureate education. The type of aid students receive and the degree to which students' financial needs are met may impact their degree expectations. Institutional type and individual characteristics should both influence financial aid measures.

Very few studies incorporate financial aid variables into their models of educational outcomes. Unfortunately, quite a few of the financial aid studies are a decade or more old, which means that we will not know for several years the effect of recent federal policies limiting financial aid: The United States government policies from the 1960s and 1970s geared toward increasing access to higher education by offering aid to financially needy students were significantly weakened in the 1980s (Baker & Vélez, 1996). The result of the weakening in financial support to low income postsecondary students is that fewer funds for grants and more aid in the form of loans were made available to students. This study does examine the effect of financial aid on the degree aspirations of college students' in the late 1980s and early 1990s.

St. John and Noell (1989) found that all types of financial aid packages had positive impacts on student enrollment decisions, particularly minority student enrollment. However, a review of the literature on access to postsecondary education noted that one reason for the decline of African American college attendees in the 1980s is that:

> African Americans are less willing to borrow for higher education for purely economic reasons . . . and for psychological reasons, given that African American students are increasingly from low-income families in which a typical $10,000–12,000 debt will often be larger than his or her annual family income. (Baker & Vélez, p. 88)

What is known about the effect of financial aid (in unspecified forms) is that it facilitates students' peer social interactions (Cabrera, Nora, & Casteñeda, 1992). "Financial aid may provide recipients with enough freedom to engage in social activities . . . [or] remove anxieties, time, and effort associated with securing additional funds to finance their education" (p. 589). Students in work study programs may benefit in particular because they tend to have more frequent contact with faculty, staff and institutional polices (Hossler, 1984). Increased interaction with faculty and staff may increase students' knowledge of degree options and may encourage students to aspire to post-baccalaureate degrees.

Some researchers have come to the conclusion that increasing tuition fees would not limit student access to institutions as long as tuition increases are accompanied by financial aid increases (Hearn & Longanecker, 1985), though students "tend to enroll at the school with the lowest net costs" (Seneca & Taussig, 1987, p. 355). There is conflicting evidence as to whether financial problems encourage students to drop out of institutions. Some researchers feel that financial difficulty is given as a reason for leaving the institution because "it is more socially acceptable and protective of self-image than the real reason" (Pantages & Creedon, 1978). Mow and Nettles (1990) feel that this explanation is less likely to be true for minority students who tend to have lower SES backgrounds and experience greater gaps between financial need and aid received than White students. Students who do not receive financial aid tend to leave college in greater numbers than other students (Mow & Nettles, 1990). There is evidence that students who are less able to pay for their college costs drop out of institutions in greater numbers (Cabrera, Stampen, & Hansen, 1990). Related to this finding, St. John et al. (1992) found that student aid has a weaker effect on persistence than does tuition cost.

Some researchers believe that financial aid programs are not structured to adequately assist low-income, nontraditional students. There are several things that financial aid programs do not pay adequate attention to: "differences in the financial resources of poor independent students; the academic progress rates of older students requiring remediation; and the additional expenses associated with having a family" (Levine & Nidiffer, 1996, p. 157). An additional problem is the unstable federal support of low-income students: "government funding levels have been erratic, yo-yoing up and down and making financial aid an undependable resource for college support for the poor" (p. 157).

Since financial aid has been found to affect access, retention, and degree progress, I expect that aid will affect students' degree expectations. Perhaps, more importantly, the form of aid (loans vs. grants) may deter students from pursuing (or wanting to pursue) advanced degrees. This will be examined in the current study.

SUMMARY

The theoretical foundations of studies of aspirations are described in Chapter Two, and this chapter discusses previous research studies and their relationship to the study of aspirations. One main gap in mobility theories is the role that institutional environments play in affecting degree aspirations.

This study tested the relationship of institutional characteristics and experiences on students' aspirations. Institutional characteristics and experiences may have greater effects on students' aspirations than SES or individual achievement. Each institution (or institutional type) has particular social environments that can independently affect academic outcomes. Specifically, certain characteristics of institutions may increase access for students from lower socioeconomic backgrounds and may particularly affect the educational goals of African American students. This study held the role of institutions as central to the process of developing students' degree goals.

African American students are a population of students who tend to come from lower income backgrounds and have lower rates of college enrollment than White students. Furthermore, researchers have not been wholly successful in explaining what affects African American students' degree aspirations. This study conceptualized the models of degree aspirations for White and African American students as unique with the main purpose of expanding current understanding of the ways in which African American college students set degree goals. The next chapter details the methodology used in the study based on the theoretical framework and previous empirical research.

4
Methodology for the Study

This study was a multi-institutional investigation of the aspirations of African American and White college students during the first two years of their college experiences. The study involved two data sets, each of which contained data from two different time periods. The longitudinal nature of the data sets was important to the investigation because pre-college characteristics and initial goals and expectations could be measured and taken into account to assess their effects on later expectations and plans. The multi-institutional nature of the data sets was important for the study because it made possible an assessment of the effects of different kinds of institutional environments on college students' educational expectations and plans.

Two different data sets were necessary for the investigation in order to shed light on a theoretical controversy: Do different measures of aspirations contribute to our understanding of the processes by which students' change their aspirations over time? Kerckhoff (1976) suggested that most measures of aspirations ask students to report educational plans abstractly, without reference to the life circumstances that may constrain their goals. Kerckhoff further hypothesized that if aspirations were measured in terms of students' degree expectations given constraints, there would be differences in the findings of the studies. Each data set measures aspirations differently: the Beginning Postsecondary Students Longitudinal Study (BPS) measured students' educational expectations given perceived structural constraints, and the Cooperative Institutional Research Program (CIRP) measured students' educational plans. Since the measurement of aspirations differs across data sets, I use the term expectations to refer to students' aspirations in BPS and plans to refer to aspirations in CIRP.

The investigation of individual and institutional contributors and inhibitors on college students' plans and expectations was conducted in three stages: Stage one focused on identifying the initial group differences in dependent and independent variables between African American and White students in both databases. Determining initial differences between groups was an important phase of the study because it addressed key theoretical controversies and established the characteristics of the students in the study in comparison to past studies. Specifically, it answers the question: How did African American students compare with White students on the relevant measures in the models?

Stage two tested a regression model across both data sets to determine the differences in predicting White and African American aspirations given different operational definitions of the dependent variable. The model regressed similar dependent variables on the same individual, institutional, involvement, achievement, and financial aid variables in both the CIRP and BPS data sets. The regression model incorporated individual and institutional characteristics as well as college involvement, achievement, and financial aid variables in order to understand better the wide variety of factors that contributed to students' goals for earning future degrees.

Stage three involved expanded regression models that were tested separately for each data set and by race/ethnicity in order to fully utilize the strengths of each database. That is, each data set had strengths and weaknesses with respect to the variables included (see the "Limitations" section at the end of this chapter). The expanded models tested the unique contribution of those measures specific to each database on the educational expectations and plans of African American and White students. For example, the BPS data set included more SES and financial aid measures than the CIRP data set, but lacked pre-college measures of academic achievement. The CIRP data set had excellent measures of pre-college achievement, perceptions of institutional priorities, and measures of college experiences including participation in school clubs and groups. However, the data set lacked some institutional and individual background variables such as size and marital status, respectively.

Many of the previous studies of educational aspirations, expectations, and plans have not explained a significant amount of the variance for African American students (Berman & Haug, 1975). Kerckhoff (1976) suggested that the difficulty in predicting the aspirations of African Americans may stem from differences in the dependent measures of aspirations used in those studies (i.e. were the studies measuring expectations or plans). This study compared models of educational expectations and plans, using similar variables across the two data sets to determine whether the relationships among the variables were consistent across the two. While the comparisons were not unproblematic, the relationships between the independent and dependent variables were revealing. By using similar regression models for the two data sets, I was able to compare how independent variables in one data set (BPS) affected educational expectations and how similar independent variables in another data set (CIRP) affected educational plans.

The main assumption of this study, supported by several researchers (Astin, 1977; 1993b; Pascarella, 1984; Smith, 1989), was that individuals' characteristics and institutional experiences could raise or lower students' educational aspirations over time. Students may begin college with lower aspirations, but institutional environments can have strong effects on students after college entry (Astin, 1977; 1993b). This study was guided by several research questions derived directly from previous research:

- Do educational aspirations differ significantly for African American and White students? Does this change over time?
- What impact does socioeconomic status (SES) have on the educational aspirations of college students—are the effects of SES lessened by particular institutional environments, or does socioeconomic status have effects that persist despite the influence of institutional characteristics?
- How do institutional characteristics, college involvement (e.g. peer and faculty interaction, participation in student organizations), achievement, and student pre-college characteristics affect students' aspirations? Do the same variables affect the racial/ethnic groups differently? Or do the significant predictors vary by group?
- In what ways do institutional characteristics, college involvement, and educational achievement mediate the effects of socioeconomic status and initial goals and expectations?
- Are the effects of the independent variables the same when the measures of the dependent variable differ? In other words, are the relationships between the independent variables and educational expectations in one data set the same as those between the independent variables and educational plans in another data set?

HYPOTHESES

Several hypotheses followed from the above research questions. Each hypothesis was tested in the analyses.

Hypothesis 1: Differences in the measurement of the educational aspirations items will not produce substantial differences in the ways the independent variables in the model affect student aspirations over time.

This hypothesis addressed one of the controversies in the aspirations literature concerning the measures used in previous studies. Some researchers felt that the wording of the survey items makes a difference with respect to fully understanding the process by which individuals attain degrees. Kerckhoff (1976) believes that the difference between measuring aspirations and expectations is the difference between conceiving of students' goals as a function of what an individual chooses to do versus conceiving of students' goals as determined by what the student is allowed to do. Therefore, a survey item that measured students' plans may capture a respondent's educational goals when he or she feels unfettered by social circumstances; while a survey item that measured students' expectations within social constraints may capture the respondents' goals as a function of perceived limitations. There are two dependent variables used in this study: In BPS, the dependent variable measures students' educational expectations "considering all practical constraints", and in CIRP, the dependent variable measures "the highest degree" students plan to complete. In this way, the BPS measure approximates students' expectations within social constraints, and the CIRP measure seems to ask for students' plans without particular attention to constraints.

Kerckhoff's hypotheses were developed for high school age students. Do Kerckhoff's assumptions hold true for college attendees who, by the mere fact they are in college, have already achieved to a significant extent? By attending college, students may have a better idea of their degree options than high school students who have limited exposure to postsecondary education. The possible effect of differences in the measures of college students' educational aspirations had not been empirically addressed in previous research. Since students who attend college are achievers in comparison to other individuals of the same age, it is possible (and perhaps even a realistic expectation) that many of the college attendees at some point will earn a post-baccalaureate degree. I believed that the regression models predicting educational plans and expectations would not be substantially different.

Hypothesis 2: Students' socioeconomic backgrounds will have strong effects on their plans and expectations two years after college entry.

This hypothesis directly addressed social allocation vs. socialization perspectives of status attainment. Several research studies showed high correlations between student SES and aspirations (Alexander & Eckland, 1975; Epps & Jackson, 1985; Sewell & Hauser, 1980). Some studies showed that the educational attainment of students' parents has a strong relationship to students' aspirations (Stage & Hossler, 1989) and to the types of colleges students attended (Astin, 1993b; Karabel & Astin, 1975; McClelland, 1990). Karabel and Astin (1975) found SES had an effect, independent of ability, on the type of institution attended. McClelland (1990) showed that higher SES students were considerably more likely than their lower SES peers to start their careers at elite institutions, and Astin (1993b) stated that students at public universities, on average, tend to come from lower socioeconomic backgrounds than those at private institutions. Higher income students and students whose parents achieved higher levels of education were expected to have higher educational aspirations, independent of race/ethnicity and ability.

This hypothesis addressed two main theoretical issues at once: the role of ascriptive factors in status attainment models and contest vs. sponsored mobility. This hypothesis tested whether ascriptive characteristics were more important in predicting aspirations than ability and social interactions within college. Also, the hypothesis tested the ongoing controversy regarding the primacy of a meritocracy in higher education.

Hypothesis 3: Financial aid measures will lessen the effect of socioeconomic status on educational aspirations.

If socioeconomic status was indeed a main factor associated with educational aspirations and eventual attainments, then particular public policies instituted over the past few decades to increase student access to higher education should mediate the effect of SES and should directly influence student aspirations. The effect of various types of financial aid on educational aspirations was not well known from past literature.

If college students had moderate to large loan debts when they began in higher education, they may have been deterred from aspiring to attend graduate school and subsequently incurring more loan debt. This may have been especially true for African American students whose families tended to earn much less than White students' families (Baker & Vélez, 1996). However, grant and scholarship aid may encourage students to seek further education. I hypothesized that students from lower income backgrounds, who had more work study, grants, and scholarships would have higher aspirations than students who had more loans (debt) and were working (non-work study) longer hours for pay.

Hypothesis 4: Ability (as measured by pre-college grade point average and academic self-concept) will affect educational aspirations and will lessen the effect of SES on educational aspirations.

This hypothesis directly tested the concept of contest mobility. If the higher education systems in the country were meritocratic, the benefits afforded students in postsecondary education should be due to ability, as theorized by Turner (1960). If ability played a minor role in the regression models of educational aspirations, or if SES had a much stronger effect than ability, the contest mobility theory of higher education could be ruled out. Additional research suggested that students of high ability tended to take more advantage of college experiences and opportunities to interact with peers (Hurtado, Carter, & Sharp, 1995). In this study, pre-college grades and college grade point average are expected to affect students' aspirations.

Hypothesis 5: Institutional characteristics will have strong effects on aspirations, independent of individual characteristics and goals.

The types of institutions students attend influence their educational outcomes. Students attending selective institutions were more likely to complete their Bachelor's degrees (McClelland, 1990), and students who attended higher cost institutions tended to have higher educational attainment and occupational status regardless of ethnicity and gender (Pascarella, Smart, & Smylie, 1992). Public postsecondary institutions—in comparison to private institutions—negatively impacted educational attainment (Astin, 1993b), and community colleges lowered aspirations and lowered degree attainment in comparison to four-year institutions (Brint & Karabel, 1989). Therefore, in the present study, each institution type was hypothesized to have different effects on students' aspirations.

In addition, this hypothesis also addressed the notion of sponsored vs. contest mobility. If community colleges constrain students' aspirations independent of academic ability as previous studies have found (Brint & Karabel, 1989; Dougherty, 1987), then this study would further support the notion that the system of postsecondary education is not based on merit. I hypothesized that particular institutional characteristics (high cost, private control, and attendance at a four-year institution) would have positive effects on students' aspirations, regardless of their individual backgrounds.

Hypothesis 6: High levels of student involvement in peer and faculty-related activities will positively affect educational aspirations.

Very little previous research was completed on the effects of college experiences on educational aspirations. However, Astin (1977, 1993b) completed a great deal of research on the effects of involvement on degree attainment, college grades, and college satisfaction. It is clear from the results of Astin's research that student participation in the college environment (particularly student-faculty interaction) could increase their satisfaction with the institution and their college grades. Frequent interaction with faculty members could raise students' aspirations in several ways. Faculty may socialize students in the skills and preparation needed for a graduate school career; and faculty may encourage the students they know well to apply to graduate school—encouragement that students with less interaction with faculty may not receive. I hypothesized that students who had frequent faculty contact or frequently participated in college activities would maintain high educational aspirations.

Hypothesis 7: The pattern of relationships between variables in the African American aspirations models will be different from those in the aspirations models for White students.

African American and White students tend to have different pre-college characteristics and college-going behaviors. For instance, African American college students tend to come from lower SES backgrounds than White college students (Baker & Vélez, 1996); do not attend their first choice colleges to the degree that White students do (Hurtado et al., 1997; Hurtado & Navia, 1997; Labovitz, 1975; Maxey et al., 1995); attend different kinds of institutions than White students, and have more negative experiences at PWIs than White students (Allen, 1992; Feagin et al., 1996). The college environments of HBCUs have been shown to be particularly effective for the educational outcomes of African Americans (Fleming, 1984).

Not surprisingly, researchers have found that educational aspirations regression models for African American and White students are quite different as well (Portes & Wilson, 1976). Based on previous research that found African Americans and White students tend to have very different experiences in and perceptions of college (Allen, 1992; Loo & Rolison, 1986), I expected the regression coefficients for African Americans would be different than the models for White students.

DATA SOURCES

This study used two data sets to investigate the educational aspirations of African American and White college students. Both data sets were national, longitudinal, and contained information from students at several different types of institutions. Each data set measured aspirations differently: The Beginning Postsecondary Students Longitudinal Study (BPS) measured students' educational expectations given perceived constraints, and the Cooperative Institutional Research Program (CIRP) measured students' educational plans. Each data set also contained data from two different time points—the first and third years of college. The longitudinal nature of the data sets was important to the investigation because pre-college characteristics and initial goals and expectations could be measured and controlled to determine their effects on changes in expectations and plans.

BPS: 90/92 Data

The data used in this study were from two main data sources: 1) National Postsecondary Student Assistance Study (NPSAS) 1990; and 2) BPS 1990 and 1992 follow-up. The BPS student sample was a sub-sample from the 1990 (NPSAS) participants. Individuals surveyed in BPS were all first-time entering students in higher education. The aim of the BPS was to gain information about a variety of students who began higher education in the 1989–90 school year. Students from a variety of ages, attending different types of institutions were interviewed by telephone. Students interviewed in 1989–90 were interviewed again in 1991–1992. The follow-up sample consisted of 10,624 students, with over 5,000 students in non-profit community colleges or four-year institutions. BPS data were merged with IPEDS data to comprise a database rich with student and institutional variables and characteristics.

The sample of the BPS:90/92 was a subset of the NPSAS:90 sample restricted to students beginning postsecondary education for the first time in the 1989–90 school year. Students who were enrolled at any time between July 1, 1989 through June 30, 1990 were eligible for inclusion in the study. In order for institutions to be eligible for the NPSAS (and thus BPS) study, they had to meet specific criteria as described in National Center for Education Statistics (NCES) (1994). If an institution only served high school students, provided short seminars, or provided education that was mainly recreational, or remedial in nature, the institution was excluded from the NPSAS sample.

The student sample of BPS was drawn over several time segments throughout the 1989–90 school year. Students were not excluded from the sample based on citizenship, part-time enrollment, or residency status. Only students who were taking courses for credit in a degree-granting program or in an "occupation-specific program" were in the BPS sample. Students who were taking courses for remediation, or for pleasure rather than an academic program and students who were auditing and/or taking courses for no credit were excluded from the BPS data set.

Detailed descriptions of the sampling frames and procedures are found in Shepard (1991) and in NCES (1994). Of the 1,533 institutions and 61,120 responding students to the NPSAS:90, 11,700 students from 1,092 institutions comprised the potential BPS:90/92 sample. Care was taken in the BPS:90/92 study to eliminate all non-first time, beginning higher education students. Individuals in the sample who were identified as graduate students or upper-division undergraduates were excluded. The number of completed or partially completed interviews was approximately 7,900 in 1989–90 and 6,500 of these students were surveyed again in 1991–92 for a 85.7% response rate (Hurtado, Kurotsuchi, & Sharp, 1996). Weights were developed to adjust for non-response on the second wave of the survey (see Shepard, 1991 for details about the weighting methodology).

There were several parts to the forty-seven-page telephone interview instrument. Interviews covered students' educational experiences in college, their educational financing of college, in-college work experiences, students' participation in other educational programs, background information (family, parents, gender, ethnicity, age, income), goals, expectations, and public service information. Most of the interviews averaged 40–60 minutes in length.

CIRP: 88/90 Data

The Cooperative Institutional Research Program (CIRP), sponsored by the American Council on Education (ACE) and the Higher Education Research Institute (HERI) at the University of California, Los Angeles conducts national studies of college students. Each year since 1966, the CIRP freshman survey program collected information about first year students using the Student Information Form (SIF; see Dey, Astin, & Korn, 1991). The sample for institutional participation in CIRP included all postsecondary institutions that participate in "Opening Fall Enrollment" (OFE) files of the IPEDS data system. Institutions were eligible for participation in CIRP if they were "operating at the time of the IPEDS survey and had a first-time full-time freshman class of at least 25 students" (Dey et al., 1991, p. 131). All of the eligible institutions are then categorized according to thirty-seven stratification groups based on institutional race (HBCU or PWI), type (two-year, four-year, or university), control (public, private, or religious), and selectivity (the average SAT score for the entering class).

Institutions with low response rates were excluded from the study: four-year colleges with less than 85% response rate, universities with lower than 75% response rate, and two-year colleges with less than a 50% response rate on the freshman survey. Therefore, the sample for 1988 was 402 institutions with 222,296 students (Dey et al., 1991).

The 1988 SIF freshman survey was administered to students during the late summer and early fall of 1988—particularly during freshman orientation and during the first weeks of fall classes. The SIF covered a range of issues including respondents' reasons for choosing their higher educational institution, high school experiences, attitudes, background characteristics, goals, and plans.

CIRP has been conducting regular follow-up surveys (FUS) of the SIF survey since 1982 (Dey, 1991). The 1990 FUS was linked with 1988 SIF to provide longitudinal information about the impacts of college on students, two years after college entry. The follow-up sample was a random, stratified sample to ensure that students from a variety of postsecondary institutions would be represented in the follow-up sample. A sample of 20,959 students was drawn from the institutions in the 1988 sample.

The 1990 follow-up survey of the 1988 Student Information Form (SIF) covered many of the issues in the 1988 survey and included items measuring self-reported changes in skill development and satisfaction with particular areas and experiences in the postsecondary institution. The instrument was sent to students in the summer of 1990 and returned by 4,695 students—22% of the sample. Admissions test scores (e.g. SAT or ACT) and registrar data were solicited for each student who was sent a follow-up survey. Because of the extensive information available on the first year student respondents, nearly 300 variables were available for developing non-response weights. Weights were developed to adjust for non-response on the follow-up of the survey (see Dey et al., 1991 for details about the weighting methodology).

SAMPLE

The samples used in this study were students from non-profit, two- and four-year institutions. Only White and African American students were selected for each data set. The data for all analyses were weighted, adjusted to maintain the sample sizes. Only students who have valid observations for the dependent variable—educational expectations for BPS and educational plans for CIRP—were selected for the analysis.

In the BPS:90/92 data set, the total number of students in the sample with valid observations for educational expectations is 3,861: 3,506 White students and 355 African American students. In the CIRP data set, the total sample is 4,164: 3,898 White students and 266 African American students. Because the numbers of White students in the data sets were so much larger, a random sample of White students was drawn to match the African American samples (see Appendix B).

Statistical tests (e.g. mean difference t-tests, correlations) take into account sample sizes between groups when calculating coefficients and levels of significance. The threshold for statistically significant relationships between variables becomes progressively lower as the sample size rises. So in regression analyses, a large sample could produce more significant predictors of the dependent variable (at the .05 level of significance) than a much smaller sample. Since White students total more than ten times the number of African American students in either sample, the original White samples in BPS and CIRP may produce significant relationships in the regression models that are more a function of the size of the samples than significant relationships between variables. Then, the regressions across groups could be more easily interpreted—independent of sample size variations.

The final sample sizes used for all analyses in the Results chapters are 355 African American students and 357 White students for BPS; 266 African American and 283 White students in CIRP. Appendix B contains a discussion of the comparisons between the reduced White student samples and the total White student samples for BPS and CIRP.

DESCRIPTION OF VARIABLES AND MEASURES

The following is a general discussion of the measures in the BPS and CIRP data sets that will be used in the regression models. Table 4.1 lists the variables in the BPS and CIRP databases across the stage of analyses. The table indicates all of the variables used in the study and whether they are used in the base regression models and/or in the full regression models. The table also shows how the variables are measured in each data set: exactly the same across data sets, measured similarly, or distinct to each data set. The purpose of the base models (which is described in more detail in the Analyses section of this chapter) is to compare how differences in the measurement of the dependent variable affect the predictors of degree

Table 4.1 Variables in BPS and CIRP Data sets by the Stages of Analyses*

Variables	Base Models	Full Models	Distinction
Dependent Variable			
Degree Expectations	•	BPS only	distinct
Degree Plans	•	CIRP only	distinct
Pre-college characteristics			
Female	•	•	exact
Age	•	•	similar
Father's Educational Attainment	•	•	similar
Mother's Educational Attainment	•	•	similar
Parent Income	•	•	exact
Number of Children		BPS only	distinct
Married		BPS only	distinct
Separated/Divorced		BPS only	distinct
Items Owned		BPS only	distinct
GPA		CIRP only	distinct
Initial Expectations/Orientations			
Degree Expectations	•	BPS only	distinct
Degree Plans	•	CIRP only	distinct
Intellectual Self-Confidence	•	•	similar
First Choice	•	•	exact
Distance From Home	•	•	exact
Good Reputation		BPS only	distinct
Close to Home		BPS only	distinct
Less Expensive		BPS only	distinct
Social Change Orientation		CIRP only	distinct
Institutional Characteristics			
Control	•	•	exact
Level	•	•	exact
Single Sex		CIRP only	distinct
HBCU†	•	•	exact
% African American Enrollment†		BPS only	distinct
Tuition Cost		BPS only	distinct
Size		BPS only	distinct
Institutional Priorities			
Commitment to Social Activism		CIRP only	distinct
Commitment to Diversity		CIRP only	distinct
Financial Aid/Work			
Borrow/Loans	•	•	similar
Scholarship	•	•	similar
Work Study	•	•	similar
Hours spent working	•	•	similar
Number of Jobs		BPS only	distinct
Involvement			
Faculty Contact	•	•	similar
Peer Contact	•	•	similar
Participated in ethnic organizations		CIRP only	distinct
Achievement			
College GPA		•	distinct

* "Exact" means that the wording of the measure and the response categories are exactly the same across both data sets; "Similar" means that the wording of the measure or the response categories are not exact, but the measures across the data sets are similar; "Distinct" means that the measure is unique to the data set.

†Note: The HBCU measure was used in the base regression model for both CIRP and BPS data sets, but only in the CIRP expanded regression models. The BPS expanded regression models used the Percent African American enrollment measure instead of the HBCU measure.

aspirations. The full regression models expand the analyses of degree aspirations to include measures that are unique to each data set. A detailed list of all the variables used in this study is in Appendix C: Table C1 for BPS measures and Table C2 for CIRP measures.

Dependent Variables

The BPS outcome measure is students' second year educational expectations. The item is worded accordingly: "Considering all practical constraints, what is the highest level of education you ever expect to complete?" The response categories for the item were coded: 1=two years or less of college or vocational education; 2=two or more years of college (including a 2-year associate's degree); 3=bachelor's degree or equivalent; 4=master's degree or equivalent; 5=M.D., D.D.S., L.L.B., or doctorate.

The CIRP outcome measure is students' second year educational plans. The survey item requests students to complete the following statement: "Please indicate the highest degree you plan to complete." The response categories for the item were coded: 1=no degree; 2=vocational certificate; 3=Associate's degree; 4=Bachelor's degree; 5=Master's degree; 6=Ph.D. or advanced professional degree.

The two dependent measures across both data sets may measure different conceptions of students' degree goals: The BPS measure reflects a student's goals as a function of what he or she is allowed to do (or can accomplish) given societal constraints. However, the CIRP measure of degree plans may measure students' goals given their choice of what they want to accomplish.

Pre-college Characteristics

Previous studies have found a number of individual characteristics impact students' educational aspirations. Background characteristics were included in the regression models to test if the relationships found in past research were similar in this sample (see Table 4.1). The pre-college measures in both CIRP and BPS data sets included gender (dichotomous, men is the comparison group), age, father's and mother's educational attainment, and parental income. In the BPS data set, additional pre-college measures are number of children (0 through 6 or more), marital status, and material conditions of students' circumstances—Items Owned. High school academic achievement is a pre-college measure specific to the CIRP data set and is a key variable in determining how far a student may go or intend to go in pursuing an education. In addition, pre-college academic achievement specifically addresses the theoretical conception of higher education as a meritocracy. Pre-college achievement is an important measure to take into account when examining the development of student's degree aspirations.

Initial Expectations/Orientations and Choice

It is also important to statistically control for initial goals and aspirations when students enter college. Controls for initial goals and aspirations are necessary in order to assess the effect of institutional environments, experiences and other factors that contribute to change over and above initial aspirations. Initial expectations and orientations include: educational expectations and plans in the first year (on the same scale as second year expectations and plans), and students' intellectual self-confidence (students were asked to compare themselves to others on categories such as academic ability, drive to achieve, emotional health, leadership ability, and intellectual confidence).

In addition, variables related to college choice were included in the model. Studies have indicated that African American students do not attend their first choice institutions at the same rate that White students do (Hurtado et al., 1997). Perhaps the inability to attend one's first choice institution is a structural constraint on students' later aspirations. Also, if a student attends his or her first choice institution, the student may be more likely to become involved in the campus community and thus have more positive institutional experiences, which may ultimately enhance the student's educational plans. The distance between a student's home and college is positively associated with educational aspirations (Astin, 1993b). Measures related to choice include whether the institution was the student's first choice, and the reasons why the student chose to attend the institution (institution has a good reputation, was close to home, and was less expensive than other institutions).

Institutional Characteristics and Perceived Institutional Priorities

Institutional structures can directly impact the future occupational outcomes and educational aspirations of students. Since there is great variation in the types of institutions students attend in both the CIRP and BPS cohorts, assessing the impact of structural characteristics becomes important to understanding the uniqueness of their experiences in different college contexts. Several researchers have found that control (public or private), size, two-year or four-year, tuition cost, selectivity and percent undergraduate minority enrollment (or attendance at an HBCU) impact a variety of educational outcomes (Allen, 1992; Astin, 1993b; McClelland, 1990; Pascarella, et. al., 1992; Smith, 1988).

Institutional climate measures have also been shown to impact student outcomes. Hurtado (1990) found that institutional commitment to diversity had a significant, negative impact on the college grade point average of Chicano students, but the same measure had a positive impact on self-concept measures. Students' (particularly African American students') perceptions of an institution's commitment to student development and diversity was assumed to facilitate their degree plans.

Involvement/Achievement/Financial Aid

Students' interactions with their college environments are important to their educational attainments and several other educational outcomes. The involvement measures that are part of this study included the number of jobs the student holds, frequency of faculty contact, participation in peer activities, and number of hours spent working each week. Participation in ethnic student organizations may be an involvement measure that enhanced African American students' involvement in college and therefore produced higher aspirations. African American students described feeling isolated in PWIs (Feagin et al., 1996), perhaps participation in organizations where they interact frequently with other minority students assisted adjustment to college and therefore facilitated higher degree plans.

Pre-college achievement (high school grade point average) has been shown to affect college aspirations (Astin, 1977; Pascarella, 1984; 1985); perhaps the same relationship is true for college achievement. Therefore, achievement in college—measured by college grade point average—was expected to affect expectations and plans.

Financial aid measures included in the regression models were the amount awarded for work-study and scholarships, and the amount borrowed and/or received in loans. St. John et al. (1992) found little relationship between aid received and educational outcomes, while Cabrera et al. (1992) found that financial aid measures impact student persistence. This suggests the possibility that student aid may compensate for SES effects, and also may determine the likelihood of students meeting their goals for attainment. Further it is not known whether receipt of particular types of aid (e.g. loans or grants) may facilitate or hinder students' plans or expectations for post-baccalaureate degree attainment. The current study can test these possibilities.

ANALYSES

This section describes the data preparation and analyses that were performed to test the hypotheses and answer the main research questions. One of the main research questions of this study centered on how the models of educational expectations and plans of African American and White students may differ. Separate analyses were conducted on both populations to allow different models of educational aspirations to emerge—one for each ethnic group—within each data set.

Table 4.2 Factor Analysis and Reliabilities by Racial Group in BPS Data set

Factor Scale Name	White Students	African American Students
Intellectual Confidence		
self-rating: leadership ability	.62	.64
self-rating: intellectual confidence	.58	.58
self-rating: drive to achieve	.52	.57
self-rating: emotional health	.49	.49
	alpha=.64	*alpha=.70*
Close to Home		
could live at home	.80	.75
school is close to home	.67	.53
can go to school and work	.61	.69
	alpha=.74	*alpha=.71*
Good Reputation		
good reputation for placing graduates	.75	.74
school has good reputation	.70	.70
offered course of study wanted	.47	.55
better chance to get job at school	.34	.36
	alpha=.69	*alpha=.69*
Less Expensive		
other living costs were less	.81	.96
tuition and other expenses were less	.62	.52
	alpha=.70	*alpha=.73*
Peer Contact/Activities		
participated in school clubs	.73	.76
intramural activities	.68	.63
go places with friends	.68	.65
attended career lecture	.62	.64
in study groups	.63	.60
in study assistance centers	.56	.66
	alpha=.73	*alpha=.73*
Faculty contact		
talk academic matters with faculty	.80	.75
contact faculty outside of class	.73	.70
meet advisors concerning academic plans	.76	.84
	alpha=.64	*alpha=.63*

Data Preparation

Missing data can greatly affect sample sizes and can limit certain types of analyses. To solve the problem of missing data in this study, mean replacements were conducted prior to analyses. Mean replacements involved replacing missing values with the mean of that variable. Only independent variables that had no more than 15% of the cases missing underwent this procedure. Means were used to replace missing responses by ethnicity and gender groups since these two variables were the focus of the multivariate analyses.

Table 4.3 Factor Analysis and Reliabilities by Racial Group in CIRP Data set

Factor Scales	White Students	African American Students
Intellectual Self-Confidence		
Self-rating: Public speaking ability	.60	.78
Self-rating: Leadership ability	.66	.75
Self-rating: Intellectual self-confidence	.49	.70
Self-rating: Drive to achieve	.72	.52
Self-rating: Competitiveness	.69	.51
	alpha=.76	alpha=.81
Social Change Orientation		
Take part in community action	.70	.77
Promote racial understanding	.69	.61
Help others in difficulty	.59	.54
Develop meaningful philosophy of life	.56	.55
Join organizations like Peace Corps	.52	.43
Influence social values	.54	.48
	alpha=.77	alpha=.74
Commitment to Social Activism		
Teach students how to change society	.58	.73
Facilitate involvement in community	.55	.66
Help students understand values	.69	.66
Develop leadership ability among students	.61	.65
Develop community among faculty and students	.70	.63
Maintain climate for airing of differences	.52	.61
Create positive undergraduate experience	.70	.57
	alpha=.84	alpha=.86
Commitment to Diversity		
Increase minorities in faculty and administration	.75	.49
Recruit more minority students	.72	.81
Develop appreciation of multi-cultural society	.49	.34
	alpha=.74	alpha=.65

Scales were constructed after mean replacements of missing data were completed. Factor analyses were used as a data reduction technique. Preliminary factor analyses were performed on several survey item sets by ethnicity in CIRP and BPS using orthogonal rotation with PAF extraction. The factors generated from the factor analyses are in Tables 4.2 and 4.3. The variables in the BPS scales had factor loadings of .34 to .84, and the reliabilities of the scales ranged from .63 to .74 (see Table 4.2). For the CIRP data set, items with factor loadings from .34 to .81 were included in the factors; the reliabilities for these factors ranged from .65 to .86 (see Table 4.3). The items included in the scales were summed to construct the factor scales.

Six factors were developed in the BPS data set. Three factors represent students' reasons for choosing their postsecondary institution: Close to Home, Good Reputation, and Less Expensive. The factors were scaled in the direction of the scale name. Therefore, the higher the scale value for Close to Home, the more likely a student decided to choose his or her postsecondary institution because it was nearby. A fourth factor in the BPS data set represents Intellectual Self-Confidence. This scale is similar to the CIRP scale of Intellectual Self-Confidence except that the BPS scale included the measure "self rating: emotional health" and the CIRP scale includes "public speaking ability" and "competitiveness."

The final scales developed in the BPS data set were Peer Contact/Activities and Faculty Contact. The Peer Contact scale measured the extent to which students were involved in clubs, study groups, intramural activities and went places with their friends. The Faculty Contact scale measured how often they met with faculty outside of class, met with advisors, and discussed academic matters with faculty. The CIRP database had two measures of peer contact and one measure of faculty contact that are similar to the BPS scales (see Appendix C). Faculty Contact in CIRP measured whether or not students assisted faculty in teaching a course, worked on a faculty member's research project, or were guests in a faculty member's home. Peer Contact in CIRP is a single-item measure that examines the degree to which students discussed course content with other students, and a final single-item measure of peer contact in the CIRP data set measured students' participation in racial/ethnic organizations (see Appendix C).

There are three additional scales in the CIRP database (see Table 4.3). Students' Social Change Orientation reflects the degree to which students entered college with the goals of promoting racial understanding, taking part in community action, helping others in difficulty, and influencing social values. There are two scales in CIRP that reflect students' perceptions of institutional priorities: Commitment to Social Activism and Commitment to Diversity. Commitment to Social Activism reflects students' perceptions that their postsecondary institution promotes student development: Helps students understand values, develops a community among faculty and students, and creates positive undergraduate experience. Commitment to Diversity is the degree to which institutions were committed to increasing minorities in faculty and administration, recruiting more minority students, and developing an appreciation of multi-cultural society.

There has not been direct evidence of student's perceptions of institutional priorities affecting degree aspirations. However, Social

Activism of college students' peer group has indirect positive effects on students' degree attainment (Astin, 1993b). Commitment to Diversity was expected to have a positive effect on the aspirations of African American students in particular. Commitment to Diversity reflects a supportive institutional climate for racial/ethnic minority students—the kind of climate in which African American students may thrive (Allen, 1992). Therefore, it was predicted that students' perceptions of institutional priorities of Social Activism and Commitment to Diversity should positively predict students' degree plans.

Bivariate relationships

Stage 1 of the analyses included examination of the bivariate relationships in the model. T-tests were used to analyze mean differences in the independent and dependent variables between White and African American students. These analyses determined if there were significant differences between the sub-samples. Mean values, sample sizes and tests of significance were the main products from the analyses.

Chi-square analyses of the first and second time point measures of educational expectations and plans were completed. These analyses illustrated the percentages of individuals whose expectations and plans have risen or lowered since college entry. Chi-square analyses were completed for each ethnicity/race in each data set.

Multivariate Relationships

The main research questions of this study were addressed using ordinary least squares regression. Regression was an appropriate statistical technique to employ because background characteristics, institutional characteristics, and entering aspirations could be controlled. As mentioned in the first part of this chapter, the investigation into differences in educational expectations and educational aspirations between African Americans and White students was conducted in several parts. The multivariate analyses were the main part of the statistical investigation that composed Stages 2 and 3 of the analyses. Table 4.1 details the variables used in each data set for each stage of the regression analyses.

Stage 2 of the analyses began with a base model investigation of students' educational expectations and plans across two data sets. In this stage, regression models were developed using variables that are common across the two data sets. Ordinary least squares hierarchical regression analysis was conducted separately by ethnicity for each data set. Each variable for BPS and CIRP was entered individually in the regression model in the sequence listed in Table 4.1. The coefficients are reported after all the variables entered the model. A comparison of the regression models showed if the independent variables in BPS had similar effects on educational expectations as the independent variables in CIRP had on educational plans.

Stage 3 of the analyses continued with an expanded regression model designed to build on the strengths of each data set. In this stage of the regression analyses, the regression models for each data set tested how measures unique to the data set (over and above the base regression models) affected White and African American students. The results of this analysis provided a comparison within data sets of how particular variables affected expectations and plans for each racial/ethnic group. The CIRP data set had much richer academic ability and involvement measures than BPS, and BPS had more SES and financial aid measures.

The Stage 3 analyses were completed hierarchically, with each variable forced entered into the equation one at a time. This allowed the researcher to observe the effects of particular variable controls with changes in betas at the entry of each variable into the regression. The betas and unstandardized regression coefficients were reported in three places: after the pre-college characteristics entered the regression; after the initial expectations/orientations entered the regression; and after the entry of the final variable. The variables were entered into the regression equation in the order listed in Table 4.1.

LIMITATIONS

Comparing the findings across data sets was the best approach to understanding how African American and White students' aspirations differ and what factors most contribute to the development of students' aspirations in college. However, a direct comparison between the data sets was complicated by the differences in the BPS and CIRP data sets—both differences in the samples and differences in the measures available for analyses.

Because BPS and CIRP survey different populations, a "pure test" of the degree to which differences in the measurement of aspirations affect the prediction of students' third-year degree aspirations was not possible. However, the following chapters detail several strong relationships that can be generalized within each data set and across populations. Therefore, this study can be thought of as a validation of the findings of one data set with the findings in another.

The timing of the surveys was not the same for the BPS and CIRP data sets. The CIRP study surveyed students prior to or during the students' first month in college; the BPS study surveyed students at the end of their first year. The follow-up survey for CIRP was administered to students before their third year in college; in BPS, students were surveyed at the end of their third year. The differences in timing of survey administration mean that students in BPS may have been exposed to a full year of college experience before they have been asked to specify their aspirations, whereas in CIRP, the students were asked their aspirations before beginning college. It is possible, then, that BPS students would experience less change in their aspirations between the two survey administrations than CIRP students because of their greater exposure to postsecondary education.

Some measures were not identical across data sets, and there are some measures that were unique to each data set (see Table 4.1). The differences in the measures may have limited the degree to which the findings in one data set can truly validate the findings in another data set. However, these limitations are not unlike the limitations of reviewing a group of published studies and concluding that similar factors had similar effects in particular outcomes—which is the case in many reviews of literature of the impact of college on students (Pascarella & Terenzini, 1991).

Each data set has weaknesses with regard to the measures available for use in a study of students' degree aspirations. The BPS data set has limited measures of students' college involvement and no measures of students' pre-college achievement; measures that have been shown to be important to take into account when examining the development of student outcomes in college (Astin, 1993b). Therefore, the extent to which ability or SES determines a student's degree expectations could not be studied definitively in the BPS data set because there is no measure of pre-college academic achievement or ability. This was why it was particularly important to attempt a similar model using the CIRP data set, which had good measures of pre-college achievement.

In contrast, the CIRP data set does not contain measures of students' marital status, nor gives more varied measures of socioeconomic status than parent income and parent education, which can aid in interpretation of findings. Students' degree expectations may be constrained by their marital status or other aspects of their socioeconomic status (e.g. material circumstances of their lifestyles) that are unmeasured in CIRP. Therefore, the BPS analyses can compensate for some of the limitations in CIRP.

An additional weakness of the CIRP data set is the response rate for the follow-up survey. Although the response rate for the freshman survey is good (75% or higher for four-year institutions; 50% or higher for community colleges), the follow-up survey had only a 22% response rate. Fortunately, response rates are developed based on over 300 entering student characteristics that could produce response bias. Although the response weights developed for this data set have been shown to adequately adjust for non-response bias in univariate distributions (Dey, 1997), it is possible that response weights could not statistically account for all non-response bias. Furthermore, African American students are less likely to respond to surveys (Dey, 1997), so the effects of institutional and individual characteristics on the aspirations of African American non-respondents may differ somewhat from the findings of this study.

A general weakness of both data sets is that neither data set measured the degree to which students' degree aspirations were affected by interactions with friends, families, and significant others who are external to the campus communities. Also, the extent to which measures that capture the unique perspectives and experiences of African Americans were present in the data set is also a limitation of this study. BPS has no measures that can bring understanding to the unique college experiences of African American students. CIRP has a few measures in the form of participation in ethnic organizations and students' goal of increasing racial understanding, and CIRP has useful institutional measures related to diversity issues. It is clear, however, that more national surveys need to incorporate items that can clearly identify aspects of the unique experiences of students of color in postsecondary institutions.

5
College Students' Degree Expectations and Plans in Two Data Sets

This chapter and the following chapter detail the results of the phases of the study as described in the previous chapter. The chapter is organized in the following fashion: First, an examination of the differences in educational expectations and plans between African American and White students in Beginning Postsecondary Students Longitudinal Study (BPS) and Cooperative Institutional Research Program (CIRP) data sets. The next section of the chapter is a discussion of student mean differences of the independent variables in the regression models—comparing racial/ethnic groups within and between the data sets. The final section of this chapter is an examination of the base regression models for African American and White students for each data set. This section involves comparisons between the regression models across data sets as well as examination of the differences in regression models for African American and White student groups.

CORRELATION ANALYSES OF INITIAL EXPECTATIONS/PLANS AND THIRD YEAR EXPECTATIONS/PLANS

Before discussing the factors that impact the educational expectations and plans of African American and White college students, it is important to discuss how (if at all) both groups of students, in both data sets, differ in terms of initial and third-year expectations/plans.

Table 5.1 shows the correlation coefficients of initial aspirations and later aspirations for African American and White students in both data sets. One might expect that the correlations between initial expectations or plans and the second time point measure (later expectations or plans) would be high, although Astin (1993b) found that the correlation between students' 1985 and 1989 degree plans was moderate at .35. It is interesting to note that the correlation between initial and later aspirations for White and African American students in CIRP is much lower for both groups in

BPS. In addition, the magnitude of the correlation coefficients for African Americans is lower in BPS and CIRP than it is for White students. That is, although the correlations remain moderate, it is more difficult to predict third year degree aspirations from initial aspirations for African American students than for White students in both data sets.

Table 5.1 Correlations between Initial Expectations/Plans and Third Year Expectations/Plans: BPS and CIRP Data sets by Racial/Ethnic Group

	African American	White
BPS (expectations)	.37**	.62**
CIRP (plans)	.24**	.46**

$^{**}p \leq .01$

Therefore, for students in the CIRP data set, factors other than initial aspirations are likely to be related to later degree aspirations. It also appears as if in comparison to White students, African American students are more likely to change their degree aspirations.

CHANGES IN DEGREE EXPECTATIONS AND PLANS BY RACIAL GROUP

The correlation analyses indicate that the students in both data sets (particularly African American students in BPS and CIRP and White students in CIRP) tend to change their degree expectations and plans over time. This section examines how students are distributed across the degree expectations/plans categories at both time points in both data sets. The final part of this section examines the trends within and between data sets with regard to expectations/plans changes over time.

BPS 90:92

Table 5.2 shows the distribution of African American and White students' educational expectations by response category in the BPS data set. Chi-square analyses were performed two ways: 1) initial expectations by racial/ethnic group; and 2) later expectations by racial/ethnic group. The first analysis revealed a significant change in degree aspirations over the early years of college for each racial/ethnic group. Over 89% (note: all percentages described in this section are rounded) of the African American students in 1990 expected to earn a Bachelor's or higher degree, with 53% expecting to earn a Master's or advanced professional/Ph.D. degree. This percentage dropped slightly in the third year of college with 87% of African American students expecting to earn a Bachelor's or higher degree, and 49% expecting to earn a Master's or more advanced degree.

For White students, fewer expected to earn a Bachelor's or higher degree (81%) in 1990, with 47% expecting to earn a Master's or advanced professional/Ph.D. degree. However, in 1992, only 77% of White students expected to earn a Bachelor's or higher degree with 42% expecting to earn a Master's or higher degree.

Chi-square analyses were also performed on African American and White students' initial expectations. The results of the analyses indicate no significant differences between African American and White students in their distribution across categories of initial expectations at college entry.

This is not true for degree expectations measured at the second time point, however. There is a statistical difference between African American and White students: African Americans tend to have higher degree expectations than White students at the second time point. Examination of Table 5.2 indicates that a much higher percentage of African American students (34%) expect to earn a Master's degree in comparison to White students (26%). In addition, a higher percentage of White students (23%) expect to earn less than a Bachelor's degree in the second time point than African American students (13%). The higher degree expectations of African American students indicate that there are particular institutional environments or other factors that may heighten the degree expectations of African American students. This may be particularly true since the correlation between initial and later expectations is so high for White students (Table 5.1), and there are no differences in the distribution of White and African American students across degree expectations category in the first time point.

Table 5.2 Educational Expectations by Racial/Ethnic Group in BPS Data set

	African American N=356		White N=357	
	1990	1992	1990	1992
Two years or less of college or vocational education	3.8	3.2	7.0	6.5
Two or more years of college/vocational education	7.0	10.2	11.6	16.1
Bachelor's Degree	36.7	37.8	34.4	35.0
Master's Degree	39.8	34.0	34.7	26.1
Professional/Ph.D.	12.7	14.8	12.3	16.3
Significance of Chi-Square for Initial Expectations[1]	ns			
Significance of Chi-Square for Later Expectations[2]	***			

1 Chi-square comparing Initial Expectations for African American and White students.
2 Chi-square comparing Later Expectations for African American and White students.
***$p \leq .001$

Overall, the pattern of changes in educational expectations is similar across both White and African American students: Compared to 1990, more students in 1992 expected to earn a doctoral or advanced professional degree, and fewer students in 1992 expected to earn a Master's degree. Slightly more students in 1992 expected to earn Bachelor's degrees, more students expected to earn two or more years of college/vocational education, and fewer students expected to earn two or less years of college or vocational education.

Since Table 5.2 shows significant differences in the distribution of White and African American students across degree expectations categories at the second time point, it is important to further investigate which students in each degree category were most likely to change their degree expectations. Table 5.3 shows the distribution of educational expectations by racial/ethnic group in the BPS data set and the degree to which students lowered or raised their expectations after two years of college. The chi-square analysis indicates that there are no significant differences between White and African American students in the overall percentages of students whose expectations were lowered, raised, or stayed the same.

Table 5.3 Changes in Educational Expectations by Racial/Ethnic Group in BPS Data set

	African Americans N=356			White N=357		
	Lowered	Same	Raised	Lowered	Same	Raised
Two years or less of college or vocational education		8.4	91.6		60.4	39.6
Two or more years of college/vocational education	.9	30.9	68.2	20.0	49.8	30.2
Bachelor's Degree	13.0	50.2	36.9	21.4	53.1	25.5
Master's Degree	40.6	43.3	16.1	34.5	39.2	26.3
Professional/Ph.D.	47.1	52.8		54.2	45.8	
Overall Changes in Expectations	28.2	44.8	27.0	24.2	47.5	28.4

Note: Chi-square analyses show no significant differences between White and African American students in the distribution of students whose expectations were lowered, raised, or stayed the same.

As expected, Table 5.3 indicates the phenomenon of "regression to the mean", whereby students at the extremes of the degree expectations categories (advanced professional/ doctoral degree or two years or fewer of postsecondary education) tend to move toward the middle. In other words, students who expect to earn two years or less of postsecondary education cannot lower their expectations (since that is the lowest category), so they either keep their expectations the same or raise them. Most of the White students (60%), who at college entry reported expecting to earn two years or fewer of college or vocational education, held the same expectations two years later. This is not true for African Americans: Nearly all African Americans (92%) who in 1990 reported expecting to earn two years or less of college or vocational education raised their expectations two years later.

Of the students who expected to earn a Bachelor's degree, about half of the White (53%) and African American (50%) students kept their expectations the same. The other half of White student Bachelor's degree aspirants were about evenly split between those who raised their expectations (26%) and those who lowered them (21%). For African American students, the half who did not keep their expectations at the same level, most (37%) raised their expectations, and 13% lowered them.

White students who had Master's degree expectations tend to be fairly evenly divided between those who lowered, raised, and kept their expectations the same, though most (39%) of the students kept their degree expectations the same. Most of the African American Master's degree aspirants tended to keep their expectations the same (43%) or lower their expectations (41%). Finally, of the doctoral/advanced professional degree aspirants, most of the White students (54%) lowered their expectations. Most of the African American students (53%) maintained the same expectations.

CIRP 88:90

Table 5.4 shows the distribution of African American and White students' educational plans by response category in the BPS data set. As with the BPS data set, chi-square analyses were performed two ways on the CIRP data set: 1) initial expectations by racial/ethnic group; and 2) later expectations by racial/ethnic group. When comparing African American and White students' initial expectations with later expectations, there is a significant difference in the distribution of students among categories of initial plans and later plans within each racial group.

Table 5.4 Degree Plans by Racial/Ethnic Group in CIRP Data set

	African American N=266		White N=283	
	1988	1990	1988	1990
No Degree	2.1	8.1	1.0	.8
Vocational Certificate	.2	.2	.2	.3
Associate Degree	1.1	2.8	1.3	4.0
Bachelor's Degree	22.9	23.5	23.3	36.4
Master's Degree	45.2	39.3	56.8	41.1
Doctorate/Advanced Professional	28.6	26.1	17.5	17.3
Significance of Chi-square for Initial/Later Plans[1]		***		***
Significance of Chi-Square for Initial Plans[2]	*			
Significance of Chi-Square for Later Plans[3]	***			

[1] Chi-square of Initial/Later Plans within each racial/ethnic group.
[2] Chi-square comparing Initial Plans for African American and White students.
[3] Chi-square comparing Later Plans for African American and White students.
*p ≤.05; ***p ≤.001

Over 96% of the African American students in 1988 planned to earn a Bachelor's or higher degree, with 74% expecting to earn a Master's or advanced professional/Ph.D. degree. These percentages changed in the third year of college (1990) with 89% of African American students expecting to earn a Bachelor's or higher degree, 65% expecting to earn a Master's or more advanced degree.

For White students in CIRP, a similar percentage plan to earn a Bachelor's or higher degree (98%) in 1988, with 74% expecting to earn a Master's or advanced professional/Ph.D. degree. However, in 1990, 95% of White students expected to earn a Bachelor's or higher degree with 58% expecting to earn a Master's or higher degree.

Chi-square analyses were performed on African American and White students' initial expectations. In contrast to BPS, the results of the analyses show significant ($p \leq .05$) differences between African American and White students in their distribution across each category of initial expectations at college entry. For instance, in 1998 more White students (57%) than African American students (45%) planned to earn Master's degrees.

This is also true for degree plans measured at the second time point. There is a statistically significant difference ($p \leq .001$) between African American and White students. Examination of Table 5.4 indicates that a higher percentage of African American students (26%) planned to earn a Doctoral/Advanced Professional degree in comparison to White students (17%). In addition, a higher percentage of African American students (11%) expected to earn less than a Bachelor's degree in the second time point than White students (5%). The main explanation for the higher percentages of students at the second time point planning to earn less than a Bachelor's degree is the sharp increase in African American students who planned to earn no degree. The percentage of African American students who expected to earn no degree increased from 2.1% in 1988 to 8.1% in 1990. In contrast, the percentage for White students decreased slightly during the same time period from 1.0% to .8%.

Far fewer African American students planned to earn only a Bachelor's degree than White students in the CIRP sample. The percentage of African American students who planned to earn a Bachelor's degree slightly increased to 23.5% in 1990, but the percentage of White students who planned to earn a Bachelor's degree increased by over 13 percentage points to 36.4%. Table 5.4 shows that the growth in the percentage of White students planning to earn only a Bachelor's degree seems to occur because students who in 1988 planned to earn a Master's degree lowered their degree plans to a Bachelor's degree. Finally, the percentages of students who planned to earn a Ph.D. or advanced professional degree remained similar over time within each racial/ethnic group. About 17% of White students in 1988 and 1990 planned to earn a Ph.D. or advanced professional degree. For African American students, 28.6% in 1988 and 26.1% in 1990 planned to earn a doctorate or advanced professional degree.

The results of the chi-square analyses are particularly interesting in light of the fact that there were no significant mean differences between White and African Americans neither in their initial degree plans nor for the later measure (see Table 5.6 later in this chapter). More African Americans in comparison to White students (at both time points) have doctoral degree plans. More White students had Bachelor's and Associate degree plans in 1990, but a much higher percentage of African American students plan to earn no degree at the second time point.

The biggest drop occurs for students who plan to earn Master's degrees. There is a 16% decrease for White students and a 6% decrease for African American students in the percentages of students who planned to earn a Master's degree in the first time point and in the second time point. Table 5.5 shows the distribution of CIRP students who raised, lowered, or kept degree plans the same. As with the BPS data set, CIRP analyses also show "regression to the mean" in the CIRP data set. All of the White and African American students who had planned to earn no degree or a vocational certificate in 1988 planned to earn a higher degree in 1990. In addition, two-thirds of the White students who planned to earn an Associate's degree kept their degree plans unchanged, the other one-third of students planned to earn a higher degree in 1990. All of the African American students who initially planned to earn an Associate's degree planned to earn a higher degree by 1990.

Nearly two-thirds of the White students (63%) who planned to earn a Bachelor's degree kept their degree plans the same in 1990; in contrast, about two-thirds of African American students (62%) who planned to earn a Bachelor's degree in 1988 raised their plans in 1990. Half of the White students (52%) who planned to earn a Master's degree kept the same degree plans two years later, but 35% lowered their plans. Of the African American CIRP Master's degree aspirants, 41% kept their plans the same, and 44% lowered their plans.

Table 5.5 Changes in Degree Plans by Racial/Ethnic Group in CIRP Data set

	African Americans N=266			White N=283		
	Lowered	Same	Raised	Lowered	Same	Raised
No Degree			100.0			100.0
Vocational Certificate			100.0			100.0
Associate Degree			100.0		66.7	33.3
Bachelor's Degree	3.7	34.7	61.6	7.5	63.6	29.0
Master's Degree	44.4	40.8	14.9	35.3	51.7	13.0
Doctorate/Advanced Professional	33.9	66.1		46.5	53.6	
Overall Changes in Plans	34.1	39.2	26.7	29.9	47.5	22.6

Note: Chi-square analyses show no significant differences between White and African American students in the distribution of students whose plans were lowered, raised, or stayed the same.

Overall, the patterns of aspirations across both data sets do not show large portions of White or African American student samples leaving higher education. However, there are particular areas that are cause for alarm. In the CIRP data set, although African Americans are more likely to raise their degree plans than White students, over one-third of the African American students lowered their plans. The main problem with the lowering of degree plans is which students lower their expectations and plans. As discussed above, 8% of African Americans in the CIRP data set plan to receive no degree. The African Americans who in 1988 planned to receive no degree, a vocational certificate, or an associate degree raised their degree plans by 1990. Thus, the 8% of African Americans who in 1990 plan to receive no degree are the students who, two years earlier planned to receive at least a Bachelor's degree.

General patterns of White and African American students' degree aspirations in BPS and CIRP are quite different (see Tables 5.2 and 5.4). CIRP students tended to have higher degree aspirations than BPS students—nearly all of the students in CIRP (more than 96%) initially planned to earn a Bachelor's or more advanced degree. For BPS students more than 81% of the students expected to earn a Bachelor's or more advanced degree. It is interesting how African American and White students' degree aspirations change over time. The percentage of White students in BPS who expected to earn a Bachelor's degree or higher decreased by 4% from 1990 to 1992, and for African American students the decrease was 3%. However, for CIRP students, there were larger between-group differences: White students who planned to earn a Bachelor's degree or higher decreased by 3% from 1988 to 1990 and for African Americans the percentage decreased by 8%. Therefore, the degree expectations of African American students in BPS seem to be supported slightly more often than the expectations of White students, but the degree plans of White students in CIRP seem to be supported to a greater extent than those for African American students in CIRP. In what ways do the groups of students differ on other variables used in the study? The next section of this chapter details the results of analyses of mean and frequency differences completed by group.

GROUP DIFFERENCES WITHIN AND BETWEEN THE DATA SETS

This section describes the characteristics of the African American and White samples in each data set and how the groups compare across the BPS and CIRP data sets. The purpose of this section is first to highlight the differences between the African American and White students in each data set and second to highlight the differences between the data sets.

Table 5.6 details the means, standard deviations, and significant differences of every variable in the BPS and CIRP regression models (base and full) in the CIRP and BPS data sets. The variables used in the base regression model are italicized in Table 5.6 with superscript notes indicating the results of cross-data set group comparisons. Group comparisons within each data set include t-test statistics for continuous variables (e.g. educational expectations/plans, intellectual self-confidence), and chi-square statistics for dichotomous variables (e.g. gender, marital status, attendance at a private university). The level of significance and the type of statistic used is indicated on the table.

Table 5.6 Frequencies, Means, and Standard Deviations of Variables in the BPS and CIRP Data sets by Race/Ethnicity

Variables	BPS					CIRP				
	African American N=355		White N=357		Mean Difference	African American N=266		White N=283		Mean Difference
	Mean	St. Dev.	Mean	St. Dev.		Mean	St. Dev.	Mean	St. Dev.	
Dependent Variable										
Degree Expectations	3.48	.94	3.30	1.15	*	—	—	—	—	
Degree Plans	—	—	—	—		4.64	1.34	4.69	.87	
Pre-college characteristics										
Female[2]	60%	.49	54%	.50		46%	.50	43%	.50	
Age[4]	20.05	4.29	22.21	9.87	***	3.20	.71	3.18	.52	
Father's Educational Attainment[4]	5.29	2.55	5.93	2.98	**	4.62	1.96	5.46	1.91	***
Mother's Educational Attainment[4]	5.12	2.70	5.53	2.80	*	4.74	1.84	4.65	1.76	
Parent Income[1]	6.33	2.79	7.92	3.16	***	6.75	3.39	9.41	2.97	***
Number of Children	.32	.71	.41	1.11		—	—	—	—	
Married	15%	.36	9%	.29		—	—	—	—	
Separated/Divorced	6%	.23	4%	.20		—	—	—	—	
Items Owned	18.50	2.04	19.42	2.11	***	—	—	—	—	
High School GPA	—	—	—	—		4.48	4.62	5.61	1.55	***
Initial Expectations/Orientations										
Degree Expectations	3.50	.92	3.43	.98		—	—	—	—	
Degree Plans	—	—	—	—		4.92	.96	4.85	.78	
Intellectual Self-Confidence[4]	2.38	.40	2.37	.37		3.70	.69	3.67	.66	
First Choice[2]	73%	.44	85%	.36	###	5%	.21	1%	.12	#
Second Choice	—	—	—	—		11%	.31	5%	.22	#
Third Choice	—	—	—	—		34%	.47	25%	.43	#
Distance From Home[1]	2.84	1.45	3.16	1.41	**	4.30	1.48	4.20	1.22	
Good reputation	2.19	.57	2.12	.50						
Close to Home	2.10	.68	1.98	.67	*	—	—	—	—	
Less Expensive	1.97	.78	1.77	.75	***	—	—	—	—	
Social Change Orientation			—	—		2.74	.58	2.32	.59	***
Institutional Characteristics										
Control[2] *(Private)*	14%	.34	25%	.43	###	55%	.50	46%	.50	#
Level[2] *(4-year)*	45%	.50	52%	.50		96%	.20	89%	.32	
Single Sex	—	—	—	—		3%	.18	3%	.16	
HBCU[3]	9%	.28	0%	.00	###	66%	.48	≤1%	.07	###

Percent African American Enrollment	.27	.30	.06	.05	***	—	—	—	—	
Tuition Cost	1894.57	2613.49	3013.34	3712.63	***	—	—	—	—	
Size	9250.34	8741.00	9975.45	10126.22		—	—	—	—	
Institutional Priorities										
Commitment to Social Activism	—	—	—	—		3.12	.65	2.98	.56	**
Commitment to Diversity	—	—	—	—		2.98	.76	2.73	.70	***
Financial Aid/Work										
Borrow/Loans[4]	803.92	1797.05	877.23	2517.14		6.01	2.63	5.44	2.41	**
Scholarship[4]	1362.73	2234.16	1155.18	2118.96		5.26	2.98	3.88	1.95	***
Work Study[4]	127.30	369.39	59.48	244.27	**	1.38	.89	1.21	.68	*
Hours spent working[4]	20.33	15.47	21.80	16.97		4.40	2.53	4.17	2.64	
Number of Jobs	1.32	.85	1.41	.96		—	—	—	—	
Involvement										
Faculty Contact[4]	2.69	.78	2.39	.80	***	1.09	.20	1.10	.20	
Peer Contact[4]	2.34	.74	2.11	.75	***	2.66	.52	2.66	.49	
Participated in ethnic organizations	—	—	—	—		24%	.43	4%	.20	###
Achievement										
College GPA	—	—	—	—		2.85	1.17	3.96	1.10	***

Note: Please see Appendix C for the scaling of the variables in each data set.

Note: Measures in italics are measures that both data sets have in common.

—: measure not in data set

* $p \leq .05$; ** $p \leq .01$; *** $p \leq .001$ for t-test analyses

$p \leq .05$; ## $p \leq .01$; ### $p \leq .001$ for chi-square analyses

1 Analyses of mean differences across data sets indicate there is a significant difference ($p \leq .001$) between African American students in BPS and CIRP and between White students in BPS and CIRP on this measure.

2 Analyses of frequency distributions across data sets indicate that there is a significant difference ($p \leq .01$) between the frequency of occurrence for African American students in BPS and CIRP and for White students in BPS and CIRP

3 Analyses of frequency distributions across data sets indicate that there is a significant difference ($p \leq .01$) between the frequency of occurrence for African American students only in BPS and CIRP.

4 Cross-data sets analyses of mean differences were not completed because measures have different scaling in BPS and CIRP. Please see Appendix C for details on scaling of measures.

The organization of this section is as follows: The differences between the African American and White student groups in the BPS data set are examined, followed by a description of the differences between African American and White students in the CIRP data set. The final part of this section describes the ways in which the samples of BPS and CIRP are similar and different—with further discussion on the ways in which the unique characteristics of the samples may influence the results of the regression analyses.

Differences Between Racial Groups in BPS: 90:92

There are a number of differences between African Americans and White students in the BPS sample. Please see Appendix C for the scaling of the measures used in each data set. Table 5.6 shows that African Americans have significantly higher degree expectations than White students at the second time point, although the mean difference is small; there is no significant difference between the groups in expectations at the first time point.

Both groups differ significantly on a number of pre-college characteristics. The most significant differences between African American and White students ($p \leq .001$) are age, parent income, and the SES measure—Items Owned. The White students in the BPS sample tend to be older than the African American students; White students' parents tend to have higher income levels than the African American students' parents; and African American students claim fewer major items owned than White students (e.g. dishwasher, own room, several books, VCR, etc.).

There are two other pre-college characteristics that are significantly different for African American and White college students in BPS: Father's and mother's educational attainment. White students' fathers ($p \leq .01$) and mothers ($p \leq .05$) tend to have earned higher levels of education than African American students' fathers and mothers. However, there are no significant differences between White and African American students in the rate at which they are married, separated or divorced, or in the number of children they had at time of attendance in a post-secondary institution.

Therefore, African Americans as a group tend to have a lower average on every measure of socioeconomic status in the BPS data set (parents' education, parents' income, major items owned by family) than White students. This finding is supported by Baker and Vélez (1996) who state that African Americans tend to come from lower SES backgrounds more often than White students. The lower SES backgrounds of African Americans could indicate that receipt of financial aid may influence their degree goals to a greater extent than White students.

The next category of independent measures in Table 5.6 is Initial Expectations/ Orientations, which include initial degree expectations, intellectual self-confidence, distance institution is from home, and reasons for choosing institution. The most significant differences between African American and White students ($p \leq .001$) is that African Americans cite lower cost as a reason they attended their college or university more often than White students. It makes sense that African Americans tended to choose less expensive institutions, given that African Americans in the BPS data set tend to be from lower SES backgrounds than the White students. This finding is supported by the research of Seneca and Taussig (1987) who found students "tend to enroll at the school with the lowest net costs" (p. 355).

The processes of choosing which postsecondary institution to attend seem to differ by racial/ethnic group in the BPS data set—particularly in the areas of attendance at first choice institution, attendance at an institution farther away from home, and choosing an institution closer to one's home. At the $p \leq .001$ level of significance, African Americans (73%) attend their first choice institution less often than White students (85%). These results support the findings of Maxey et al. (1995) and Hurtado et al. (1997). One explanation given for African Americans attending their first choice institution in lower proportions than White students is that African Americans tend to spend a shorter amount of time preparing for college attendance than White students (Maxey et al., 1995).

A larger proportion of White students compared to African American students also tend to go to institutions farther away from home ($p \leq .01$). Similar to this finding, African Americans tend to mention more often that one of the reasons for attending their current postsecondary institution is because it is close to their homes. The groups do not significantly differ in terms of their levels of intellectual self-confidence, their initial degree expectations, or the extent to which they selected their postsecondary institution because it has a good reputation.

The results of the chi-square and t-test analyses also show that African Americans and White students attend different kinds of institutions. White students (25%) attend private institutions in greater proportions than African American students (14%). Not surprisingly, African Americans attend HBCUs in greater numbers than White students, and African Americans attend institutions with higher enrollments of African American students than White students do. Indeed, no White students in the sample attend HBCUs, while 9% of the African Americans attend HBCUs. Although there is no significant difference in the rate with which both racial/ethnic groups attend two-year vs. four-year institutions, or size of institution, White students tend to attend higher-cost institutions in much greater numbers than African American students do. Since African Americans in this data set tend to have fewer financial resources compared to White students, it is expected that African Americans would attend lower cost institutions.

Despite the fact that African Americans and White students vary significantly in socioeconomic status, these differences are not uniformly reflected in the levels of financial aid received. There is only one significant difference between the groups in financial aid variables: African Americans tend to receive more financial aid in the form of work study than White students. However, it is interesting to note that African American students tend to have more contact with faculty and their peers than White students do. This may have much to do with the type of colleges they have chosen.

Differences Within CIRP: 88:90

The differences between African American and White students in the CIRP data set are also shown in Table 5.6. There are no significant mean differences between African American and White students' degree plans after their second year of college, nor are there significant mean differences between the groups' degree plans before college. However, earlier in this chapter (Table 5.4) is a discussion of the differences between the distribution of students between the categories of degree plans. Although the means between the groups are not statistically different, a higher percentage of African Americans plan to earn a doctorate at college entry and at the third year of college in comparison to White students. A higher percentage of White students plan to earn a Master's degree at both points in time.

In terms of pre-college characteristics (gender, age, SES measures, and high school GPA), White students tend to have higher parental income and higher father educational attainments than African American students ($p \leq .001$). The other SES measure in the CIRP data set, mother's educational attainment, is not significantly different for African American and White students. Therefore, as with BPS, the African American students in CIRP tend to be lower socioeconomic status compared to White students.

The pre-college achievement measure in CIRP is high school grade point average. White students in this data set have a much higher high school GPA than African American students in the sample. Given African Americans' lower SES and lower GPA in comparison to White students, analyses in the CIRP data set provided a direct test of the extent to which pre-college academic performance and SES (contest or sponsored mobility) affect later degree plans.

In terms of the Initial Expectations/Orientations measures (Intellectual Self-Confidence, choice of institution, distance institution is from home, and students' Social Change Orientation), the measure with the most significant mean difference ($p \leq .001$) is Social Change Orientation. African American students more often perceive themselves as having a social change orientation—taking part in community action, promoting racial understanding, helping others in difficulty—than White students. The other variables that are significantly different for African American and White students are the choice measures. African Americans tended to report more often that they are currently attending their first choice (5%

vs. 1%), second choice (11% vs. 5%) or third choice (34% vs. 25%) institution in comparison to White students. Therefore, 50% of the African American students (as compared to 31% of White students) in the CIRP sample are attending an institution they ranked as first through third. This finding indicates several things. First, that African Americans and White students in CIRP tend to apply to many colleges; obviously, in order to attend a school that is lower than 3rd choice, a student must have applied to at least 4 institutions.

Second, the fact that African Americans more often attend their first through third choice institutions may reflect their lower pre-college academic credentials and their lower SES. In BPS, the students tend to apply to only one institution (Hurtado et al., 1997), and they tend to be lower SES than the students in CIRP (see Table 5.6). Therefore, it may be that students who have higher pre-college achievement and those who are from higher SES backgrounds have more choices of institutions to attend and therefore attend a fourth or lower choice institution. Although the relatively low frequency with which White and African American students in CIRP attend their first choice institution indicates that students: either are not accepted into their institutions of top choice; or students changed their minds between the time they were accepted and when attendance decisions needed to be made (Maxey et al., 1995).

White and African American students tended to go to different types of institutions in the CIRP data set. African American students (55%) attended private institutions in greater numbers than White students (46%). Again, very few White students (less than 1%) attended HBCUs while, the majority of African American students the CIRP sample attended HBCUs (66%). There are no significant differences between the racial/ethnic groups in the rates at which they attend single-sex institutions, however. Compared to White students, African Americans tend to characterize their institutions as being more committed to social activism and diversity.

There are significant differences between White and African American students in the financial aid variables. African American students were more likely to borrow funds or receive loans than White students. African American students also were more likely to receive more funds in the form of scholarships and work study awards than White students. Since African American students have much lower parental income levels than White students in CIRP, this is not a surprising finding.

Although there were no significant differences in the frequencies with which African American and White students interact with faculty members and their peers, far more African American students participated in ethnic organizations than White students. Finally, on average, White students reported higher college grade point averages than African American students. White students tended to report having an A average in college, African American students report having an average of B. Given the significantly higher levels of high school grade point averages reported by White students, the higher college GPAs is not a surprising finding. Therefore, White students in the CIRP sample were higher achieving than African American students—both pre-college and after two years in college, and yet have degree plans that were similar. The next section discusses how the samples in the CIRP and BPS data sets compare to each other.

Differences Between BPS and CIRP Samples

This section discusses the similarities and differences between African American and White students in the BPS and CIRP data sets. The independent measures in Table 5.6 that are italicized are the measures that are similar across data sets. Measures with a superscript notation indicate which cross-data set analyses of mean and frequency differences were completed.

Four pre-college characteristics are similar across BPS and CIRP—gender, age, parent's education and parents' income. There are more women in the BPS sample than in the CIRP sample ($p \leq .01$). In the BPS sample 60% of the African American students and 54% of the White students are women. Less than half (46% of African Americans, 43% of White students) of the CIRP sample are women. There are stark differences in the levels of parental income between BPS and CIRP. African Americans' parent income in CIRP is significantly higher ($p \leq .01$) than African Americans' parent income in BPS, though African Americans across both data sets tend to report levels of parental income between $25,000 and $30,000. White students in CIRP also have a much higher income ($p \leq .01$) than White students in BPS. White students in CIRP report parental income levels of $40,000–$50,000 in comparison to the average parental income levels of White students in BPS close to the $35,000 to $40,000 range. Therefore, on at least one of the SES measures, the CIRP students have much higher mean averages than BPS students.

The variables age and parent's educational attainment were measured on different scales in BPS and CIRP (see Appendix C for details on scaling), so no cross-data set analyses were completed. However, some comparisons can be made. The students in CIRP tend to be younger in comparison to the students in BPS. The average age for African Americans in BPS is just over 20, and just over 22 for White students. For CIRP, the average age for White and African American students is about 18 (category 3 indicates student is 18 years old). Therefore, the CIRP data may represent a more traditional-aged population than the BPS data.

The levels of parental education in the BPS and the CIRP tend to be similar, with White and African American students in BPS reporting their parents as having 1–2 years of vocational education on average (5=1–2 years of vocational school; 6=more than two years of vocational education). White and African American students in CIRP report their parents as having some postsecondary education (4=postsecondary school other than college; 5=some college; 6=college degree). However, it seems the White students in CIRP report more often that their fathers have some college education or more compared to African Americans in CIRP or either racial group in BPS. The BPS students, therefore, tend to be of lower SES status than the CIRP students. Perhaps financial aid measures for BPS students will have a greater impact on their degree expectations given their lower resources for postsecondary institution attendance.

More students in BPS than CIRP stated they attended their first choice institutions ($p \leq .01$), with 85% of the White students and 73% of the African American students attending their first choice college or university. The students in CIRP attended their first choice institution in much smaller numbers (5% for African Americans and 11% for White students). One explanation for this finding is that students in CIRP seem to apply to more institutions. Previous studies using BPS data have found that the students tend to apply to fewer institutions (Hurtado et al., 1997). Most of the White students in CIRP (69%) and half of the African American students (50%) indicated that the postsecondary institution they attended is their fourth choice or lower. Therefore, most of the CIRP students applied to at least 4 institutions, which is a much higher number than the BPS average number of one institution as reported by Hurtado et al. (1997).

Students in CIRP typically attend institutions that are much farther away from home than students in BPS ($p \leq .01$). CIRP students tend to go to colleges and universities that are more than 50 miles away. African American BPS students attend institutions less than 11 miles away, White students in BPS attend institutions that are 11–50 miles away. Since students in BPS are older, come from lower SES backgrounds, and tend to apply to only one institution (Hurtado et al., 1997), it seems consistent that students in BPS would be attending institutions closer to their homes. Students living 50 miles or less away from their postsecondary institution could live at home and commute to school if necessary. This may be one way students can minimize the costs of college.

The CIRP sample is quite different from the BPS sample in terms of the type of institutions the students attend. Most of the students in CIRP attend 4-year institutions (96% for African Americans, 89% for White students). In BPS, about half the students attend four-year institutions (46% for African Americans, 52% for White students). More CIRP students (55% of African American students, 46% of White students) attend private institutions than BPS students do (14% African American and 25% White students). Seven times as many African Americans in CIRP attend HBCUs (66%) than African Americans in BPS (9%). These findings are consistent with the earlier comparisons between BPS and CIRP students' socioeconomic status. Several researchers have found that a student's SES is significantly related to the type of postsecondary institution he or she attends. Lower SES students far more often attend two-year (rather than four-year) institutions (Karabel & Astin, 1975). Lower SES students are also more likely to attend public (rather than private) institutions (Pascarella et al., 1992). BPS students tend to be lower SES than CIRP students are and attend public institutions in greater proportions than CIRP students do. BPS students also attend two-year institutions in greater proportions.

The rates at which students receive work-study awards across the data sets are similar. Both groups in each data set average up to $500 in work study awards. One final difference between the groups in each data set with regard to financial aid/work is in the hours students spent working. Students in BPS averaged 20 or more hours of week working. CIRP students averaged only approximately 3–5 hours of work a week.

The comparisons between the CIRP and BPS samples suggest a few ways in which the base regression models may differ: The role of institutional characteristics and experiences and the role of financial aid measures in affecting students' aspirations. Since the students in the BPS sample attend their first choice institution in greater numbers (and thus may not have the variety of institutional options available to them like many of the CIRP students), the characteristics of their postsecondary institutions may impact the BPS students to a greater extent. Also, CIRP students in general tend to receive more financial aid and work more hours per week than BPS students do. Therefore, the financial aid/work of students in CIRP may affect their degree plans to a greater extent compared to the students in BPS.

Earlier in this chapter I discussed that the degree aspirations of the students in the Beginning Postsecondary Students Longitudinal Study (BPS) are lower than the aspirations of the students in the Cooperative Institutional Research Program (CIRP) study. A central question I sought to investigate is if the lower degree expectations of students in BPS are a result of their lower socioeconomic status, the types of institutions the students attend, or other factors? The last section of this chapter investigates a base regression model for African American and White students to examine if variables that are consistent across both data sets affect degree plans and expectations.

BASE REGRESSION MODEL OF BPS AND CIRP DATA SETS BY RACE

This section examines students' pre-college characteristics and college experiences that affect their later aspirations. I discuss the base regression model in the BPS data set, and follow this with a discussion of the regression model in the CIRP data sets. The chapter concludes with a comparison of the regression models in both data sets.

Table 5.7 shows the results of the base regression models by race/ethnicity for the BPS and CIRP data sets. The R^2 for each racial/ethnic group across both data sets ranges from .28 and .29 (for African American and White students respectively in the CIRP data set) to .34 and .59 for African

American and White students respectively in BPS. The table shows the standardized regression coefficients (Betas) for the models. Please see Table D1 in Appendix D for unstandardized coefficients.

BPS Base Regression Model

Of the pre-college characteristics—gender, age, parents' education, and parents' income—only mother's education and student's age significantly

Table 5.7 Base Regression Model of BPS and CIRP Data sets by Race/Ethnicity on Educational Expectations and Plans[1]

	BPS		CIRP	
Variables	African American N=356	White N=357	African American N=266	White N=283
Pre-college characteristics				
Female	-.04	.06	.10	.08
Age	.00	-.25***	-.12*	-.10
Father's Educational Attainment	.07	.07	.12	.05
Mother's Educational Attainment	.16**	.10*	-.02	-.01
Parent Income	-.02	-.05	-.11	.05
Initial Expectations/Orientations				
Educational Plans/Expectations	.20***	.38***	.16*	.48***
Intellectual Self-Confidence	-.14**	.13***	.09	-.00
First Choice	-.11*	-.07*	.03	.03
Distance From Home	-.02	-.02	.21**	.09
Institutional Characteristics				
Control (private)	-.06	.10*	-.09	-.05
Level (4-year institution)	.27***	.17***	-.04	-.05
HBCU	.14**	—	-.06	.08
Financial Aid/Work				
Borrow/Loans	.09	.01	.12	.10
Scholarship	.08	-.02	-.38***	.06
Work Study	-.03	-.03	.16**	.06
Hours spent working	-.00	-.04	.02	-.18**
Involvement				
Faculty Contact	.15**	-.04	-.01	-.02
Peer Contact	-.06	.05	.18**	.00
R^2	.34	.59	.28	.29

[1] Standardized regression coefficients (Betas) are reported. Please see Table D1 in Appendix D for unstandardized coefficients.
—: Variable did not enter regression. No White students attended HBCUs in the BPS sample.
* p≤.05; **p≤.01; ***p≤.001

affect either African American or White students' degree expectations. The only pre-college characteristic that significantly predicts third year educational expectations for African Americans is mother's educational attainment (p≤.01). African American students whose mothers have higher educational attainment tend to have higher educational expectations. The same is true for White students. White students whose mothers have higher educational attainment tend to have higher degree expectations (p≤.05).

A much stronger pre-college predictor of degree expectations for White students is age. Younger White students are much more likely to have higher degree expectations than older students ($p \leq .001$).

All but one of the initial expectations/orientations measures (degree expectations, intellectual self-confidence, choice of institution, distance institution is from home) significantly predicts degree expectations after the third year of college. Initial degree expectations is the strongest predictor of any of the independent variables for White students and the second strongest predictor for African American students ($p \leq .001$). Those students who have higher degree expectations their first year of college tend to have higher degree expectations in the third year. Intellectual Self-Confidence has opposite effects for African American and White students: negative effects for African American students and positive effects for White students. Therefore, African American students with lower levels of Intellectual Self-Confidence the first year of college tend to have higher levels of degree expectations two years later. White students with higher levels of Intellectual Self-Confidence the first year of college tend to have higher levels of degree expectations.

The explanation for the opposite effect of Intellectual Self-Confidence for African American and White students can be determined from close examination of the correlation matrix (see Appendix E) and the regression models for BPS students. The significant effect of Intellectual Self-Confidence on second-time-point degree expectations is the result of a suppressor effect (Astin, 1993a; Pedhazur, 1997).

Suppressor effect is a phenomenon by which an independent variable that has close to zero correlation with the dependent variable becomes a significant predictor of the dependent variable when it is included in the multiple regression analysis (Pedhazur, 1997). The independent variable may have a low correlation with the dependent variable, but a moderate to strong correlation with another of the predictor variables and therefore appears to be a significant predictor in the regression analysis. Therefore, for African American students another independent measure is "suppressing" the observed relationship between the independent variable in question and the dependent variable (Astin, 1993a). Intellectual Self-Confidence is correlated with degree expectations at the first time point. Both of these measures are positively correlated with degree expectations at the second time point. The negative relationship of Intellectual Self-Confidence on degree expectations at the second time point seems to be an artifact of the relationship of Intellectual Self-Confidence and degree expectations in the first time point.

African American and White students who attended their first choice institution tended to have lower degree expectations than other students. As was discussed in the mean differences section of this chapter, many of the students in BPS applied to only one institution (Hurtado et al., 1997).

Perhaps students who applied to many institutions and had more options of postsecondary institutions to attend are those who have higher degree expectations.

All of the institutional characteristics are significant predictors of African American or White students' degree expectations after the third year of college. The strongest predictor of degree expectations for African American students ($p \leq .001$) and the third strongest predictor for White students ($p \leq .001$) is level of institution. Students who attend four-year institutions tend to have higher degree expectations than students attending two-year institutions. Clark (1960) and Brint and Karabel (1989) believe that community colleges tend to "cool out" the hopes and aspirations of students by managing students' ambitions. These findings are supported in the BPS data set.

Control—or attendance at a private institution—is a positive predictor of White students' degree expectations only. Attendance at a historically Black college or university (HBCU) is a positive predictor of African American students' degree expectations. It should be noted that none of the White students in BPS attended a HBCU. Astin et al. (1996) found that private universities have the highest degree attainment rates, and several researchers have found positive effects of HBCU attendance on African American students' academic development and future goals (Fleming, 1984; Darden et al., 1996). The combination of the significant impact of institutional characteristics on the degree expectations of African American and White students indicate that although initial expectations and pre-college characteristics impact later expectations, institutional environments play a major role in the development of college students' educational expectations.

None of the financial aid measures significantly impact degree expectations of White or African American students. The only involvement measure that significantly impacts degree expectations is Faculty Contact. African American students who interact frequently with faculty members tend to have higher degree expectations than African American students who have fewer interactions with faculty members.

The regression results in BPS indicate that African American college students' degree expectations are a function of individual characteristics and institutional experiences. However, for White students, college students' degree expectations are mostly a function of individual characteristics. The implications of the regression analyses are many. First, although African American students tended to have lower SES backgrounds than White students, mother's educational attainment is the only SES measure that significantly impacts students' expectations. Further, the BPS base regression model shows—particularly for African American students—that both groups of students are constrained by society and are relatively free to pursue their dreams. Evidence that the development of degree expectations is a function of constraints is indicated by the statistical significance of mother's educational attainment on students' expectations. Although Faculty Contact may not be an element of societal constraints, it may illustrate Turner's (1960) concept of sponsored mobility, whereby particular faculty members and advisors take certain African American students under their tutelage and encourage their hopes, dreams, and application to graduate school. Indications that individuals are relatively free in society to do what they want and achieve their dreams unconstrained are that initial degree expectations have such a significant effect on later expectations. There is strong evidence that students' expectations are shaped (and perhaps constrained) by the postsecondary institutions they attend. Students in four-year institutions, White students in private institutions, and African Americans attending HBCUs tended to have higher degree expectations. Therefore, there are ways in which institutional structures can develop or constrain students' hopes for degree attainment.

The next section discusses the base regression model in the CIRP data set and discusses the patterns of relationships in CIRP regression models.

CIRP Base Regression Model

In the CIRP data set, none of the pre-college characteristics (gender, age, parents' education and income) has a significant effect on the changing degree plans of White students. For African American students, age has a negative effect on degree plans. African American students who are younger tend to have higher degree plans.

Of the initial expectations/orientations measures (first year degree plans, Intellectual Self-Confidence, choice of institution, distance institution is from home), first-year degree plans is the strongest predictor of White students' third-year degree plans ($p \leq .001$), and the fourth strongest predictor of African American students' later degree plans ($p \leq .05$). Students who enter college with high degree plans tend to have high degree plans two year later. The other variable in this group that is significantly related to students' degree plans is distance from home. In general, the farther away African American students go to college, the higher their degree plans ($p \leq .01$). Levels of Intellectual Self-Confidence and choice of institution do not significantly affect African American or White students' degree plans, and distance from home does not significantly affect White students' plans.

None of the institutional characteristics significantly affect students' degree plans. Therefore, structural elements and characteristics of institutions are not key elements for students' development of degree plans in the base regressions in the CIRP data set, which supports Pascarella's (1984) findings that institutional characteristics seem to have indirect effects on students' aspirations. However, there are indications that students' experiences do play a significant role in the development of their degree plans.

Table 5.7 shows that all of the financial aid measures except amount of loans received significantly affect African American or White students' degree plans. White students' degree plans are affected by hours-spent working. White students who work more hours a week tend to have lower degree plans than students who work fewer hours a week. Table E2 of Appendix E shows the results of the correlation analysis of the variables in the regression models for African American and White students. From examining the correlation coefficients, it is clear that there is a significant, negative correlation between working many hours a week and SES. In addition, there is a positive, significant correlation between working more hours a week and amount of loans and work-study received. Therefore, White students who work more hours a week seem to have already received financial aid and may need to work additional hours a week because financial aid assistance was not enough to meet their expenses. Students who work many hours a week could be making the decision that they could not plan to earn a graduate degree given the number of hours they are working in order to get through undergraduate education.

African Americans' degree plans are affected by different financial aid measures. The strongest predictor of African American students' degree plans is receipt of scholarships and grants. Students who receive more scholarships and grants tend to have lower degree plans than other African American students. Table E2 shows that the bivariate correlation between receipt of scholarship/grants and third year degree plans is strong (-.32), and that parents' income also has a strong negative correlation with receipt of scholarships (-.25). However, receipt of scholarships is significant after parent income is controlled—or held constant. This may mean that, given the recent cutbacks in federal and state grants (Baker & Vélez, 1996), African American students are not receiving enough scholarship/grant aid to encourage them to continue their education beyond undergraduate work. The mean differences between White and African American student groups in CIRP (see Table 5.6 and coding schemes in Appendix C) indicate a $15,000–$20,000 difference between the groups' parental incomes, although African American students attend institutions with tuitions approximately $1000 less per year than the institutions White students attend. However, the means for receipt of scholarship and grants indicate that African American students receive only about $500 more in scholarships and grants than White students. Therefore, African American students have far fewer resources than White students, and the award of scholarships and grants may not be enough to meet their needs. African American students may acknowledge that their financial situations are tolerable for completion of undergraduate education (or not, considering the much higher numbers of African American students who plan to earn no degree in the third year—see Table 5.4). However, African American students cannot pursue graduate education given their current financial circumstances.

African American students who have more work study awards tend to have higher degree plans. Hossler (1984) discussed the possibility that a positive effect of work-study on student outcomes was due to work-study students having more interactions with faculty, staff and institutional policies. This seems to be the case for African American students in CIRP. Work-study students may have more interactions with the campus facilities and policies and thus may become more aware of their educational options.

Finally, only one of the involvement measures—Peer Contact—significantly affects African American students' degree plans. Students who interact with their peers tend to have higher degree plans than their peers who have fewer interactions. Neither the Faculty Contact measure nor the Peer Contact measure significantly affected White students degree plans, however.

The regression results in CIRP indicate that White college students' degree plans are mostly a function of degree plans at college entry, although hours spent working are also significant predictors of White students' third year degree plans. However, for African Americans, degree plans are a function of individual characteristics and institutional experiences/support. Results of the regression analyses indicate that views of students as constrained by society and as free to move through society without constraints are both accurate descriptions of students' degree plans development. In terms of constraints, the effects of financial aid/work measures show that African American scholarship/grant recipients tend to have lower degree plans and White students who work more tend to have lower degree plans. Therefore, the lower economic strata of both student populations are having their degree plans constrained. The White students who work longer hours tend to have lower parent income and may have to work longer hours to pay for expenses; and African American students who are scholarship recipients may not be receiving enough aid to pay expenses and thus they adjust their degree plans to reflect what they think is possible given their financial constraints.

In terms of individuals being able to move through society unconstrained, there are several indications of this in the CIRP base regression models. None of the SES measures is a significant predictor of degree plans for African American or White students. Thus, SES measures are not the most important factors in determining students' degree plans for this sample of traditional-aged students. In addition, African Americans who have greater contact with their peers tend to have higher degree plans. Therefore, the African American students may be developing their goals for the future through their peer interactions. Perhaps students who informally discuss academic material with each other discover their facility with academic coursework and thus raise their degree goals over time.

COMPARISON BETWEEN THE CIRP AND BPS BASE REGRESSION MODELS

In what ways are the results of the base regression analyses in CIRP and BPS similar or different? The predictive values of the BPS regression models—particularly for White students—are much higher than the models in CIRP (see R^2 in Table 5.7). Table 5.8 shows a summary of the significant predictors of degree aspirations for African American and White students in BPS and CIRP. From this summary table, it is apparent that the regression models between the BPS and CIRP student samples are quite different. The models for African American and White students within each data set are similar, but more similar for BPS than for CIRP.

Table 5.8 Summary of Regression Model of BPS and CIRP Data sets by Race/Ethnicity on Educational Expectations and Plans

Variables	BPS		CIRP	
	African American	White	African American	White
Pre-college characteristics				
Female	—	—	—	—
Age	—	**neg**	**neg**	—
Father's Educational Attainment	—	—	—	—
Mother's Educational Attainment	**pos**	**pos**	—	—
Parent Income	—	—	—	—
Initial Aspirations/Orientations				
Educational Plans/Expectations	**pos**	**pos**	**pos**	**pos**
Intellectual Self-Confidence	**neg**	**pos**	—	—
First Choice	**neg**	**neg**	—	—
Distance From Home	—	—	**pos**	—
Institutional Characteristics				
Control (private)	—	**pos**	—	—
Level (4-year institution)	**pos**	**pos**	—	—
HBCU	**pos**	—	—	—
Financial Aid/Work				
Borrow/Loans	—	—	—	—
Scholarship	—	—	**neg**	—
Work Study	—	—	**pos**	—
Hours spent working	—	—	—	**neg**
Involvement				
Faculty Contact	**pos**	—	—	—
Peer Contact	—	—	**pos**	—

In both BPS and CIRP data sets, initial degree aspirations are strong predictors of third year degree aspirations: however, intellectual self-confidence and attendance at first choice institution are also strong predictors of students' aspirations in BPS only. In addition, the types of institutions students attended had strong effects on their degree aspirations in BPS, but institutional characteristics were not significant predictors of degree aspirations for students in CIRP. Thus, there are greater impacts of different institutional environments on the degree expectations of students in BPS than on the degree plans of students in CIRP. This could in part be due to that students in BPS are attending more diverse types of institutions than students in CIRP.

The involvement measures have different effects on African American students across the data sets. Faculty Contact affects African American students' aspirations in BPS, but Peer Contact affects African American students' aspirations in CIRP. Since more of the students in CIRP attend four-year institutions and therefore more of them may live on campus, they probably have greater interactions with their peers than do the BPS students. The BPS students may commute to their campuses more often and frequent interaction with faculty members may be their main means of academic support.

None of the SES measures are significant for predicting CIRP students' degree aspirations, but mothers' educational attainment is a significant predictor of White and African American students' degree expectations in BPS. Therefore, the development of degree expectations in BPS is clearly a function of students' SES, initial expectations, and type of institution attended. The results in the BPS data set suggest that students' expectations are constrained by their backgrounds (particularly those from lower socioeconomic backgrounds) and yet their future goals can be enhanced by their experiences in certain types of institutions.

In CIRP, a different kind of process of degree plan development is noticeable. White students' third-year degree plans are almost totally a function of their degree plans at college entry, although the fact that students who work more tend to have lower degree plans gives an indication that White students in CIRP are constrained somewhat by their financial circumstances. African American students' degree plans in CIRP are mostly a function of institutional support and experiences (in the form of financial aid and contact with peers) and their attendance at an institution farther away from home. Thus, for African American students in BPS and CIRP, more than for White students in either data set, it is clear that institutional choices and experiences have greater effects on their degree goals.

The next chapter investigates the development of degree expectations and plans in full regression models in BPS and CIRP data sets. Each data set provides unique variables that can expand the understanding of degree aspirations development. In addition, as has been established through mean differences, the data sets are quite different, so full regression models can inform how the development of degree plans differ in a more traditionally-aged, higher SES sample versus a more nationally representative sample of postsecondary institutional attendees.

6
What Affects College Students' Degree Expectations and Plans?

The previous chapter detailed the first stages of statistical analyses for this study. First, I examined the bivariate relationships of the variables in each data set and between African American and White students. Second, I performed ordinary least squares regression analyses using a base model investigation of students' educational expectations and plans across the two data sets. I tested a regression model using variables that were common across the two data sets.

This chapter describes the results of the last stage of data analyses: expanded regression analyses. These regression analyses were designed to build on the strengths of each data set. That is, the regression models for each data set tested how measures unique to the data set (over and above the base regression models) affected White and African American students. The results of this analysis provide a comparison within data sets of how particular variables affected expectations and plans for each racial/ethnic group. Chapter 4 specifies how the analyses were completed.

The first part of the chapter details the Beginning Postsecondary Students Longitudinal Study (BPS) regression analyses, followed by the results of the analyses using the Cooperative Institutional Research Program (CIRP) data set. The chapter concludes with a summary of the regression analyses across both data sets—highlighting the comparisons between African American and White students in both data sets.

BPS FULL REGRESSION MODEL BY RACE

This chapter discusses full regression models for each dataset and examines the effect of additional predictors on the dependent variables—revealing how variables unique to each dataset affect the educational plans and expectations of students. The additional variables included in the BPS full regression model are: *additional student background characteristics* (marital status, number of children, and an SES measure—number of major items owned by household); *reasons for choosing a postsecondary institution* (close to home, good reputation, less expensive); *additional institutional characteristics* (size, tuition cost, and percent minority enrollment instead of the HBCU measure included in the BPS base regression model); and *the number of jobs students had while attending college.*

The results of the full regression model are discussed after the entry of each of the four categories of variables: (1) the pre-college characteristics enter the regression; (2) expectations at the first time point enter the regression; (3) the institutional characteristics enter the regression; and (4) entry of all the variables. Examination of the regression model at these four points is important and addresses the main research questions in this study: What are the main predictors of degree expectations after SES and initial degree expectations are controlled; after SES, initial expectations, and institutional characteristics are taken into account; and when all measures in the full model are entered? Table 6.1 shows the results of the full regression model in the BPS dataset and includes the standardized regression coefficients (betas) for each variable entering. Table 6.1 also shows the betas of variables that were not yet entered into the regression model. For unstandardized regression coefficients, please see Table D2 in Appendix D.

Table 6.1 shows the R^2 and significant predictors after the pre-college characteristics enter the regression. The R^2 for African American students is .12 and it is .38 for White students. Mother's educational attainment and number of children are significant predictors of African American and White students' degree expectations. The more education students' mothers received the higher the students' degree expectations. However, students who have children tend to lower their degree expectations. Students could be assessing the degree to which they can invest large amounts of time and money toward their degree achievement in light of responsibilities to their children. Having children may constrain the expectations of students to achieve higher degrees.

There are two other significant predictors of White students' degree expectations: Age and Items Owned. The younger the student is the higher his or her degree expectations. In addition, Items Owned is a scale comprised of items that indicate the material circumstances of students' lives prior to college. These include such items as: Did students' families have the newspaper delivered, a dishwasher, reference books, personal computer, did the student have a room of his or her own, etc. (see Table C1 for details about the measure). Although White students' parental income is not a significant predictor of degree expectations after the initial group of variables entered the regression, the material circumstances of students' lives prior to college is a significant predictor of degree expectations. The better students' circumstances the higher the students' degree expectations.

Table 6.1 shows the R^2 and significant predictors after the initial degree expectations enter the regression. The R^2 for African American students is

.21; it is .54 for White students. The following paragraphs discuss the ways in which the model changed after entry of initial expectations into the regression model.

Table 6.1 Regression Model of BPS Dataset by Race/Ethnicity and Regression Step[1]

Variables	Pre-college Characteristics		Pre-college Characteristics and Expectations at First Timepoint		Institutional Characteristics		Full Model	
	African America n N=266	White N=283	African America n	White	African America n	White	African America n	White
Pre-college Characteristics								
Female	.01	.10*	.00	.05	-.00	.07*	.00	.07
Age	.05	-.23***	.10	-.24***	.17**	-.18***	.16*	-.19***
Father's Educational Attainment	.08	.10	.08	.07	.03	.02	.04	.02
Mother's Educational Attainment	.22***	.26***	.17**	.14**	.12*	.10*	.12*	.10*
Parent Income	-.05	-.00	-.05	-.05	-.03	-.07	-.01	-.08*
Number of Children	-.24***	-.16**	-.20**	-.04	-.18**	-.03	-.18**	-.02
Married	-.05	.01	-.08	.14**	.02	-.03	-.01	-.04
Separated/Divorced	.03	-.06	-.01	-.04	.04	-.07	.04	-.08*
Items Owned	.03	.15**	-.01	.14**	-.06	.09*	-.05	.09*
Initial Expectations/Orientations								
Educational Plans/Expectations	*.31****	*.46****	.31***	.46***	.19***	.39***	.19***	.39***
Intellectual Self-Confidence	*.05*	*.22****	*.00*	*.15****	-.11*	.12***	-.13*	.13**
First Choice	*-.19****	*-.12***	*-.16***	*-.08**	-.13**	-.07	-.11*	-.07
Distance From Home	*.20****	*.15****	*.15***	*.06*	.00	-.06	-.02	-.05
Good reputation	*-.09*	*.12***	*-.10*	*.08**	-.14*	.02	-.12*	.01
Close to Home	*-.27****	*-.13***	*-.21****	*-.11***	-.14*	-.06	-.11	-.06
Less Expensive	*-.02*	*-.01*	*-.01*	*-.04*	.06	.01	.05	.01
Institutional Characteristics								
Control (Private)	*.14***	*.18****	*.10**	*.14****	.06	.17**	.04	.18**
Level (4-year)	*.36****	*.30****	*.29****	*.20****	.20**	.13**	.20**	.14**
Per. African American Enroll.	*.11**	*-.09**	*.07*	*-.06*	.12*	-.07	.12*	-.07
Tuition Cost	*.21****	*.19****	*.17****	*.14****	.04	-.05	.01	-.04
Size	*.16***	*.08*	*.16***	*.07*	.20***	.14**	.19***	.13**
Financial Aid/Work								
Borrow/Loans	*.16***	*.06*	*.15***	*.04*	*.07*	*.01*	.07	.01
Scholarship	*.21****	*.12***	*.16***	*.06*	*.06*	*-.02*	.04	-.01
Work Study	*.04*	*.06*	*.02*	*.02*	*.00*	*-.03*	-.02	-.03
Hours spent working	*-.07*	*-.11**	*-.06*	*-.07*	*-.00*	*-.04*	.00	-.05
Number of Jobs	*.06*	*.02*	*.02*	*.00*	*.00*	*.00*	.02	.03
Involvement								
Faculty Contact	*.25****	*.12***	*.22****	*.04*	*.15***	*-.04*	.16**	-.03
Peer Contact	*.16***	*.22****	*.13**	*.13***	*.01*	*-.03*	-.06	-.01
R^2	.12	.38	.21	.54	.36	.61	.38	.61

[1] Standardized regression coefficients (betas) are reported. Please see Table D2 in Appendix D for unstandardized coefficients.

Note: Italicized coefficients below the solid lines in the table indicate that variables have not yet entered the regression equation.

* p<.05; **p<.01; ***p<.001

Not surprisingly, the strongest predictor of African American and White students' expectations is initial expectations (.31 beta for African Americans, .46 beta for White students). The other significant predictor that both African American and White students have in common is again mother's educational attainment (.17 for African Americans, .14 for White students). The other significant predictors at entry of the previous group of variables remain significant. However, there is one difference: Being married is a positive predictor of third year degree expectations for White students.

The third group of variables included in the regression model is Intellectual Self-Confidence, choice of institution, distance the institution is from home, reasons for choosing institution, and institutional characteristics. After this group of variables enters the regression, the R^2 for White students is .61 and for African American students it is .36. After institutional characteristics and choice measures are controlled, one of the predictors of African American students' degree expectations changes: Age becomes a significant predictor (.17). Unlike White students at entry of this group of variables and at the entry of the previous two groups of variables, where age is a negative predictor of expectations, for African Americans, the older the student, the higher the students' expectations. Therefore, taking into account institutional characteristics and reasons for choosing their institutions, it seems that younger White students and older African American students have higher degree expectations. Table 5.6 shows that White students in BPS tend to be older than African American students. Therefore, given that African American students are a year or so younger in BPS, perhaps the opposite effects of age for African American and White students actually indicate that overall, students who are about 19 or 20 years old tend to have higher degree expectations.

The opposite effects of age on degree expectations is another indication of the fact that different processes are at work in terms of the development of African American and White students' degree expectations. Older African American students may have higher degree expectations because they more clearly understand what will be involved in earning graduate degrees. Younger White students may have higher degree expectations because youth may represent fewer family commitments and thus an ability to strive for more education without needing to manage families as well. Astin et al. (1996) concludes that African Americans take longer to complete degrees. Institutional policies that are supportive of students who are a bit older may help to increase the numbers of African Americans who expect to pursue graduate degrees.

The other difference in pre-college predictors of degree expectations between the entry of the first two groups of variables and the third group of variables is that being married is no longer a significant predictor of degree expectations. When institutional characteristics and choice variables are taken into account, marital status no longer significantly affects expectations. This indicates that the effect of marital status may be dependent on the type of institution the student attends. The other significant pre-college characteristics discussed after entry of the previous groups of variables remain significant after entering the second group of variables.

In the Initial Expectations/Orientations and Institutional Characteristics groups of measures there are a number of significant predictors of African

American and White students' expectations. Intellectual Self-Confidence has a significant effect on degree expectations for White students (.12). Students with more positive perceptions of their academic abilities tend to have higher degree expectations in the third year of college. However, the opposite is true for African American students. African American students who enter with higher levels of self-confidence tend to have *lower* degree expectations (-.11) two years later. These findings are similar to the BPS base regression model findings (Table 5.7), and again this is a suppressor effect. The negative effect of Intellectual Self-Confidence on African American students' degree expectations is an artifact of the relationship between Intellectual Self-Confidence and initial degree expectations. Therefore, for African American students, initial degree aspirations are strongly tied to Intellectual Self-Confidence.

There are other significant predictors of degree expectations for African American students: attending one's first choice institution (-.13), attending an institution because it has a good reputation (-.14), and attending an institution because it is close to home (-.14) are all negative predictors of degree expectations for African American students. Therefore, students who attend their first choice institution tend to have lower degree expectations than students who do not attend their first choice institution. This finding is similar to the BPS base regression finding (Table 5.7). It is possible that because fewer students apply to more than one institution, the first choice variable represents students who applied to only one institution and thus were constrained by their institutional choice. Students who have several options in terms of postsecondary institution attendance may be in a better position to choose which institutional environment may best suit their needs. However, if students do not (cannot) have several choices of institutions their experiences may be restricted by cost—or which institution is closer to their homes. This is an explanation of processes that reflect how students can be constrained by social circumstances.

From the mean differences between African American and White students (see Table 5.6) it is clear that African Americans students tend to go to institutions that are closer to their homes than White students. Also, African American students mention more often that a main reason they chose to attend their postsecondary institutions is because it is closer to their homes. However, the fact that African American students are attending institutions closer to their homes and are attending an institution *because* it is close to home indicates that African Americans' degree expectations are constrained by their choices of institutional attendance. Presumably, African American students are choosing institutions close to home because of a host of social and economic reasons. Perhaps if African Americans were able to choose from among more institutions—including those away from home—the type of institution attended could increase both their opportunities and their degrees.

Attending an institution because it has a Good Reputation is a negative predictor of degree expectations for African American students, after controlling for institutional characteristics and other choice variables. The Good Reputation measure may approximate selectivity. Therefore, the more selective an institution is concerning its incoming classes, the higher the educational expectations for African American students. A competitive, selective, college environment may facilitate academic achievement and educational aspirations (Astin, 1977), but for African Americans this college environment constrain their educational expectations over time. It may be more important for African American students to attend institutions that are supportive of their development and achievement. Selective and competitive institutions (which are PWIs for the most part) may strive for the academic achievement of "all", but may be destructive to the development and maintenance of high educational goals of African American students (Feagin & Sikes, 1995).

The relationship between the Good Reputation measure and the degree expectations of African American also seems to be the result of suppressor effects. Table E1 in Appendix E shows the correlation coefficients for the measures in the BPS regression models. The correlation between Good Reputation and degree expectations is of low magnitude, and the Good Reputation measure is moderately correlated with the other choice measures (attending an institution because it is less expensive, and attending an institution because it is close to home). Therefore, other measures in the regression model are correlated with the Good Reputation measure and degree expectations, which strengthened the relationship between Good Reputation and degree expectations in the regression model.

For African American and White students there are two institutional characteristics that significantly predict both groups' degree expectations: Attendance at a four-year institution, and attendance at a large institution. Students who attend a four-year institution (in comparison to a two-year institution), or students who attend a larger institution tend to have higher degree expectations. The finding of attendance at four-year institutions supporting the development of degree expectations is supported by the results of the BPS base regression models (Table 5.7). Again, prior research shows that four-year institutions tend to support higher degree goals than two-year institutions (Brint & Karabel, 1989; Dougherty, 1987). The results of the full BPS regression model also support this finding. Larger institutions may have more resources and provide more support for a broad range of students' interests. Also, larger institutions tend to have more graduate programs and thus, students' exposure to more graduate students may influence their expectations of earning graduate degrees.

Percent African American enrollment is a significant predictor of African American degree expectations (.12). African Americans who attend institutions with more African American students tend to have higher degree expectations. This is a finding similar to the base regression model (Table 5.7) where African Americans attending HBCUs tend to have higher degree expectations. Institutions with higher enrollments of African Americans may be more committed to the academic development of African American students and thus African Americans may have higher degree goals. White students who attend private institutions tend to have higher degree expectations (.17). This is supported by previous research that found attendance at private institutions has positive impacts on a variety of educational outcomes (Astin et al., 1996).

The final group of variables included in the regression includes all of the independent variables in the full regression model. The R^2 for African Americans is .38, and .61 for White students, which is unchanged from the R^2 after the second group of variables entered the regression model. The final step of the regression is similar to the previous step of the regression; the next few paragraphs will focus on the ways in which the regression model after the final group of variables differs from the regression model after the previous group of variables was entered.

There are no differences in the pre-college characteristics affecting African American students' third-year degree expectations between the entry of the third group of variables and the final group of variables in the regression analysis. However, for White students, two pre-college characteristics measures become significant after financial aid and involvement measures are controlled. Parent income (-.08) and being separated/divorced (-.08) become significant negative predictors of White students' degree expectations. Students who are separated or divorced (in comparison to single, never married students) tend to have lower degree expectations. This measure becomes significant after financial aid measures and institutional characteristics are controlled, as a result of a suppressor effect. Individuals who are separated and divorced tend to be older (see Table E1) and therefore may be returning to school for a terminal degree only. Thus, they would be less likely to expect to earn graduate degrees.

The negative effect of parent income on White students' degree expectations is also the result of several suppressor effects. When examining the regression model after the entry of each variable, it is clear that parent income becomes significant after the entry of the involvement measures. In addition, because the involvement measures were part of the base regression model, and parent income is not a significant predictor of degree expectations in Table 5.7, it seems that controlling institutional characteristics and financial aid measures in particular seem to affect the relationship of parent income and degree expectations. Therefore, once institutional characteristics and financial aid and involvement measures are taken into account, students with higher incomes tend to have lower degree expectations.

The initial correlation between parent income and degree expectations is .24 (see Table E1). After controlling for all the variables in the model, the effect of parent income is negative and significant. This suggests that receiving financial aid may have an indirect effect on degree expectations. In this way, receiving financial aid can provide increased access to postsecondary education for White students and thus may reverse the effects of low income. In addition taking into account the type of postsecondary institution a student attends also seems to change the relationship of parent income on degree expectations.

As with the regression model when the second group of variables is entered, initial expectations are strong predictors of students' third year expectations (.19 for African American students, .39 for White students). The opposite relationship of Intellectual Self-Confidence to the degree expectations of White students and African American students noted at the entry of the second group of measures—when institutional characteristics, Intellectual Self-Confidence, and choice measures are controlled—is still evident after financial aid and involvement measures are controlled: African American students with higher levels of Intellectual Self-Confidence tend to have lower degree expectations; White students with higher levels of Intellectual Self-Confidence tend to have higher degree expectations. One difference in the choice measures, once financial aid measures and involvement are taken into account, is that students' reasons for attending an institution because it is close to home is no longer a significant, negative predictor of African American degree expectations. This clearly indicates that the receipt of financial aid is tied to the choice of college a student attends (Somers & St. John, 1993).

None of the financial aid measures significantly predict African American or White students' degree expectations, and of the involvement measures, only Faculty Contact positively affects African American students degree expectations. African American students who have frequent interactions with faculty tend to have higher degree expectations in their third year of college. This confirms the finding in the BPS base regression model (see Table 5.7). African American students who interact with faculty may have more access to information concerning applying to graduate school and their options post-baccalaureate. In addition, since faculty members select the students with whom they interact frequently, the significant effect of Faculty Contact on students' degree expectations may indicate the faculty's role in the socialization of college students. The effect of Faculty Contact may also indicate the important role of faculty in encouraging the degree expectations of African American students. In contrast, neither the peer nor faculty contact measures significantly affect White students' degree expectations, perhaps because the White students in the BPS sample are less likely to live on campus and therefore their degree expectations are less affected by peer and faculty interactions.

There are no differences in the effects of the institutional characteristics between the entry of the third and final group of variables in the regression model. Attendance at a four-year institution and attendance at a larger institution tend to positively affect White and African American students' degree expectations. The findings of this study seem to counter past findings in this regard. Larger institutions seem to facilitate students' degree expectations, which is counter to the findings of Astin (1993b). Larger institutions in Astin's study had negative effects on several cognitive measures (grade point average and test scores) and negative effects on degree aspirations. However, in the expanded BPS regression model, size of institution seems to facilitate students' degree expectations. BPS students' attending larger institutions could be attending institutions with more graduate students and programs and thus have more access to graduate degree options than BPS students attending smaller institutions. This seems particularly plausible given the more nontraditional sample of the BPS population, and the more varied types of institutions BPS students attend (see Table 5.6).

Attendance at a private institution affects White students' degree expectations, and attendance at four-year institutions particularly seems to positively affect the educational expectations of both African American and White students. This is also supported by previous research that found community colleges tend to limit the educational achievement of students (Brint & Karabel, 1989; Clark, 1960). Figure 6.1 shows the mean differences between African American and White students' degree expectations at 2-year and 4-year institutions in 1990 and 1992. In 1990, African American and White students' degree expectations are higher at 4-year institutions than at 2-year institutions. White students attending two-year institutions have the lowest expectations; African American students at four-year institutions have the highest expectations. In 1992, the degree expectations of African American and White students attending four-year institutions increased slightly, but the expectations of students attending two-year institutions declined—this decline is particularly sharp for White students at two-year institutions. Therefore, the findings of this study show that four-year institutions seem—at the least—to hold students' degree goals steady, while two-year institutions seem to constrain students' dreams and expectations for earning post-baccalaureate degrees.

For African American students particularly, institutions with larger African American enrollments may provide environments in which African American students can more easily develop social relationships and build social support systems. However, peer support is not a significant predictor of expectations, so perhaps the percentage of African American enrollment is a structural measure that reflects particular institutional practices and policies that encourage the academic development of African American students. Frequent faculty contact by African Americans positively impacts educational expectations. African American students who are able to meet frequently with faculty and advisors may have access to more information about possible career and academic paths than students who do not have as much access to faculty and advisors.

In summary, the BPS expanded regression model shows that individual and institutional characteristics are important in predicting students' third

Figure 6.1 African American and White Students' Initial and Third-year Degree Aspirations by Level of College in BPS Dataset.

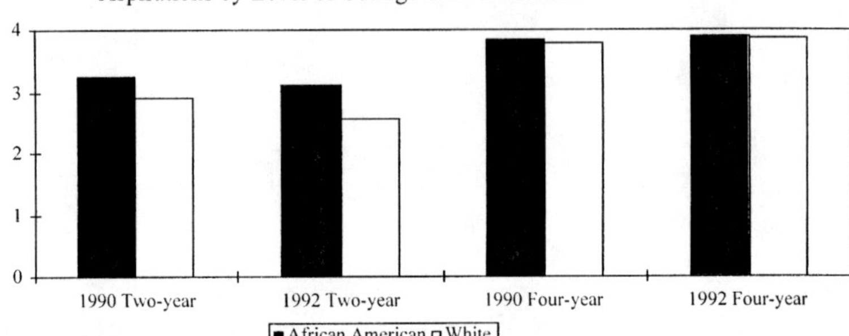

year degree expectations. As with the BPS base regression model, White and African American students' degree expectations are affected by individual characteristics (SES measures, age, marital status, Intellectual Self-Confidence, choice measures) as well as institutional characteristics. Individual students bring particular backgrounds, previous experiences, and different levels of initial plans, but institutional environments can raise or constrain the students' expectations. In addition, first-year degree expectation is a much larger predictor of third year expectations for White students than for African American students. This supports the research of Maxey et al. (1995): African American students may not have the same access to information concerning post-secondary education and therefore seem to attend their first choice institution less often than White students (Table 5.6). In addition, African American students change their degree expectations from first year to third year of college more often than White students (Table 5.3). It seems that institutional characteristics and exposure to faculty, and post-baccalaureate options are important for the development of college student degree expectations.

CIRP FULL REGRESSION MODEL BY RACE

This section details the full regression model of the CIRP dataset by race. The measures added in the full regression model include indications of whether students attended their second or third choice institution, Social Change Orientation—a measure of students' commitment to promoting racial understanding and influencing social values. Also, two measures of students' perceived institutional priorities—Commitment to Social

Activism and Commitment to Diversity are added to the full regression model. Two final measures, participation in ethnic organizations and students' college achievement, are additions to the CIRP full regression model.

Table 6.2 reports the results of the regression after four groups of variables enter the regression: The results of the full regression model are discussed at four points of the regression model: (1) the pre-college characteristics enter the regression; (2) degree plans at the first time point enter the regression; (3) the institutional characteristics enter the regression; and (4) after entry of the final variables. Thus, the structure of this section of the chapter is similar to the discussion of the BPS full regression model. The table includes the standardized coefficients for the independent variables after entry of each group of variables. In addition, standardized coefficients for measures not yet entered into the regression are included in the table—they are italicized and below the bold line. Please see Table D3 in Appendix D for unstandardized regression coefficients.

The table shows the R^2 and significant predictors after the pre-college characteristics and initial degree plans enter the regression. The R^2 for African American students after entry of these variables is .05, and it is .09 for White students. There are no significant predictors of African American students' degree plans at entry of the pre-college characteristics and only one significant predictor of White students' degree plans: high school grade point average (beta is .19). Therefore, students with the highest high school GPAs tend to have higher degree plans two years later in college. This finding supports the theoretically predicted relationship of academic performance and degree aspirations. In a meritocratic educational system, those students who have higher grade point averages should have higher degree plans—the most "able" will be the most likely to achieve additional degrees. This indicates that the secondary school system may support the degree plans of academically high-performing White students.

The R^2 for African American students after entry of initial degree plans is .09 and it is .26 for White students. The only significant predictor of African American students' degree plans at this group of variables is initial degree plans (beta is .22). Initial degree plans is also the strongest predictor of White students' degree plans (.43), and high school grade point average continues to significantly predict degree plans (.19).

The third group of independent measures entered into the regression is college choice measures and institutional characteristics. The R^2 at this point in the regression analyses is .20 for African Americans and .30 for White students. After institutional characteristics and college choice measures are controlled, two pre-college characteristics for African American students become significant predictors of degree plans: Age becomes a significant negative predictor of degree plans (-.14), and high school grade point average becomes a significant negative predictor of degree plans (–.18). Therefore, younger African American students tend to have higher degree plans after two years of college than older African American students, and African American students with lower high school GPAs tend to have higher degree plans.

As with the results after the first two groups of measures entered the regression, the opposite is still true for White students: Students with higher high school grade point averages tend to have higher degree plans. Therefore, the relationship of secondary school academic performance has opposite relationships for African American and White students in the CIRP sample. For White students, the relationship is in the theoretically predicted direction—students who have high academic performance will have higher degree plans. However, for African American students, the relationship between pre-college academic performance and degree plans remains negative.

Given that high school GPA becomes a significant predictor of degree plans after institutional characteristics are controlled, the degree plans of African American students seem to be dependent upon the kinds of institutions they attend. The opposite relationship of high school GPA on degree plans in CIRP is also similar to the relationship of Intellectual Self-Confidence on the degree expectations of African American and White students in BPS (see Table 6.1). Intellectual Self-Confidence has a negative effect on African American students' degree expectations and a positive effect on White students' degree expectations. Perhaps Intellectual Self-Confidence in BPS is behaving similarly as a predictor of aspirations to high school grade point average in CIRP.

Initial degree plans remain the strongest predictors of African American and White students' degree plans, with their standardized coefficients unchanged from the entry of the first group of independent variables. When institutional characteristics and choice measures are controlled, the institution's distance from home becomes a significant predictor of degree plans for African American (.14) and White students (.12). Students who go farther away from home tend to have higher aspirations (degree plans). In addition, White students who attend their second choice institution tend to have higher degree plans than students attending their fourth or lower choice institution (reference category). While, attendance at their first choice institution is not significantly predictive of degree plans from the referent category, it seems that White students who are able to attend their second choice institution tend to have somewhat higher degree plans.

Only one of the institutional characteristics has an effect on students' degree plans after the second year of college: Attendance at an HBCU for African American students has a negative effect on student's degree plans (-.15). Therefore, at this stage of the regression analyses there seems to be something about the institutional environment of HBCUs that seem to constrain the degree plans of African American students in CIRP after entry of this group of variables. This effect disappears after controlling for institutional priorities, financial aid, and involvement measures; therefore, this seems to be a minor finding.

The fourth and final group of variables entered into the regression includes all of the independent variables in the regression model: Pre-college characteristics, college choice measures, institutional characteristics, perceived institutional priorities, financial aid/work measures, and involvement variables. The final R^2 for the regression model is .40 for African American students and .35 for White students. Given the significant change in R^2 between the entry of the second group of variables and the entry of

Table 6.2 Regression Model of CIRP Dataset by Race/Ethnicity and Regression Step[1]

	Pre-college Characteristics		Pre-college Characteristics and Plans at First Timepoint		Institutional Characteristics		Full Model	
Variables	African American N=266	White N=283	African American	White	African American	White	African American	White
Pre-college Characteristics								
Female	.10	.06	.04	.05	.02	.03	.02	.06
Age	-.10	-.05	-.11	-.03	-.14*	-.08	-.08	-.08
Father's Educational Attainment	.07	.10	.04	.04	.07	.03	.16*	.04
Mother's Educational Attainment	.08	-.07	.06	-.04	.05	-.07	-.02	-.01
Parent Income	-.01	.09	-.03	.03	-.04	.04	-.08	.04
High School GPA	-.06	.25***	-.10	.19***	-.18**	.20***	-.26***	.12
Initial Expectations/Orientations								
Educational Plans/Expectations	*.22****	*.43****	.22***	.43***	.22**	.43***	.14*	.48***
Intellectual Self-Confidence	*.21***	*.08*	.15*	-.04	.12	-.07	.11	-.08
First Choice	*-.01*	*.03*	*.02*	*.02*	.06	.02	.06	.04
Second Choice	*.07*	*.12**	*.12*	*.10*	.13	.11*	.13*	.12*
Third Choice	*-.19***	*-.02*	*-.21****	*-.05*	-.12	-.01	-.07	-.01
Distance From Home	*.10*	*.09*	*.07*	*.11*	.14*	.12*	.14*	.10
Social Change Orientation	*.13**	*.12**	*.11*	*.03*	.05	.04	.01	.07
Institutional Characteristics								
Control (private)	*-.09*	*.03*	*-.10*	*.04*	-.09	.00	-.11	-.09
Level (four-year)	*.01*	*-.02*	*-.06*	*-.05*	-.03	-.06	-.01	-.05
Single Sex	*.14**	*.00*	*.12*	*.00*	.11	-.01	.05	-.02
HBCU	*-.13**	*.15*	*-.14**	*.10*	-.15*	.09	-.03	.06
Institutional Priorities								
Commitment to Social Activism	*-.04*	*.02*	*-.04*	*.03*	*-.04*	*.01*	.10	.06
Commitment to Diversity	*-.14**	*-.05*	*-.13**	*-.07*	*-.13**	*-.09*	-.12	-.11
Financial Aid/Work								
Borrow/Loans	*.08*	*.11*	*.10*	*.09*	*.13**	*.09*	.04	.11
Scholarship	*-.30***	*.05*	*-.29****	*.05*	*-.29****	*.05*	-.29***	.03
Work Study	*.14**	*.03*	*.14**	*.04*	*.12**	*.05*	.16**	.06
Hours spent working	*-.00*	*-.08*	*-.01*	*-.16***	*-.05*	*-.13**	.01	-.15**
Involvement								
Faculty Contact	*.04*	*.03*	*.05*	*.02*	*.02*	*-.04*	-.05	-.04
Peer Contact	*.15**	*.05*	*.14**	*.02*	*.15**	*.02*	.18**	-.01
Participated in ethnic organizations	*.21****	*-.04*	*.18***	*-.07*	*.12*	*-.08*	.09	-.09
Achievement								
College GPA	*.41****	*.06*	*.39****	*.11*	*.35****	*.10*	.26***	.11
R^2	.05	.09	.09	.26	.20	.30	.40	.35

[1] Standardized regression coefficients (Betas) are reported. Please see Table D3 in Appendix D for unstandardized coefficients.

Note: Italicized coefficients below the solid lines in the table indicate that variables have not yet entered the regression equation.

* p<.05; **p<.01; ***p<.001

the final group of variables, taking into account financial aid, work, and involvement measures produces several significant changes in the regression models for African American and White students.

There are notable differences in the significant pre-college measure predictors of degree plans between the entry of the third group of variables and the entry of all the measures in the regression model. For African Americans, age is no longer a significant predictor of degree plans, but father's educational attainment becomes a positive predictor of degree plans (.16). African American students whose fathers have earned more education tend to have higher degree plans. As with the regression model after entry of the third group of variables, high school GPA is a negative predictor of African American students' degree plans (-.26). For White students, none of the pre-college characteristics significantly predict degree plans. The positive relationship of high school grade point average on degree plans is no longer significant in the final regression model.

How have the relationships of initial degree plans and college choice measures on second year degree plans been affected when taking receipt of financial aid, involvement, and college achievement into account? Degree plans at college entry is no longer the strongest predictor of African American students' second year degree plans (.14). However, for White students, initial degree plans remains the strongest predictor of later degree plans (.48). Attendance at a second choice institution is still a significant predictor of White students' degree plans (.12), but it becomes a significant predictor of African American student plans when financial aid, involvement, and college achievement are controlled (.13). Therefore, it seems that focusing attention on financial aid, involvement, and college achievement that contributes to initial and continued enrollment at the institution may be more important than focusing on attendance at first or second choice institutions.

Distance from home is still a positive predictor of degree plans for African American students, but is no longer a significant predictor of degree plans for White students. None of the institutional characteristics and none of the perceived institutional priorities is a significant predictor of students' degree plans. Therefore, obtaining particular college experiences, achieving in college, and frequent interaction with faculty and peers are more important for the development of degree plans than any of the institutional characteristics.

The effect of financial aid on students' degree plans is quite strong for African American and White students. Receiving scholarships or grants is a negative predictor of African American students' degree plans (-.29); however, receiving work study awards is a positive predictor of African American students' degree plans (.16). This is a similar finding to the CIRP base regression. Since African American students' have fewer financial resources than White students (see Table 5.6), and yet receive only about

$500 more than White students in terms of scholarship/grant aid, there may be a significant amount of unmet need for African American students. African American students who are scholarship and grant recipients may realize that they cannot afford tuition and related costs of attending graduate school and are thus less likely to aspire to advanced degrees.

A finding also similar to the CIRP base regression (see Table 5.7) is the positive effect of work-study awards on African American students' degree plans. Students who are awarded work-study may be able to interact with campus officials and faculty more often and thus may gain more information about their options after receiving their baccalaureate. For White students, only the number of hours spent working significantly affects students' degree plans. The White students who work longer hours tend to have lower degree plans. This confirms the relationship found in the CIRP base regression. White students who work more, probably because they have received less financial aid than needed, seem to have lowered their degree plans during college. The amount of loan indebtedness has no significant effects on White or African American students degree plans, however.

Peer contact is a positive predictor of African American students' degree plans (.18). This finding is consistent with the CIRP base regression (see Table 5.7). African American students who have more contact with their peers in terms of discussing course content tend to have higher degree plans. This finding indicates that there are ways in which interaction with peers facilitates the academic development and degree planning of African American students. None of the other involvement measures had significant impacts on students' degree plans.

College achievement is a positive predictor of African American students' degree plans. Students with higher college achievement have higher degree plans. This finding supports the predicted relationship between achievement and degree plans. It seems that the highest achievers in college are encouraged (or directed) to pursue advanced degrees. However, because high school GPA is a negative, significant predictor of degree plans, the positive relationship of college GPA on degree plans may indicate that the degree aspirations process for African American college students is a complex matter. It seems that the processes affecting African Americans' third-year degree plans seem to approximate sponsored mobility whereby the college achievers interact more frequently with faculty and peers and have their degree plans reinforced. The negative relationship of pre-college achievement on African American students' degree plans also indicates that taking into account institutional characteristics and experiences is important in examining the effects on students' changing degree plans.

In summary, the CIRP expanded regression analyses indicate that the regression models between White and African Americans are distinct in terms of the significant predictors of degree plans. Only two measures in the final stage of the regression models are significant predictors for both White and African American groups of students: Initial degree plans is a positive predictor for both groups, and attending the second choice institution is also a positive predictor for both groups.

Of the institutional characteristics, none is significantly related to the students' degree plans. Additionally, none of the students' perceptions of institutional priorities is significantly related to degree plans, but the financial aid/work measures do affect students' degree plans. The findings in the CIRP dataset seem to support Pascarella's (1984) conclusions that degree aspirations may be indirectly affected by institutional characteristics, although the analyses in this book are only of direct effects.

It seems, then, that African Americans' degree plans in CIRP are a function of individual characteristics (high school grade point average, and father's educational attainment), institutional choices, support and experiences (in the forms of financial aid and peer interactions), and college achievement. The degree to which notions of contest or sponsored mobility are characteristic of the process by which African American students develop their degree plans is very clearly mixed in the CIRP dataset. Elements of sponsored mobility seem to be evident in the fact that father's educational attainment impacts students' degree plans.

In this way, African American students are somewhat constrained by their social circumstances (the SES of their fathers) and yet free to move through society unconstrained—by "choosing" an institution farther away from home; by interacting more with their peers, they tend to maintain or develop high degree plans. However, there is one way in which students are constrained by circumstances: the degree to which lower income students get the financial support they need to attend college. Although income is not a significant predictor of degree plans, receiving scholarships and grants is a significant predictor. African American students are much more likely than White students to be lower income, and they are more likely to receive scholarship funds. And yet, the amount of scholarship aid negatively affects their degree plans. The next section explores the relationship of financial aid, parental income, and achievement of students' aspirations in CIRP.

SCHOLARSHIP AID AND THE DEGREE PLANS OF AFRICAN AMERICAN STUDENTS

To further investigate the relationship of income, achievement (pre-college and college) and scholarship/grant award on African American students' degree aspirations in CIRP, several additional analyses were performed. For the purpose of composing figures, the scholarship measure was reduced into three categories: No scholarships received; some scholarship aid received— approximately \$1 to \$1000 of aid; and high amount of scholarship awards—\$1000 or more of aid. The parental income measure was also reduced into three categories: Low—less than $6000 to $15,000; medium—$15,000 to $35,000; and high—above $35,000. The reason for the category groupings was to maximize the numbers of African American and White students in each of the three income categories. It should be noted that the high-income category is not comprised of wealthy students; most of the students in this category are middle class.

Table 6.3 shows the numbers of White and African American students in each scholarship and income category. Most of the African American and White students in the sample received no scholarship aid; however, far more White students received no scholarship aid than did African American students. The following figures in this section focus on the relationship of schoarship aid and African American students' aspirations.

Figure 6.2 shows the degree aspirations of African American and White college students in CIRP by scholarship level. The levels of White and African American students' degree aspirations for both the no scholarship and some scholarship categories are similar with African American students having slightly higher aspirations than White students, but African American students with some scholarship awards having slightly lower aspirations than White students. However, in the high scholarship category, there are much greater gaps between African American and White students: White students who have high scholarship awards tend to have higher aspirations than African American high scholarship award recipients.

To further explain why African American high scholarship recipients have lower degree aspirations, mean differences of scholarship award by income were completed. Figure 6.3 shows African American students' degree aspirations by income category and scholarship/grant aid.

Table 6.3 Numbers of African American and White Students in CIRP Dataset by Income and Scholarship Award Categories

	African American (n=266)			White (n=283)		
	None	Some	High	None	Some	High
Low Income	12	22	20	3	6	3
Medium Income	47	21	40	26	15	13
High Income	74	14	17	189	12	16
Total	132	57	77	218	33	33

The degree aspirations of African American students who received no scholarships or some scholarship awards both follow the same pattern. Those students who are low income tend to have lower aspirations for both scholarship groups. However, the aspirations of the high scholarship recipients follow the opposite pattern. Students who are from low-income backgrounds but receive high amounts of scholarship tend to have higher aspirations, while the high income and high scholarship aid individuals have far lower aspirations.

Therefore, parents' income, for the most part, plays a significant and linear role in students' degree aspirations in the third year of college. One thing that seems to mediate this relationship for low-income students is scholarship aid. The receipt of high amounts of scholarship aid is provid-

Figure 6.2 African American and White Students' Third Year Aspirations by Scholarship Award

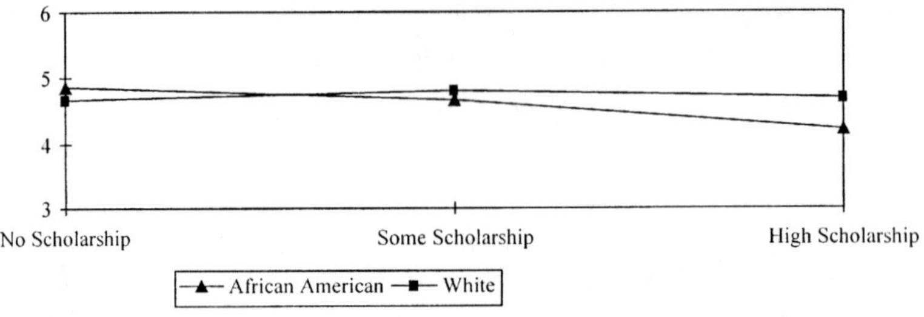

ing opportunities for lower income students—their aspirations are the highest in the African American student sample.

Figure 6.4 shows the initial and third year aspirations of African American students. The initial aspirations of lower income students are similar in 1988 when the students begin college, but the low income students receiving high amounts of scholarship aid increase their degree aspi-

Figure 6.3 African American Students' Third Year Aspirations by Income and Scholarship Award

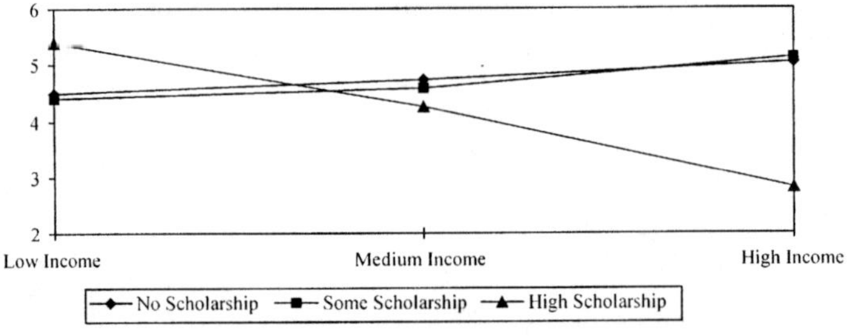

rations two years later, while the aspirations of low income students receiving no or some scholarship aid decreased. The aspirations of the medium income students are quite similar initially, but the high scholarship recipients' aspirations decrease slightly two years later. The most interesting and complex pattern of relationships is with the higher income students: Students who have high amounts of scholarship awards and students who have no scholarship awards begin with high degree aspirations in 1988, but the high scholarship students have far lower aspirations in 1990. However, the students receiving some scholarship dramatically increase their aspirations over time. Figures 6.3 and 6.4 show that the main individuals whose degree plans decrease are the high income, high scholarship aid recipients who previously had planned to earn post-baccalaureate degrees.

This seems to indicate that scholarship aid plays a mixed role in encouraging African American students' aspirations. On the one hand, low income students with high levels of scholarship aid have high levels of aspirations but the receipt of high levels of scholarship aid tends to depress the degree aspirations of students from the medium and high income ranges—particularly the high income range.

Perhaps the reason that high scholarship receipt tends to negatively impact degree aspirations is related to students' academic achievement. Figure 6.5 shows the relationship of parents' income and scholarship aid on African American students' high school GPA. The students with the highest and the lowest high school GPAs are students with high levels of parental income. Students with some scholarship aid and high income have the lowest high school grade point averages, while students with high levels of scholarship aid and high income have the highest high school grade point average. Low-income students of all scholarship receipt types tend to have similar levels of high school achievement.

The results of Figure 6.5 show that high-income students with high levels of scholarship aid are also high achievers in high school. Together with Figure 6.3 it seems that high income, high scholarship individuals have higher pre-college achievement and low degree aspirations. These students are among the most "talented" of the African American students—the tal-

Figure 6.4 African American Students' Initial and Third Year Aspirations by Income and Scholarship Award Categories

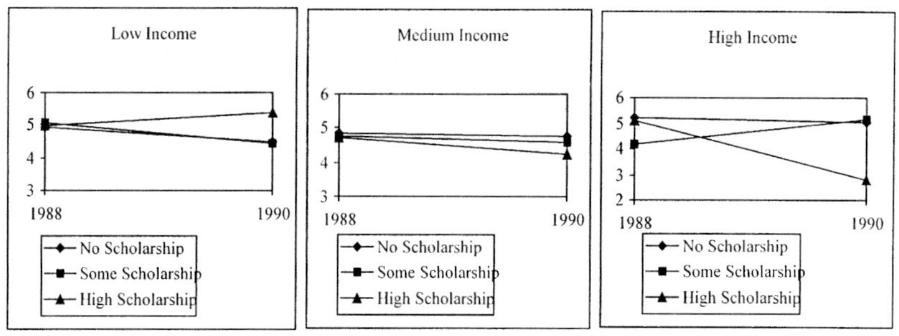

ented 6% as it were. They are the most able when taking academic performance into account and given their higher levels of parental income, they are also the most likely to achieve. Paradoxically, their degree aspirations are the lowest.

What is the relationship of African American students' income and scholarship aid receipt on their college performance? Figure 6.6 shows the students' college grade point average by income and scholarship award. As with degree aspirations (see Figure 6.3), the high income, high scholarship group of students have the lowest college grade point average. Thus it could be the high income/high scholarship students are not performing with high enough grade point averages to consider advanced degrees, since a minimum 3.0 undergraduate GPA is required by many graduate programs. Therefore, it seems that the positive relationship of college grade point average on African American students' degree aspirations (see Table 6.2) differs by scholarship award group: Those in most need of financial assistance and who receive it (low income, high scholarship) have higher college GPAs and those who least need financial assistance and receive it (high income, high scholarship) have the lowest college GPAs.

The analyses of the relationships of scholarship aid, income, and achievement on African American students' degree plans shows areas that are cause for concern and areas of hope for African American students' aspirations. Low-income students with higher levels of scholarship/grant aid are having their dreams supported and developed over time. This shows the importance of grant and scholarship aid to low income students. It can

Figure 6.5 African American Students' High School GPA by Income and Scholarship Award

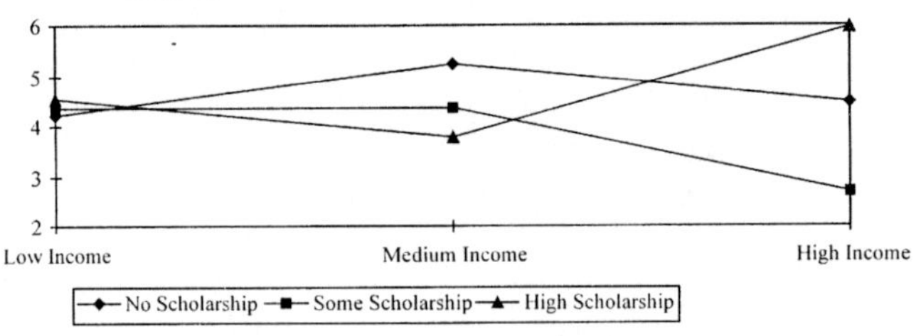

facilitate their matriculation in institutions and their degree goals over time.

It appears that some high scholarship students (medium and high income) have lowered their degree aspirations during college, which may be the cause of the negative relationship between scholarship aid and third year degree aspirations. Why have high scholarship students with higher levels of income lowered their degree aspirations during college? One reason is that African American students who are higher income may be attending higher cost institutions (a variable unmeasured in this dataset). The higher scholarships may assist students during their first year of enrollment, but the high cost of tuition fees over time may negatively affect the students' degree goals.

In addition, the higher income, African American students who receive large amounts of scholarship aid may be receiving merit-based aid given their high levels of academic achievement in high school (see Figure 6.5). If the students are indeed attending higher cost institutions and these institutions are competitive, the African American students may not be able to maintain high enough college GPAs so they can maintain their levels of aid. Since financial aid awards are measured at college entry for students in

Figure 6.6 African American Students' College GPA by Income and Scholarship Award

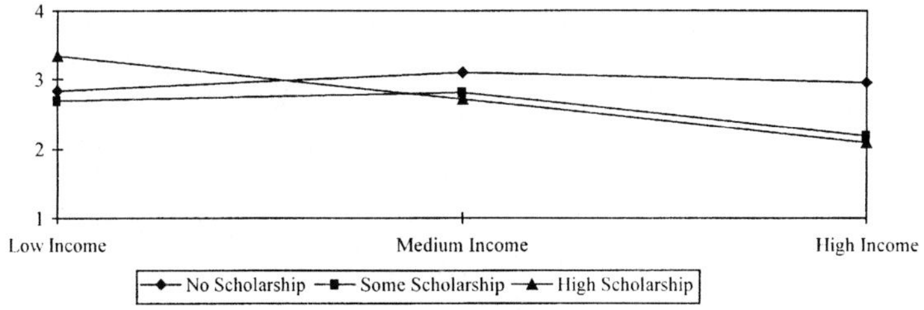

CIRP, it cannot be determined if the high scholarship, high-income students had decreased levels of financial aid later in college.

COMPARISONS BETWEEN THE CIRP AND BPS FULL REGRESSION MODELS

There are distinct differences between the full regression models of BPS and CIRP—and many of the distinctions seem to have little to do with the unique variables introduced into the regression models. Table 6.4 shows a summary of the significant predictors of degree aspirations for African American and White students in BPS and CIRP full regression models. As with the base regression model (see Table 5.7), the regression model for White students in BPS (R^2 of .61) has the highest predictive value of the separate group analyses. However, the regression model for African Americans in CIRP (R^2 of .40) has a higher predictive value than the regression model for African Americans in BPS (R^2 of .35). The higher amount of variance explained by the African American CIRP regression model seems due to the additional measures added in the full model. Since many of the significant predictors of aspirations across BPS and CIRP are similar to the base regression models (see Tables 5.7 and 5.8), the following paragraphs highlight the most important differences between the regression models in each dataset after unique variables are taken into account.

Although none of the SES measures in the CIRP dataset significantly affect students' degree aspirations in the base regression model, father's educational attainment is a significant, positive predictor of African American students' aspirations. High school GPA is a negative predictor of African American students' degree aspirations, which seems to indicate that high achieving African American high school students are not receiving the support (academic or otherwise) they need to succeed in college and ultimately lower their degree aspirations.

Intellectual Self-Confidence continues to have opposite effects on White and African American students' aspirations in BPS. African American students with high levels of Intellectual Self-Confidence have lower degree aspirations over time, while White students with high levels of Intellectual Self-Confidence have higher degree aspirations over time. These findings (for African American students) are similar to the relationship of high school grade point average on students' aspirations in CIRP. Perhaps Intellectual Self-Confidence in BPS is a proxy for high school grade point

	BPS—Degree Expectations		CIRP—Degree Plans	
Variables	African American	White	African American	White
Pre-college characteristics				
Female	—	—	—	—
Age	**pos**	**neg**	—	—
Father's Educational Attainment	—	—	**pos**	—
Mother's Educational Attainment	**pos**	**pos**	—	—
Parent Income	—	**neg**	—	—
Number of Children	**neg**	—	*NA*	*NA*
Married	—	—	*NA*	*NA*
Separated/Divorced	—	**neg**	*NA*	*NA*
Items Owned	—	**pos**	*NA*	*NA*
High School GPA	*NA*	*NA*	**neg**	—
Initial Expectations/Orientations				
Degree Expectations	**pos**	**pos**	*NA*	*NA*
Degree Plans	*NA*	*NA*	**pos**	**pos**
Intellectual Self-Confidence	**neg**	**pos**	—	—
First Choice	**neg**	—	—	—
Second Choice	*NA*	*NA*	**pos**	**pos**
Third Choice	*NA*	*NA*	—	—
Distance From Home	—	—	**pos**	—
Good Reputation	**neg**	—	*NA*	*NA*
Close to Home	—	—	*NA*	*NA*
Less Expensive	—	—	*NA*	*NA*
Social Change Orientation	*NA*	*NA*	—	—
Institutional Characteristics				
Control (Private)	—	**pos**	—	—
Level (4-year)	**pos**	**pos**	—	—
Single Sex	*NA*	*NA*	—	—
HBCU	*NA*	*NA*	—	—
Perc. Afr. Am Enrollmt	**pos**	—	*NA*	*NA*
Tuition Cost	—	—	*NA*	*NA*
Size	**pos**	**pos**	*NA*	*NA*
Institutional Priorities				
Commitment to Social Activism	*NA*	*NA*	—	—
Commitment to Diversity	*NA*	*NA*	—	—
Financial Aid/Work				
Borrow/Loans	—	—	—	—
Scholarship	—	—	**neg**	—
Work Study	—	—	**pos**	—
Hours spent working	—	—	—	**neg**
Number of Jobs	—	—	*NA*	*NA*
Involvement				
Faculty Contact	**pos**	—	—	—
Peer Contact	—	—	**pos**	—
Participated in ethnic organizations	*NA*	*NA*	—	—
Achievement				
College GPA	*NA*	*NA*	**pos**	—

Note: NA indicates that variable was not available in dataset and thus not entered into full regression models.

average. Since the BPS dataset does not contain a pre-college achievement measure, the use of Intellectual Self-Confidence in absence of high school grade point average may be adequate.

Findings are mixed with regard to the impact of college choice on students' degree aspirations. African American students attending their first choice institution in BPS have lower aspirations over time, while African American and White students in CIRP attending their second choice institutions have higher aspirations over time. These findings seem to reflect that the BPS and CIRP samples are quite different and therefore processes by which the students in each sample chose postsecondary institutions differed dramatically. Most of the BPS students attended their first choice institutions and attended institutions closer to their homes than CIRP students (see Table 5.6). Other studies have indicated that BPS students' choice sets (the number of institutions to which they apply) are composed of only one institution (Hurtado et al., 1997), and many of the CIRP students applied to more than 3 institutions (see Table 5.6). Thus, the students in CIRP begin preparing for postsecondary education from a position of having a lot of options of college attendance. The first choice measure in BPS may reflect the students who had fewer options of institutions to attend. While the second choice measure in CIRP may reflect students being able to attend an institution that would offer them the best experience given the other two or more institutions on their list.

Institutional characteristics remain strong predictors of students' aspirations in BPS. Institutional size is a measure added to the BPS full model and it too is a significant predictor of African American and White students' aspirations. None of the institutional characteristics are significant predictors of aspirations for students in CIRP. As in the base regression model, financial aid measures are significant predictors of the aspirations of CIRP students but are not significant predictors of the aspirations of students in BPS.

One of the main distinctions in the pattern of predictors of degree aspirations for African American and White students across both datasets is the function of SES measures. In BPS, SES has direct effects on students' aspirations and seems to indirectly affect aspirations through the choice measures and the kinds of institutions students are able to attend. However, in CIRP, SES has primarily indirect effects on students' aspirations through financial aid and work measures.

Therefore, in BPS the pattern of relationships seems to function like this: Students' socioeconomic statuses affect the kinds of institutions students choose, their degree aspirations, and the institutions they attend. The kinds of institutions they attend affect their interactions and experiences, which then affect their third year aspirations.

In CIRP, students' aspirations are a function of pre-college achievement, initial aspirations, choice measures, financial aid/work, contact with peers, and college achievement. Students begin college with initial degree aspirations, which affect the kinds of colleges that are in their choice set, which affect the college they attend and the financial aid they receive. The colleges they attend affect their interactions and their college achievement, which affects their degree aspirations. In CIRP, the aspirations development process seems mostly as a result of students' individual choices, but in BPS, the aspirations development process seems to be mostly a result of what students are allowed to do given the constraints of their parents' education levels, individual circumstances, and the kinds of institutions they are able to attend.

7
Conclusion: Dreams Deferred?

A REVIEW OF APPROACH TO STUDYING EDUCATIONAL ASPIRATIONS

Langston Hughes (1958) once asked, "What happens to a dream deferred? Does it dry up like a raisin in the sun?" The main research question of this study was to discover how is it that dreams are deferred? What are the processes by which students' aspirations grow or decline over time? Given African American students' lower rates of college attendance, college graduation, and graduate school attendance in comparison to White students, it is important to understand how African American students develop their educational aspirations and degree goals and address the factors that impede their progress toward realizing their dreams.

The theoretical basis for the study comes from Blau and Duncan's (1967) status attainment model, the assumptions of the Wisconsin attainment model (Sewell et al., 1969), and Turner's (1960) notion of contest vs. sponsored mobility. The study attempted to resolve some theoretical controversies in the assumptions of the Wisconsin attainment model. Some researchers assert that the model assumes students are free to move through society choosing their paths, but that a true conceptualization of students' attainment is that students are constrained by society and are "allowed" to achieve based on their socioeconomic (SES) backgrounds (Kerckhoff, 1976). In addition, the processes by which students develop their degree goals can be described as resulting from an educational contest whereby the most able students have the highest goals, or via sponsorship whereby individuals in powerful positions sponsor particular students and therefore influence their achievement and attainment (Turner, 1960). The objective of this study was to identify the individual and institutional factors involved in the development of degree aspirations for African American and White students.

This study used two national, longitudinal databases of college student data—Beginning Postsecondary Students Longitudinal Study BPS:90/92) and Cooperative Institutional Research Program (CIRP:88/90) to examine the roles of individual characteristics and institutional factors on educational aspirations. The BPS database includes students who entered higher education for the first time in the 1989–90 school year and surveyed students at the end of their first year, with the first follow-up of students occurring at the end of their third year of college. CIRP includes students who entered higher education in the 1988–89 school year and surveyed students before college entry or during Fall orientation of their first year, with the first follow-up occurring before or at the beginning of their third year of college.

The use of both data sets was necessary because each database has strengths and weaknesses with respect to the measures used and because they measure educational aspirations differently. BPS also has more varied and complete measures of socioeconomic status, while CIRP contains measures of pre-college achievement and several more measures of students' experiences in the campus community. With regard to the dependent measures used in the study: The BPS data set asks students to report their degree expectations and the CIRP data set asks students to report their degree plans. Kerckhoff (1976) hypothesizes that the different measurements of aspirations represent theoretically distinct conceptions of the status attainment process. Expectations measure students' degree goals within social constraints and plans may measure students' aspirations without taking into account constraints. The different measurements of educational aspirations may have contributed to different findings for the data sets and a similar regression model was tested on both data sets to determine if the measurement of aspirations contributes to different findings. Since there are differences between the samples and measures in the data sets, it is difficult to precisely determine whether the difference between groups (and the factors that influence their aspirations) can be attributed to different dependent variables or distinct samples. BPS represents a wider range of college attendees and CIRP represents a more traditional student sample.

Each data set is comprised of a different sample of students. The BPS sample had older students, more students attending two-year institutions and students from a wider range of backgrounds and experiences than the students in CIRP. The CIRP samples were more traditional-aged (attending college a year or two after high school graduation), more HBCU attendees among the African American students, and CIRP students tended to have more postsecondary institutional choices than the students in BPS. Given the different backgrounds of the students in CIRP and BPS, the students also attended different kinds of institutions, and had different kinds of college experiences. Therefore, the regression results for the students in BPS and CIRP were quite different.

The use of both data sets informed the investigation of the development of degree aspirations in several ways. First, if only the BPS data set had been used, no effect of financial aid measures on students' degree aspirations would have been found. Apparently, financial aid measures are more important to traditional college students (like those in CIRP) who have greater choices about the colleges they attend. Second, only using the BPS data set, the effect of academic achievement (before college or in college) on the development of students' future degree plans would have been impossible to determine. Third, if only the CIRP data set had been used, there would be no evidence of the effect of institutional characteristics on degree aspirations. It seems that when students have several choices of the institutions they can attend as in CIRP, the characteristics of the institution they attend do not significantly impact aspirations. However, if students have only one institution they can attend (because it is nearby and it is an institution they can afford to attend), the characteristics of that institution do impact the students' aspirations. Finally, using only CIRP, there would have been no evidence of the ways in which marital status and the number of children seems to constrain students' aspirations over time as in the BPS sample. These data allowed the investigation of those students with multiple roles and responsibilities.

Ideally, the use of both BPS and CIRP could have provided a direct test of the ways in which the measurement of aspirations affects regression results. However, many of the findings in each data set can be tied to the unique differences in the BPS and CIRP samples. The institutional choices of BPS students seem directly tied to their comparatively lower SES backgrounds and the more nontraditional (older, married, having children) students in the sample. The traditional age, perhaps residential, students in CIRP have more options of institutions to attend and therefore the institutional characteristics seem not to significantly impact their degree aspirations.

Therefore, the use of both data sets (and therefore both samples) informs the understanding of degree aspirations that the use of only one data set cannot. The results from the BPS analyses paint a portrait of students being constrained by their backgrounds in terms of the types of institutions they were able to attend, and their ability to conceive of themselves as future post-baccalaureate degree earners given their parents' attainment and material circumstances. In contrast, the results of the CIRP analyses (with some exceptions) mostly seem to represent students as freely making choices about their future with less regard for constraints.

Overall, this study provides considerable evidence to support the notion that students' degree aspirations—their dreams—are affected by their individual characteristics, the kinds of institutions students attend, the types of interactions students have and the financial support they receive. The following section provides a detailed summary of the results of this study and a discussion of the hypotheses in terms of what both data sets contribute to the understanding of aspirations development.

SUMMARY OF RESULTS AND HYPOTHESES

The results of this study are mixed with regard to the confirmation of the hypotheses (see Chapter 4 for discussion of the hypotheses). The theoretical framework for most studies of educational aspirations is grounded in either the assumption of higher education as a meritocracy or in the primacy of socioeconomic disadvantages affecting students' outcomes. This study finds that both characterizations are accurate. In particular, the next few pages discuss the results of the study with regard to roles of status attainment, contest vs. sponsored mobility, institutional environments and experiences, and financial aid in shaping students' degree goals. The final paragraphs of this section describe the distinctiveness of the models for the BPS and CIRP data sets and for African American and White students within the data sets.

Status Attainment

Hypotheses 2 and 4 specifically addressed the assumptions of the status attainment model. Hypothesis 2 asserted that students' SES would have strong effects on their degree goals. Overall, the results of the study support this hypothesis, but there are mixed results with regard to Hypothesis 4—that measures of ability would affect aspirations and would lessen the effect of SES on aspirations. The following paragraphs discuss both hypotheses in the context of the perspectives of status attainment and Turner's (1960) concepts of contest vs. sponsored mobility.

Sewell, Haller, and Portes (1969) first developed the social psychological status attainment model to explain some of the relationships in Blau and Duncan's original model. In addition, Sewell et al. purport that a student's socioeconomic status and academic (or intellectual) ability affect the degree to which he or she receives encouragement and support from others, which in turn affects the student's goals and aspirations (Kerckhoff, 1976). Critiques of the social psychological perspective of status attainment have questioned the theoretical foundation for the social psychological view of status attainment. The social psychological perspective views aspirations as resulting from an individual's social interactions and abilities. Students are not constrained by society and their successes are determined by their abilities. A competing perspective is that of social allocation. Individuals only have the expectations that they think they can achieve given the social constraints in which they live.

This study provides support for both the social psychological and the social allocation views of status attainment: however, social allocation processes seem to dominate the development of students' aspirations. In support of the social allocation view, the full BPS regression model shows several significant effects of SES measures on students' aspirations. One measure of SES—mother's educational attainment—has strong effects on the educational expectations of both African American and White students, and the material circumstances of White students also affect their degree expectations. For CIRP, only one SES measure affects students' degree plans—father's educational attainment affects African American students' degree plans.

There are other pre-college characteristics that have much stronger effects for BPS respondents: number of children for African American students and age for White students. Therefore the results of the study give some credence to Kerckhoff's (1976) notion that students' educational expectations are a function of perceived constraints. These findings show that there are some real constraints for particular groups of students and researchers must account for them in future studies. Clearly, the fact that African American students with children in BPS have much lower degree expectations than African American students without children suggests that students are making decisions about their future degree goals based on their responsibilities and socioeconomic circumstances. There is no measure of number of children in the CIRP data set, so it cannot be determined if the same relationships would be true for CIRP respondents.

The social psychological perspective of status attainment (and aspirations development) views aspirations as a product of individual's abilities, interactions with others, and the individual's perceptions of their skills. The role that Intellectual Self-Confidence plays in affecting African American students' aspirations contradicts the theoretically expected direction of the relationship. Intellectual Self-Confidence has opposite effects on the educational expectations of African American and White college students in the BPS data set. For African American students, Intellectual Self-Confidence is a negative predictor of degree expectations, and it is a positive predictor of degree expectations for White college students. Intellectually self-confident African American students who did not enter with higher degree aspirations are likely to have somewhat lower aspirations. Never having had "the dream" to begin with almost ensures these students will not aspire to advanced degrees.

In support of the social psychological view of attainment, is the positive relationship of Intellectual Self-Confidence on White students' aspirations in BPS, and that African American students tend to benefit from interaction with peers (BPS) and interaction with faculty members (CIRP). These findings indicate that for African American students, their fellow students and faculty seem to respond to the students' high degree goals and ability and thus may encourage high degree aspirations. In addition, college choice perspectives assume that students are free and unconstrained from attending the types of institutions they may want to choose. The choice measures used in this study are significant predictors of degree aspirations indicating that attendance at first or second choice institutions influence their degree aspirations. However, there are also indications that the college choice measures represent the limited number of institutions (one institution for most of the students in BPS) students were able to consider attending. Therefore, as Kerckhoff (1976) suggests, students adjust (or set) their degree goals commensurate with their circumstances.

Contest and Sponsored Mobility

Turner's (1960) conceptions of contest and sponsored mobility are appropriate frameworks for understanding educational aspirations. This study provides support for both of Turner's notions. On one hand, students' educational aspirations are a function of their parents' educational attainments. Thus, the educational system seems not to function solely as a meritocracy, but also as a sponsorship. On the other hand, there are no significant effects of SES on the degree plans of White students in the CIRP data set, suggesting little evidence of sponsorship. In addition, there was a strong effect of college achievement on African American students' degree plans, showing that contest mobility processes are at work.

The most "able"— defined as students who have higher college achievement—tend to have the highest degree aspirations. However, those African American students who had higher pre-college achievement tend to have lower aspirations. Achievement in college is most important for African American students' advanced degree plans. These findings indicate that the processes of postsecondary institutions may be supporting the aspirations of college achievers to a greater extent than high school achievers—all other things being equal.

The social psychological view of social mobility assumes that the ways in which students perform affect how people around them behave and support their interests. Perhaps college achievers are having their dreams facilitated through interactions with faculty. This is an indication that the college achievers may be "sponsored" (or directed) toward advanced degrees. The reason that faculty interaction in particular seems to affect African American students' degree goals may be because African American students seem to have less information about higher education than White students (Maxey et al., 1995), and that particular institutional environments seem to facilitate faculty/student interactions. Interaction with faculty members can assist African American students in increasing their knowledge about graduate degrees and in developing degree goals.

Financial Aid

The relationship between financial aid variables and students' degree goals represents institutional support of students and students' individual financial circumstances. Hypothesis 3 asserted that financial aid measures would lessen the effects of SES on aspirations. The results of this study are mixed in support of this hypothesis. I expected that when financial aid variables were controlled in the regression models, the effects of SES would be diminished.

In the CIRP data set, father's educational attainment became a significant predictor of African American students' degree plans after financial aid measures were controlled, as did parental income for White students in BPS. However, in the BPS data set, mother's education remained a significant predictor of both groups' educational expectations at all steps of the regression models.

In terms of financial aid measures significantly predicting aspirations, the results depended upon the data set used. In BPS, none of the financial aid measures significantly affected expectations. In CIRP, African American, high scholarship recipients tended to have lower educational plans, while African American work-study students had higher educational plans. White students who worked longer hours had lower educational plans. Thus the type of aid received was important in terms of its effects on different student groups.

These findings point to the fact that financial aid has conflicting effects on the outcomes of students. Additional analyses of African American scholarship/grant aid recipients in CIRP showed that low-income African American students tended to have higher aspirations over time. So in this way, scholarship aid was helping low income students plan to earn post-baccalaureate degrees. However, the higher income students who were high scholarship recipients tended to lower their degree goals. Perhaps these students attended more expensive institutions (a variable unmeasured in the CIRP data set). It may also be that African American students who were high-income receiving high scholarships received merit-based aid and attended selective institutions. The students may not have been able to maintain the college grade point averages to keep their aid. The results suggest that the roles of selectivity and tuition cost in conjunction with financial aid awards need to be examined.

In addition, the finding that White students who work longer hours tend to have lower degree plans indicates that White students who are not awarded enough financial aid tend to work longer hours to pay expenses. Therefore their decisions to earn graduate degrees may be constrained by their financial circumstances. Except for the positive effects of work-study among African American students in BPS, the awarding of financial aid does not uniformly show a positive effect on the degree aspirations of students.

Institutional Environments and Involvement

Students' experiences in particular institutional environments seem to affect their degree expectations and plans. Hypotheses 5 and 6 addressed the role that institutional characteristics and involvements have in the development of students' aspirations. Hypothesis 5 stated that institutional characteristics would have strong effects on aspirations, and Hypothesis 6 asserted that high levels of student involvement in student and peer-related activities would positively affect aspirations. Both hypotheses were confirmed with portions of the BPS and CIRP samples.

Institutional characteristics have strong effects on students' degree expectations in BPS only. Therefore, this hypothesis was partially confirmed. Perhaps the nature of the CIRP sample (mostly traditional-age, four-year college attendees, from middle-class backgrounds) affected the degree to which institutional differences influenced students' degree aspirations. Institutional environments can provide particular interactions and experiences that tend to constrain or develop students' dreams. Larger institutions tend to positively influence the aspirations of students, perhaps because larger institutions tend to have more graduate programs and undergraduate students may have more access to graduate students and therefore increase their knowledge about post-baccalaureate degree options.

Four-year institutions seem to develop the degree goals of students more than two-year institutions. Dougherty (1987) and Brint and Karabel (1989) support this finding. The structural elements of community colleges seem to "cool out" students from pursuing higher degree goals, a concept proposed by Clark (1960). Therefore, Clark's statement that faculty, peers, institutional structures, and administrative procedures diminish higher degree goals may be supported by this study.

Institutions with higher percentages of African Americans positively affect the expectations of African American students which may suggest that the students may receive more peer support and may experience less social isolation than at less racially/ethnically diverse institutions. The results of the BPS analyses also support previous research (Bohr et al., 1995; Fleming, 1984) that HBCUs (historically Black colleges and universities) in particular support students' aspirations more than PWIs (predominately White institutions)—though this is not a significant effect in the CIRP sample. CIRP students at HBCUs are attending institutions that are more selective and enroll higher achieving students than the high African American enrollment institutions that BPS students attended. Therefore, controlling for initially high aspirations and achievement essentially supplants a HBCU effect.

It seems that what is necessary for the development of African American aspirations is an environment that is supportive of African Americans. Although the results of the CIRP analyses did not show a significant effect of perceived Commitment to Diversity on students' aspirations, structural measures of high African American enrollments are important predictors of African American post-baccalaureate degree goals. A structural indication of a supportive environment is the percentage of African Americans enrolled. It seems that these institutions tend to facilitate students' academic goals in many of the ways that Fleming (1984) mentioned: friendship among peers, faculty and staff; participation in the life of the campus; and feelings of academic success. This may be enhanced on campuses with more African American students. This is an aspect of students' college experiences that significantly affects their degree expectations (in the BPS data set) and perhaps is one way that HBCUs and institutions with higher numbers of African American students positively affect students' degree goals.

The student involvement measures used in this study only affected the degree plans and expectations of African American students. Therefore, Hypothesis 6 is confirmed for African American students. In BPS, faculty contact affects the expectations of African American students, while in CIRP, peer contact affects the African American students' degree plans. African American students who interact with their peers in academic-related activities and students who interact with faculty frequently tend to have their aspirations supported and developed. Faculty interaction may socialize African American students into future occupations and advanced degree options. Perhaps the type of institutions African Americans attend influence the kind of faculty interactions they have. African American students in BPS tend to be commuter students and spend less time on campus interacting with peers. Faculty interaction, more than peer interaction, therefore affected their degree aspirations.

The fact that no involvement measures are significantly related to White students' degree aspirations is counter to the findings of Astin (1993b) that peer and student-faculty interaction significantly affects degree aspirations. Astin's (1993b) study focused on student outcomes after four years of college. Perhaps involvement measures are key predictors of African American students' aspirations in the early years of college, but for White students, involvement measures may be more important during the later years of college. Given that African Americans tend to have less knowledge about postsecondary options, it may be more important for them to become involved in the campus community early so they can clarify their goals. This may be particularly true for African American students at predominantly White institutions who may be marginal to the mainstream campus life and need to find ways to maintain their high degree goals by interacting with key faculty or peers.

The results of the BPS and CIRP regression models indicate that initial degree aspirations have the strongest effects on students' later degree aspirations of all factors included in the models. White students enter much surer of their degree goals than African American students. White students tend to have much more access to pre-college information about degree goals and options than African American students and therefore attend their first choice institution in greater numbers (in BPS) and change their degree goals much less often (in BPS and CIRP) than African American students. Therefore it may be that college experiences have less of an effect on the aspirations of White students than on the aspirations of African American students.

Distinctiveness of the Models by Race and Between Data Sets

Hypotheses 1 and 7 addressed the ways in which the models predicting degree aspirations would differ across data sets and for African American and White student groups within each data set. Hypothesis 1 stated that differences in the measurement of aspirations items would not produce substantial differences in the ways the independent variables affect aspirations over time. This hypothesis can neither be clearly confirmed nor disconfirmed.

There are substantial differences in the regression models across both data sets. Whether this difference is due to the measurement of aspirations or the differences in the student samples is an issue that cannot be determined. The samples of BPS and CIRP are significantly different from each other in areas of students' pre-college characteristics and institutional characteristics. For instance, there are more women in the BPS sample, younger students in the CIRP sample, more students at two-year institutions in BPS, more students at private institutions and HBCUs in CIRP). The differences in the regression results are not only because of different measures of educational aspirations. The only significant predictor of third-year plans or expectations for both groups is students' initial plans or expectations.

While previous studies of educational aspirations have inconclusive findings with regard to the predictors of educational aspirations, it may be that some of the conflicting findings are attributable to differences in the measurement of aspirations. However, after analysis of two data sets, I conclude that it is also possible that the conflicting findings of previous studies are due to the different samples used and the different measurement of degree aspirations. Pascarella (1984) found that institutional characteristics had only indirect effects on students' degree plans using the CIRP data. If this study had used only CIRP data (despite the data being more recent than that used in Pascarella's study), the same conclusions would have been drawn. In contrast, the use of BPS data shows strong effects of institutional characteristics on degree expectations. The endurance of the lack of direct effects of institutional characteristics on CIRP students' degree plans may indicate that the measurement of degree aspirations—despite sample differences—is the main reason for the different findings between BPS and CIRP. However, the results of this study can neither clearly confirm nor disconfirm this hypothesis. Future research should clarify the results of the study by testing different measurements of aspirations on the same population of students. This would be a direct test of the hypothesis.

Hypothesis 7 was that the pattern of relationships between variables in the African American models would be significantly different from the models for White students. This hypothesis is confirmed. Not only are the predictors of educational expectations and plans different for each racial/ethnic group in each data set, in some cases, the significant predictors of expectations/plans for African American and White students have opposite effects. For instance, age is a positive predictor of African American students' degree expectations in BPS, but a negative predictor of White students' degree expectations. The opposite effects of age may reflect the social constraints on each group. White students who are traditional age tend to have higher aspirations, but older African American students, those who may not have been able to go directly to postsecondary education after high school seek opportunities later in life to pursue their dreams. The tendency to delay college entry among African American students has been noted by other researchers (Hearn, 1992).

There are several reasons for the differences between the predictors of African American and White students' degree aspirations. First, African American students are more likely to change their degree aspirations than White students in both BPS and CIRP. Therefore, African American degree aspirations are somewhat more dependent upon their college experiences than White students' aspirations. Second, African American students tend to go to different types of institutions (e.g. attendance at HBCUs; attendance at two-year institutions in greater numbers) than White students because of their race/ethnicity and their lower income backgrounds. Thus both groups have different kinds of college experiences, which contribute to the development of their degree aspirations. The finding for African American students in BPS that attendance at institutions with high enrollments of African American students positively affects their degree expectations indicates that there are particular environments that are more supportive of the degree goals of African American students. In addition, involvement with faculty and peers are much stronger predictors of African American students' aspirations than White students' aspirations. Although African American students may come from comparatively lower income backgrounds, the interactions they have with members of the campus community seem particularly important in developing their degree goals.

The final reason for the different regression models between African American and White students is the difference in the students' SES backgrounds and individual characteristics. African American students have much lower levels of SES than White students in both the BPS and CIRP samples and therefore the SES measures explain far more of the variance for African American students than White students across both data sets. Perhaps because of the lower levels of SES, the results of the CIRP analyses show that financial aid variables affect the degree aspirations of African American students to a greater degree than White students in the CIRP data set. Financial aid, in part, is able to provide access to lower income students and is associated with higher aspirations among lower income, African American students. Despite the fact that institutional characteristics and experiences affect student's degree goals, it is clear that the financial circumstances of students have strong effects on the goals of students, at the point of college entry and after two years of college.

The results of the study do not support previous findings that African American students have higher aspirations than White students (Agnew & Jones, 1988; Astin, 1990). Only the third year aspirations of African American and White students in BPS are significantly different—with African American students having higher aspirations. There is no significant difference in the means of White and African American students' initial aspirations in BPS or CIRP data sets, or in the third year aspirations of students in CIRP. Therefore, it cannot be concluded from this study that African American students have unrealistic aspirations (at least not more so than White students). The higher aspirations of African American students compared to White students in BPS seems to be due to the influences of the students' college experiences.

IMPLICATIONS FOR THEORY, RESEARCH, AND PRACTICE

Theory

The competing assumptions of status attainment models have focused on conceptions of individual students' aspirations and attainment being the function of social constraints or that students are individual actors able to fulfill their goals unconstrained by society. This study provides considerable support for the view of aspirations resulting from social constraints and some support for the notion that students are able to fulfill their goals without constraints.

In particular, the differences in the BPS and CIRP samples seem to reflect the processes differently. For the traditional students in CIRP, it seems that individual choices and actions seem to most affect students' aspirations, where in BPS, social constraints mostly affect students' degree goals. Students with low levels of mother's educational attainment, White students who are older, divorced, or separated, and African American students having several children—individuals who are considered "nontraditional" students (Bean & Metzner, 1985)—all experience constraints on their degree expectations.

The processes affecting aspirations are different for African American and White students. The college experiences and achievement of African American students are strong predictors of their third year degree aspirations, but neither significantly predicts White students' aspirations. The results of this study suggest that, although it may be possible to develop a theoretical model of aspirations development that encompasses the experiences of both African American and White students, the model should be tested separately for each group. This is particularly true because African American and White students begin college with different backgrounds, attend different types of institutions, and have different experiences in college.

In addition, the theoretical conceptualizations of college students' degree goals have been lacking in terms of the role of institutions in the development of students' aspirations. Pascarella (1984) critiqued educational aspirations research as being atheoretical, and found few direct effects of institutional measures on students' degree aspirations. This study shows that the structural characteristics of institutions do have direct effects on students' aspirations and that the role of institutional characteristics in the development of students' degree goals needs to be theoretically linked with the theoretical perspectives of status attainment. In particular, the social psychological (socialization) view of attainment purports that teachers, parents, and peers respond to students based on students' ambition and ability. Past research suggests that the socializing influences on students' degree aspirations also differ by institution. Clark's (1960) notions of community college attendees being "cooled out" from the pursuit of a Bachelor's degree are based on the idea that community colleges socialize students—through students' interactions with other students, faculty, staff, and the administrative policies and procedures—to lower their degree goals over time.

Therefore, students' degree goals are a function of their own individual backgrounds and circumstances, their institutional choices (such as they are), and the socializing influences of institutions. Theories of students' degree aspirations development and achievement that encapsulate the multi-faceted nature of student decision-making as well as the ways in which institutional environments affect students' decisions can better conceptualize the processes by which students make decisions about their futures.

Figure 7.1 shows a theoretical model based on the findings of the study and some suggested indirect effects of groups of variables in the model on aspirations. First, individual characteristics (background measures) in the form of SES, race/ethnicity, age, family status, and pre-college achievement affect initial aspirations, students' career and life goals, levels of intellectual self-confidence, and college choices.

The results of this study show that the factors influencing third year college students' degree aspirations differ quite a bit for African American and White students. Therefore, students' racial/ethnic backgrounds must be taken into account when examining degree goals, as should students' socioeconomic statuses. Both contest and sponsored mobility processes

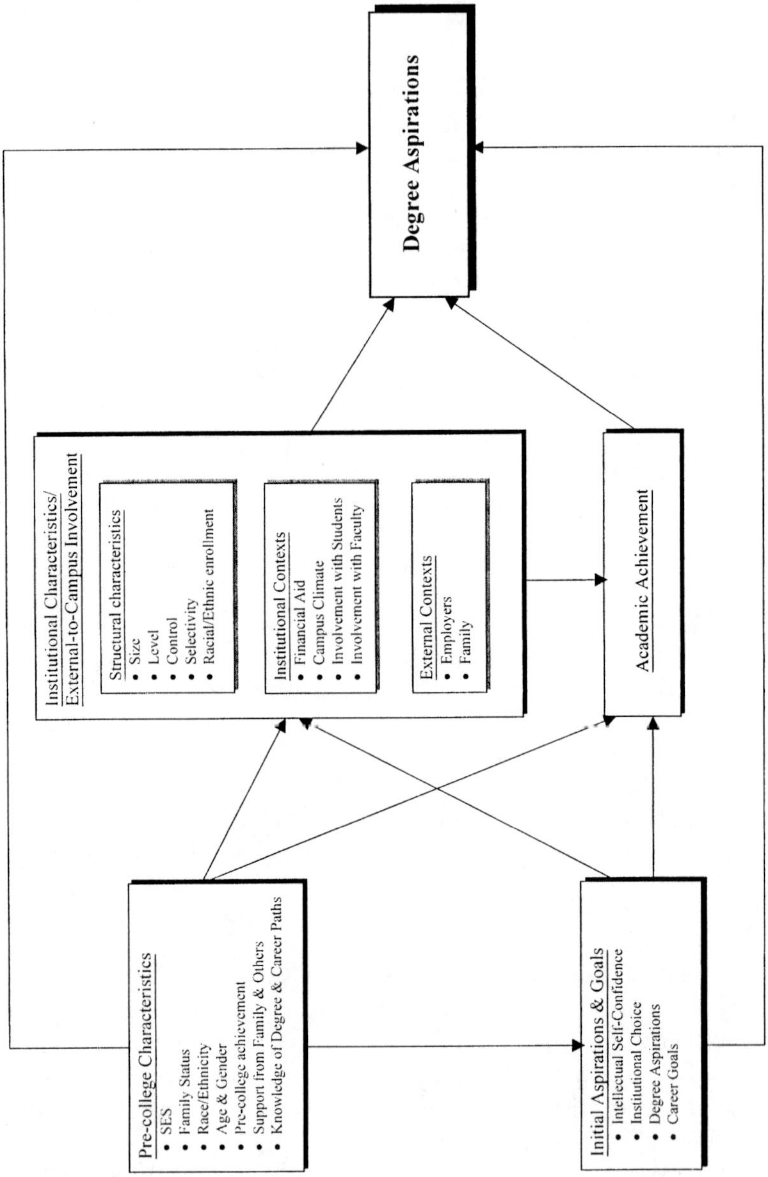

Figure 7.1 Theoretical Model of Factors Influencing College Students' Degree Aspirations

affect the ways in which students develop their aspirations. However, some high-income African American students who achieved in high school tended not to do as well in college and subsequently lowered their aspirations. This runs counter to the expected relationship of SES to achievement and seems to indicate that there are specific elements of the college environment that can work against African American students regardless of the "advantages" in their backgrounds.

Initial orientations, goals, aspirations, and college choice measures are important to incorporate into a model of degree aspirations because they show the degree to which students have knowledge about their options, are confident about their abilities, and are constrained by financial or social circumstances. The results of this study also suggest that students' initial orientation toward wanting to improve society may provide strong indirect effects on aspirations later in college.

Knowledge of career and degree paths is another important element to consider in aspirations models. If students are not knowledgeable about the paths to postsecondary degrees and/or the necessary educational requirements for certain professions their aspirations may change considerably over time.

Individual characteristics and initial aspirations/orientations affect the postsecondary institutions students attend. The results of this study and of previous studies (reviewed in Chapters 2 and 3) show that students interact in particular institutional contexts that influence their aspirations. For instance, the type of institution students' attend (four-year or two-year, high cost vs. low cost) affects the kind of financial assistance they can receive. The financial aid students receive (especially students with work-study awards) affect the students' involvement with faculty, staff, and students on campus.

Two sets of variables that are important for understanding students' degree aspirations but were unmeasured in this study are climate and external-to-college contexts. Perceptions of the campus climate for minority students and perceptions of the degree to which the institution supports students' academic goals are important predictors of outcomes. Perceptions of campus climate may have indirect effects on aspirations by affecting the level of involvement students have with other students, faculty, and staff. In addition, students' involvements in communities that are external to the campus community also may be important factors affecting students' aspirations. In predominantly White institutions, African American students may have frequent interactions with their families, friends, and others that may buffer them from negative experiences.

Students' experiences in institutional and external-to-the-institution contexts may affect their levels of college achievement. Finally, individual measures, experiences in- and out- of the institutional context, and college achievement all affect aspirations.

Future Research

The results of this study indicate several implications for future research in the area of student degree goal formation. First, the results of the study suggest that there are quite a few indirect effects on students' degree goals (see Figure 7.1). Financial aid measures seem to have some direct effects on the educational aspirations of students, but students' income is connected to the amount of financial aid they receive. Further investigation into indirect effects of financial aid measures on students' degree goals is an important direction for future research. For example, investigating the indirect effects of SES can also inform an understanding of how initial aspirations are formed and how initial aspirations are related to students' aspirations after three or more years of college. Measuring college achievement and experiences at a time point prior to the measurement of aspirations may aid the theoretical and empirical understandings of the role college experiences play in the development of degree goals.

The findings in this study do indicate the need for multiple measures of SES to be used in research studies. If the parental education and material circumstances measures were combined into one SES measure, the separate effects of mother's education and material circumstances on White students' degree expectations in BPS would not have been evident. Similarly, father's education was significant in the CIRP sample. This indicates that different measures of SES can result in slightly different effects.

The final research implication of the study is the linking of aspirations to degree attainment. These links have been made in previous literature, but there is a need to clearly establish these links in future research. Clearly aspirations is a precursor for attainment, but how do the processes that affect aspirations affect attainment? Given that African American students have less knowledge about postsecondary education opportunities than White students and may develop their post-baccalaureate knowledge while attending college, it is important for researchers to identify the points in the education attainment process that are most important for students' goal-setting and goal attaining.

Although one of the strengths of this study is that I could examine aspirations development across several institutions and compare how different institutional characteristics affect aspirations, there is a need for qualitative research into the processes of degree goal development as well. The roles of family members and individuals external to the campus community in supporting students' goals are unexamined in most survey research studies, particularly for African American students who delay college entry. Intensive interviewing can explore the degree to which students themselves feel constrained or hopeful of their ability to achieve.

Implications for Educational Practices

The results of the study suggest that campus leaders and administrators need to create and maintain environments that are supportive of African American students' academic development and degree goals. African American students' are currently making choices of which institutions to attend based upon their perceptions of how supportive the university climates will be to their needs and development. Feagin et al. (1996) report that African Americans decided not to attend particular prestigious universities because they perceived that the campus climate was not supportive of African American students.

Frequent interactions with faculty and staff and in particular offices on campus that help students maneuver through the institutional bureaucracy also aid students' goal development. Designing programs and interactions with faculty so that students, particularly African American students, have access to information about their educational options is important for students to consider and plan for graduate education in the early years of college. Since this study examined the development of students' aspirations in the first two years of college, it seems particularly important for students to have productive interactions with faculty and peers early in their college careers.

Particular kinds of programs that would serve this purpose are undergraduate research programs where students are able to receive academic credit while working with faculty members on research projects. These programs can provide students access to faculty that they may not ordinarily have on large college campuses (in particular) and can expose students to the type of work that may be required of them in graduate school. In addition, students who work closely with faculty are in better positions to receive encouragement from faculty members for pursuing advanced degrees. Also, the organization of structured peer study groups can assist students academically and help students develop the skills for the rigors of graduate work.

Financial aid seems to be important for students in considering the amount of education they can earn. Financial aid that links students with their institutions (e.g. work-study) and prevents them from taking on too many work responsibilities is crucial. In addition, need-based aid is also important for enabling lower income students to attend colleges and universities. Campus policies that are geared to evaluating and meeting students' financial needs are important in ensuring access to college and in ensuring that more students consider themselves able to pursue graduate education. A commitment to increased access for students means that not only must students be admitted to college, but must be provided with financial resources to support their attendance.

Degree aspiration is an important predictor of student persistence in college. Having a greater understanding of the kinds of campus programs that positively influence students' degree aspirations may also influence persistence. It is of critical importance that students have adequate information about their postsecondary educational opportunities, know the services provided by campus units, and understand how to meet career goals through coursework and co-curricular experiences. Universities are under increased pressure to meet economic goals by increasing enrollments, and distance education is becoming a cost-efficient way for colleges and universities to provide course content. Faculty, staff, and administrators will need to think creatively about how to best meet the individual developmental needs of traditional and nontraditional students.

There are segments of the adult population that higher education institutions currently are not serving well. Once students get to college, they must feel welcome and supported in their campus environments. Without the proper support and assistance, students leave college with their dreams deferred and may have their impulses to dream beaten out of them by experience. If the educational attainment rates of African American students are to continue to improve, campus faculty, staff, and administrators are necessary in assisting students to "hold fast to their dreams."

Appendix A
Previous Empirical Research on Aspirations

Chapter 2 provides a brief discussion of the operational definitions of aspirations in previous research. This Appendix shows more detailed tables of previous research. Tables A-1 and A-2 list fifty-three studies, with each table organizing the studies in different ways. Table A-1 is a summary table in which I show the author-defined definitions and my own definition category for the aspirations studies. Table A-2 is organized by my own definition category and the author-defined definitions are also indicated.

Author-defined operational definitions are indicated next to each study in the tables. *Author-defined* means that I have indicated the terms the authors themselves used to refer to the measure of aspirations in the study. Next to each research study in Table A-2 is an indication .of the author-defined operational definition category: Studies of "aspirations" are marked with an "a"; studies of "expectations" are marked with a "b"; studies of "plans" are marked with a "c"; studies of "aspirations" and "expectations" are marked with a "d"; and studies of "aspirations" and "educational plans" are marked with an "e."

Thirty-seven of the 52 articles study aspirations according to the *author's* description of the concepts used, ten study expectations, eight study educational plans, and three study "other" concepts that are operationally defined similarly to aspirations *and* expectations (see Table A-1). It should be noted that five of the studies include measures of multiple concepts (e.g. studies of aspirations and expectations), and they have been double-counted where appropriate. Table A-1 shows multiple categories for some studies (e.g. Agnew & Jones, 1988). This is an indication that the study was counted both as a study of aspirations and expectations (author-defined categories), and also in the "educational likes or wants" and the "educational plans" categories that I developed.

Although many of the studies use similar operational definitions of aspirations and expectations, there remain several inconsistencies. Twenty-six of the 52 studies used survey items that include the word "plan" in the survey question; therefore, it seems that one of the most common ways to operationalize "aspirations" or "expectations" is to measure students' educational plans. Of the twenty-six studies using language regarding educational plans, authors in sixteen studies described the survey item as "aspirations," two as "expectations", and seven as "plans."

Within the broad category of "educational plans, there are a handful of specific survey items used: "highest academic degree planned" (Pascarella, 1984); "how far student plans to go in school" (Allen, 1992); "plans to continue education after high school" (Sewell, Haller, & Ohlendorf, 1970); "plans to pursue graduate study" (Isaac, Malaney, & Karras, 1992); and "the highest level of education the student plans to attain" (Vélez, 1985). The greatest similarities between survey questions are CIRP's "highest academic degree planned" and the National Study of Black College Students' (NSBCS) "how far student plans to go in school", although NSBCS has four response categories while CIRP has seven. In addition, both surveys were administered to undergraduate students and measure the students' graduate school plans. The Wisconsin Study's measure of aspirations is somewhat dated given that survey administration was in 1957, and the aspirations survey item limits students' response choices to what they plan to do after high school. If students planned to attend graduate school or even *finish* college, they could not indicate this on the survey. Finally, Isaac, et al. (1992) specifically studies the graduate school plans of college seniors and not the specific level of degree students plan to achieve.

The other twenty "aspirations" studies ask students to indicate their likes or preferences ("the highest degree you would like to have"); intentions ("highest degree that you intend to obtain"); level of satisfaction ("the lowest level of education with which you'd be satisfied"); predictions ("how far do you think you will get?"), other ("the highest level of education they expect to achieve"; "highest degree aspired to"); or give no detail of the survey item used. There is a final type of measurement of aspirations that does not neatly fit into the other categories of operational definitions: a factor comprised of several items. Friesen's (1983) study is an example of this: aspirations are described as "wishing to be remembered as outstanding student", "expecting to earn a university degree", and "expected median income ten years after high school graduation."

As can be noted from this appendix, fewer studies were found concerning educational expectations. Of the eleven expectations studies, three use "expect" in the wording of the survey item (although one study—Kerchoff & Campbell, 1977—identifies the construct as "ambition"); two ask what students think they will achieve; two use educational plans; and three do not state the survey item used. Three of the studies concentrate on college students while the other six surveyed high school students. All but three of the studies involved data compiled prior to 1980.

Table A-1. Aspirations, Expectations and Educational Plans Studies by Author

Article	Aspirations, Expectations, or Plans (Author-Defined)	Definition Category
Agnew and Jones (1988)	Aspirations and Expectations	L,P
Alexander and Eckland (1975)	Expectations	T
Allen (1992)	Aspirations	P
Allen and Haniff (1991)	Aspirations	P
Alwin (1974)	Aspirations	P
Ashar and Skenes (1993)	Other	P
Astin (1977)	Aspirations	P
Astin (1993b)	Aspirations	O
Bateman and Hossler (1996)	Plans	ND
Berman and Haug (1975)	Aspirations and Expectations	L,T
Braddock and Trent (1991)	Aspirations	P
Braddock, et al. (1991)	Aspirations	P
Burke and Hoelter (1988)	Expectations	E
Cranston and Leonard (1990)	Aspirations	L
Davis (1995)	Aspirations	O
Dawkins and Braddock (1982)	Plans	P
Drew and Astin (1972)	Aspirations	I
Friesen (1983)	Aspirations and Plans	P,F
Hanson (1994)	Aspirations and Expectations	ND
Hauser and Anderson (1991)	Aspirations	L
Hearn (1984)	Aspirations	D
Hearn (1987)	Aspirations	I
Hearn (1991)	Expectations	ND
Hearn (1992)	Aspirations	O
Isaac, Malaney, and Karras (1992)	Plans	P
Kamens (1979)	Aspirations and Expectations	ND,ND
Kao & Tienda (1998)	Aspirations	P
Kempner and Kinnick (1990)	Aspirations	ND
Kerchoff and Campbell (1977)	Expectations	E
Labovitz (1975)	Aspirations	P
Lee, Mackie-Lewis, and Marks (1993)	Aspirations	F
Marini (1984)	Expectations	P
Nettles, Thoeny and Gosman (1986)	Aspirations	E
Pascarella (1984)	Aspirations	P
Pascarella (1985)	Aspirations	P
Pascarella, Duby, and Iverson (1983)	Other	E

Peng and Fetters (1978)	Aspirations	P
Phillips and Asbury (1993)	Aspirations	F
Portes and Wilson (1976)	Aspirations	P
Quilter (1995)	Aspirations	ND
Riehl (1994)	Aspirations	I
Schmidt and Hunt (1994)	Aspirations	ND
Sewell and Shah (1967)	Plans	P
Sewell, Haller, and Ohlendorf (1970)	Aspirations	P
Sewell, Haller, and Portes (1969)	Aspirations	P
Solorzano (1992)	Aspirations	T
St. John (1991)	Aspirations	P
Stage and Hossler (1989)	Plans	P
Stage and Rushin (1993)	Aspirations	O
Thomas (1991)	Expectations	E
Velez (1985)	Plans	P
Weiler (1993)	Expectations	E
Wilson-Sadberry, et al. (1991)	Aspirations	T

E=expectations; F=factor of aspirations items; I=intentions; L=educational likes or wants; ND=no detail; O=other; P=educational plans; T=educational predictions.

Table A-2. Studies using Educational Aspirations by Construct

Educational Plans Studies			
Construct*	Article	Sample	Operational Definitions
P	Sewell and Shah (1967)c	1957 study of all Wisconsin high school seniors	College plans is "based on a statement by the student when he was a senior in high school that he definitely planned to enroll in a degree-granting college or university."
P	Sewell, Haller, and Portes (1969)a	1957 study of all Wisconsin high school seniors	"a dichotomous variable corresponding to the respondent's statement in 1957 of whether or not he planned to attend college after graduating from high school."
P	Sewell, Haller, and Ohlendorf (1970)a	1957 study of all Wisconsin high school seniors	"the respondent's 1957 plans to continue education after high school are coded arbitrarily zero to two, as follows: not continuing, vocational school, and college."
P	Alwin (1974)a	1957 study of all Wisconsin high school seniors	"a dummy variable indicating whether the respondent planned to attend college." Variable is also referred to as college plans.
P	Labovitz (1975)a	San Diego public high school seniors in 1966 and 1967	the student's response to "whether he or she definitely plans to attend college" in the pre-graduation survey upon graduation from high school. The variable is coded as "four-year college", "two-year college", "unidentified college", and "no college plans."
P	Portes and Wilson (1976)a	national sample of male high school students in 1966	No detail about actual survey question. Item was coded on a four-point scale ranging from "plans to drop out of high school" to "plans to attend graduate or professional school"
P	Astin (1977)a	CIRP 1961-1969	Degree Aspirations: "Highest degree planned as freshman." "Degree aspirations" and "degree plans" are used interchangeably. Categories of response are "Associate", "None", "Bachelor's", "Master's", "Ph.D. or Ed.D.", "M.D., D.D.S., D.V.M.", and "L.L.B., or J.D."
P	Peng and Fetters (1978)a	NLS 1972	Aspirations: "This variable tapped the educational level planned during his [sic] senior year in high school to have." high school or less=1; some vocational studies=2; two-year college=3; four-year college or graduate school=4
P	Dawkins and Braddock (1982)c	1968 CIRP and 1972 followup study	college degree plans: five-point scale ranging from "1"=none to "5"=Ph.D., M.D., or J.D.
P	Friesen (1983)e	1969 and 1981 survey of high school students in Canada	Plans is described as "students who plan to attend university or related institutions"

*See codes for Table A-1.

"a"; studies of "expectations" are marked with a "b"; studies of "plans" are marked with a "c"; studies of "aspirations" and "expectations" are marked with a "d"; and studies of "aspirations" and "educational plans" are marked with an "e."

Table A-2. Studies using Educational Aspirations by Construct (continued

Educational Plans Studies

Construct*	Article	Sample	Operational Definitions
P	Hearn (1984)a	1975 CIRP survey	"educational aspirations...were obtained from the CIRP survey." Coded: 1=none; 2=associate's degree; 3=bachelor's degree; 4=master's or divinity degree; 5=doctoral or professional degree.
P	Marini (1984)b	1957-58 and 1973-74 study of Illinois HS students	"measures whether respondent planned to go to college" (1=planned to go; 0=other)
P	Pascarella (1984)a	1975-1977 CIRP surveys	"highest academic degree planned. At first timepoint, coded 1=none to 5=Ph.D., M.D., D.D.S., L.L.B., J.D., or equivalent. At second timepoint coded: 1 (vocational diploma/certificate) to 6 (Ph.D., M.D., D.D.S., L.L.B., J.D., or equivalent)."
P	Pascarella (1985)a	1975-1977 CIRP surveys	"highest academic degree planned. At first timepoint, coded 1=none to 5=Ph.D., M.D., D.D.S., L.L.B., J.D., or equivalent. At second timepoint coded: 1 (vocational diploma/certificate) to 6 (Ph.D., M.D., D.D.S., L.L.B., J.D., or equivalent)."
P	Velez (1985)c	NLS 1972	Plans: the highest level of education the student plans to attain. 0=high school, vocational school, less, or non-answer to question; 1=respondent plans to obtain a two-year degree; 2=respondent plans to complete four years of college, graduate school, or professional school.
P	Agnew and Jones (1988)d	NLS 1972	Expectations are "the highest level of education the student plans to attain" (1= four year degree or more; 0=less than four year degree)
P	Stage and Hossler (1989)c	1987 survey of Indiana 9th graders	"educational level plans" coded 1=high school diploma; 2=vocational certificate; 3=two-year degree; 4=four-year degree; 5=master's degree; 6=professional degree.
P	Allen and Haniff (1991)a	National Study of Black College Students. 1981-1985 study of Black undergraduate and graduate students at PWIs and HBCUs	no survey item provided. Assuming item is similar to Allen (1992).

*See codes for Table A-1.

"a"; studies of "expectations" are marked with a "b"; studies of "plans" are marked with a "c"; studies of "aspirations" and "expectations" are marked with a "d"; and studies of "aspirations" and "educational plans" are marked with an "e."

Table A-2. Studies using Educational Aspirations by Construct (continued

Educational Plans Studies			
Construct*	Article	Sample	Operational Definitions
P	Braddock, Royster, Winfield, and Hawkins (1991)a	NELS 1988 African American males	Aspirations is considered a measure of academic resilience. Aspirations has three dimensions of aspirations: a) plans to enroll in a high school academic program or college preparatory program (1=yes; 0=no); b) plans to graduate from high school (1=definitely graduate; 0=no); c) plans to attend college (1=college attendance as minimum educational goal; 0=otherwise).
P	Braddock and Trent (1991)a	National Study of Black College Students. 1981-1985 study of Black undergraduate and graduate students at PWIs and HBCUs	no survey item provided. Assuming item is similar to Allen (1992).
P	St. John (1991)a	HSB sophomore cohort. High school seniors in 1981-1982	postsecondary aspirations are described as postsecondary plans. 5 item scale ranging from "1" for no postsecondary plans to "5" for advanced degree.
P	Allen (1992)a	National Study of Black College Students. 1981-1985 study of Black undergraduate and graduate students at PWIs and HBCUs	described as "how far the student plans to go in school" and is coded 1=some college to 4=J.D., M.D., Ph.D.
P	Isaac, Malaney, and Karras (1992)c	1986 study of seniors in a large midwestern public research university	Further educational plans: includes four response categories—"students who had no plans or were unsure of their plans to pursue graduate study", "students who had not applied to graduate school but planned to pursue graduate student at a future, undetermined time", "applied to graduate school" for the year after the study", and "attending professional school."
P	Ashar and Skenes (1993)c	1989-90 sample of adult learners in a major metropolitan area	academic integration/commitment to learning: whether the student had furhter educational plans beyond B.A.
P	Kao & Tienda (1998)a	NELS:88	highest grade students planned to earn

*See codes for Table A-1.

"a"; studies of "expectations" are marked with a "b"; studies of "plans" are marked with a "c"; studies of "aspirations" and "expectations" are marked with a "d"; and studies of "aspirations" and "educational plans" are marked with an "e."

Table A-2. Studies using Educational Aspirations by Construct (continued)

Educational Expectations Studies

Construct*	Article	Sample	Operational Definitions
E	Kerchoff and Campbell (1977)b	1969 sample of twelfth grade boys in Fort Wayne, Indiana	Ambition: "how much education do you really expect to get?" The responses to the question ranged from "I'll quit high school before graduating" to "I'll go to profession or graduate school after college."
E	Pascarella, Duby, and Iverson (1983)b	1979 sample of a large, midwestern university	goal commitment: highest expected academic degree (2=master's degree; 1=bachelor's degree or below)
E	Nettles, Thoeny and Gosman (1986)a	stratified national sample of students and faculty in 30 postsecondary institutions	degree aspirations: highest expected degree (0=Bachelor's or less; 1=Master's or more)
E	Burke and Hoelter (1988)b	12th grade students on Louisville Public School System prior to 1975	Student responses to the question "realistically, when you consider the obstacles of money, grades, family responsibilities, and so on, what is the highest level of education you expect to attain?" Student responses were coded as "high school", "vocational school or community or junior college", "four-year college", and "graduate or professional degree."
E	Hearn (1991)	HSB 1980 and 1982	No detail about survey item. Coded 1=less than high school graduation; 2=high school graduation only; 3=vocational, trade, or business school fewer than 2 years; 4=vocational, trade, or business school 2 years or more; 5=college program, fewer than 2 years; 6=college program, 2-4 years; 7=college program, bachelor's degree; 8=master's degree or equivalent; 9=Ph.D., M.D., or another advanced professional degree.
E	Thomas (1991)b	1982 study of African American and White college juniors and seniors in the Southern Atlantic States	"highest level of education they expect to obtain (ranging from 1='do not expect to graduate from college' to 'expect to obtain and advanced graduate or professional degree')"
E	Weiler (1993)b	HSB 1980 high school graduates who graduated from college by 1985.	1=expects to attend graduate school; 0=lesser education expectations

*See codes for Table A-1.

"a"; studies of "expectations" are marked with a "b"; studies of "plans" are marked with a "c"; studies of "aspirations" and "expectations" are marked with a "d"; and studies of "aspirations" and "educational plans" are marked with an "e."

Table A-2. Studies using Educational Aspirations by Construct (continued

Construct*	Article	Sample	Operational Definitions
		Factor of Aspirations Items	
F	Friesen (1983)e	1969 and 1981 survey of high school students in Canada	aspirations described as "wishing to be remembered as outstanding students"; "expecting to earn a university degree"; "expected median income ten years after high school graduation"
F	Lee, Mackie-Lewis, and Marks (1993)a	NELS	construct referred to as "graduate school aspirations" and "expectations of graduate school." Measures taken from a battery of questions that ask students whether they have considered various degree programs.
F	Phillips and Asbury (1993)a	1986 CIRP participants at a HBCU	4 components comprise aspirations measure: highest degree planned anywhere; number of colleges applied to; reasons given for going to college; expects to graduate with honors
		Educational Likes or Wants	
L	Berman and Haug (1975)d	1970 undergraduate students in urban midwestern cities	Aspirations: "what is the highest amount of education you would like to have? That is, given ideal conditions, how far in school would you like to go?" The responses to this question could be anything from "some college courses" to "graduate or professional degree beyond the master's level."
L	Agnew and Jones (1988)d	NLS 1972	Aspirations are "the highest level of education the student would like to attain" (2=four year degree or more, 1=less than four-year degree)
L	Cranston and Leonard (1990)a	1987 study of undergraduate students at a midatlantic university	"What is the highest educational degree you would like to obtain eventually?" Coded 1=associate's degree; 2=bachelor's degree; 3=master's degree; 4=doctoral or professional degree.
L	Hauser and Anderson (1991)a	nationally representative sample of high school seniors from 1975-1986	defined as students' responses to the question "suppose you could do just what you'd like, and nothing stood in your way. How many of the following things would you want to do?" Responses included attending a technical-vocational college, enlisting in the armed services, attending a two-year college, and attending a four-year college.

*See codes for Table A-1.

"a"; studies of "expectations" are marked with a "b"; studies of "plans" are marked with a "c"; studies of "aspirations" and "expectations" are marked with a "d"; and studies of "aspirations" and "educational plans" are marked with an "e."

Table A-2. Studies using Educational Aspirations by Construct (continued)

Educational Intentions			
Construct*	Article	Sample	Operational Definitions
I	Drew and Astin (1972)a	CIRP freshmen cohort of 1966	"What is the highest academic degree that you intend to obtain?" Coded: 1=none; 2=associate; 3=bachelor's; 4=master's; 5=all others (e.g. Ph.D., Ed.D., M.D., J.D.)
I	Hearn (1987)a	1972 and 1976 study of undergraduate students at two selective universities	same survey item used at two timepoints: "the highest academic degree that you intend to obtain" coded as 1=none; 2=associate or equivalent; 3=bachelors; 4=masters or law; 5=Ph.D., D.D.S., M.D., or other doctoral)
I	Riehl (1994)a	1992 college freshmen at Indiana State University	"What is the highest academic degree that you intend to attain?" Categories include: none, associate, bachelor's, master's, Ph.D., M.D., Law Degree, Divinity Degree. In addition, the author also described that a measure of self-predicted first-semester college grades was also a measure of academic aspirations.
Educational Predictions			
T	Alexander and Eckland (1975)b	1955 nationally representative sample of sophomore and senior high school students	"what do you think you will do when you finish high school?" The original set of eight response categories was reduced to three categories "college goers", "possible college", and "non-college-goers."
T	Berman and Haug (1975)d	1970 undergraduate students in urban midwestern cities	Expectations are measured by "realistically, what is the highest education you think you will actually get? That is, how far in school do you really expect to go?"
T	Wilson-Sadberry, Winfield, and Royster (1991)a	HSB senior surveys: 1980,1982, 1984	"As things stand now, how far in school do you think you will get?" Responses to the question range from "none", "vocational/technical", "less than a four-years degree", "college degree", and "advanced degree"
T	Solorzano (1992)a	NELS 8th graders	"As things stand now, how far in school do you think you will get?" Coded: 1="greater than college"; 0=otherwise.

*See codes for Table A-1.

"a"; studies of "expectations" are marked with a "b"; studies of "plans" are marked with a "c"; studies of "aspirations" and "expectations" are marked with a "d"; and studies of "aspirations" and "educational plans" are marked with an "e."

Table A-2. Studies using Educational Aspirations by Construct (continued)

Construct*	Article	Sample	Operational Definitions
Other Operational Definitions			
O	Hearn (1992)a	HSB 1980 seniors	"lowest level of education with which they would be satisfied." 9=Ph.D., M.D., or another advanced professional degree; 8=master's degree; 7=Bachelor's degree; 6=two or more years of college; 5=less than two years of college; 4=two or more years of vocational, trade, or business school; 3=less than two years of vocational, trade, or business school, 2=high-school graduation; 1=less than high-school graduation.
O	Astin (1993b)a	1985 and 1989 CIRP study of college students	Degree Aspirations: "Highest degree aspired to" coded as "none or less than Bachelor's", "Bachelor's", "Master's", "Doctoral or advanced professional"
O	Davis (1995)	1988 survey of 4,094 college students attending 30 colleges and universities in the southern and mid-Atlantic states	"Highest academic degree aspired to by respondent" coded as 1=none; 2=associate degree; 3=bachelor's degree; 4=master's degree; 5=doctorate; 6=professional degree
O	Stage and Rushin (1993)a	HSB 1980-86	degree aspiration (also describe as a measure of predisposition): "lowest level of education student would be satisified with"
No Detail Given			
ND	Kamens (1979)d	1965 college students	independent measure is referred to as "aspirations", dependent measure is referred to as "expectations", no detail on survey items
ND	Kempner and Kinnick (1990)a	1974 survey of Oregon high school seniors	"educational goals or aspirations." No survey item provided; coded "less than BA" or "BA or higher"
ND	Hanson (1994)d	HSB 1986	no detail. aspirations coded if student had aspirations for a college degree or not; expectations coded if student had expectations for a college degree or not
ND	Schmidt and Hunt (1994)a	Maryland longitudinal study of 1980 entering freshmen, younger than 22	aspirations: when first declared a college major: "not yet", "freshmen year", "senior year of high school", "prior to senior year of high school"; educational aspirations: categories BA, MA, Ph.D. or professional degree.
ND	Quilter (1995)a	42 first-year college students at Eastern Michigan University	no detail. Refers to aspirations as a dimension of academic self-concept.
ND	Bateman and Hossler (1996)	Indiana high school students in 1987-1988	no detail. Refer to postsecondary educational plans.

*See codes for Table A-1.

"a"; studies of "expectations" are marked with a "b"; studies of "plans" are marked with a "c"; studies of "aspirations" and "expectations" are marked with a "d"; and studies of "aspirations" and "educational plans" are marked with an "e."

Appendix B
Differences Between Reduced and Full White Student Samples

Chapter Four describes the methodology used for the study. For most of the analyses in the study, I used a reduced sample of White students. This reduced sample was drawn randomly from the full White sample in the BPS and CIRP data sets. It was necessary to draw a reduced sample because the total numbers of African American students in BPS and CIRP are approximately one-tenth of the numbers of White students. As discussed in Chapter Four, large sample size differences can skew the results of multivariate and bivariate statistical analyses. This section describes the procedure used to draw the reduced sample and shows comparisons between the reduced sample and the original sample.

Table B-1 shows the frequencies, means, and standard deviations of the measures for the White student full and reduced samples in the BPS and CIRP data sets. For all but six of the measures, there are no significant differences between the full White student BPS sample and the reduced sample used for regression analyses. For the most part, the reduced White sample of BPS is representative of the full White student sample.

However, there are significant differences between the two samples in the following measures that should be noted: Age, attendance at an institution because it is less expensive, attendance at a private institution, tuition cost, scholarship aid, and hours spent working.

The reduced White student sample tends to be a bit older (by one year) than the full BPS White student sample. In addition, the White students in the reduced sample tend to mention less often than the full sample that they attended their postsecondary institutions because they are less expensive. White students in the full sample attend institutions with lower tuition costs than White students in the reduced sample and the students in the full sample tend to receive less tuition aid than students in the reduced sample. The students in the full sample tend to spend more hours a week working than students in the reduced sample. One final difference between the

White students in the BPS full sample vs. students in the reduced sample is that students in the reduced sample attend private institutions in a slightly higher proportion in comparison to the students in the full sample (25% vs. 19%).

For the CIRP data set, there are no significant differences between the full White student sample and the reduced sample except for three of the measures. Again, for the most part the reduced sample is representative of the full White student sample. The White student reduced sample tends to have higher parental income than the full sample, and the students in the reduced sample attend their first choice institution less often in comparison to the students in the full sample. Finally, students in the reduced sample more often tend to regard their institutions as having a commitment to social activism than do students in the full sample.

Table B-1. Frequencies, Means, and Standard Deviations of Variables in the BPS and CIRP Full and Reduced White Student Samples

Variables	BPS				CIRP			
	Full N=3506		Reduced N=357		Full N=3898		Reduced N=283	
	Mean	St. Dev.	Mean	St. Dev.	Mean	St. Dev.	Mean	St. Dev.
Dependent Variable								
Degree Expectations	3.31	1.09	3.30	1.15	—	—	—	—
Degree Plans	—	—	—	—	4.69	.94	4.69	.87
Pre-college characteristics								
Female	51%	.50	54%	.50	39%	.49	43%	.50
Age	21.03*	7.08	22.21*	9.87	3.23	.61	3.18	.52
Father's Educational Attainment	5.84	3.17	5.93	2.98	5.30	2.03	5.46	1.91
Mother's Educational Attainment	5.23	2.84	5.53	2.80	4.83	1.79	4.65	1.76
Parent Income	7.80	3.33	7.92	3.16	8.84**	3.18	9.41**	2.97
Number of Children	.32	.84	.41	1.11	—	—	—	—
Married	11%	.31	9%	.29	—	—	—	—
Separated/Divorced	5%	.21	4%	.20	—	—	—	—
Items Owned	19.51	1.99	19.42	2.11	—	—	—	—
GPA	—	—	—	—	5.45	1.69	5.61	1.55
Initial Expectations/Orientations								
Degree Expectations	3.35	1.00	3.43	.98	—	—	—	—
Degree Plans	—	—	—	—	4.90	.87	4.85	.78
Intellectual Self-Confidence	2.38	.37	2.37	.37	3.60	.61	3.67	.66
First Choice	82%	.38	85%	.36	3%#	.17	1%#	.12
Second Choice	—	—	—	—	5%	.22	5%	.22
Third Choice	—	—	—	—	23%	.42	25%	.43
Distance From Home	3.09	1.42	3.16	1.41	4.14	1.31	4.20	1.22
Good Reputation	2.09	.50	2.12	.50	—	—	—	—
Close to Home	2.05	.72	1.98	.67	—	—	—	—
Less Expensive	1.87*	.75	1.77*	.75	—	—	—	—

Social Change Orientation	—	—	—	—	2.35	.61	2.32	.59
Institutional Characteristics								
Control (private)	19%##	.39	25%##	.43	49%	.50	46%	.50
Level (four-year)	48%	.50	52%	.50	88%	.33	89%	.32
Single Sex	—	—	—	—	3%	.18	3%	.16
HBCU	0%	.00	0%	.00	<1%	.02	<1%	.07
Percent African American Enrollment	.06	.06	.06	.05	—	—	—	—
Tuition Cost	2475.57**	3367.01	3013.34**	3712.63	—	—	—	—
Size	10122.10	10175.70	9975.45	10126.22	—	—	—	—
Institutional Priorities								
Commitment to Social Activism	—	—	—	—	2.91*	.61	2.98*	.56
Commitment to Diversity	—	—	—	—	2.76	.72	2.73	.70
Financial Aid/Work								
Borrow/Loans	693.70	1894.59	877.23	2517.14	5.57	2.56	5.44	2.41
Scholarship	890.44*	1942.83	1155.18*	2118.96	3.96	1.98	3.88	1.95
Work Study	60.03	271.63	59.48	244.27	1.23	.75	1.21	.68
Hours spent working	23.96*	16.27	21.80*	16.97	4.32	2.66	4.17	2.64
Number of Jobs	1.49	.97	1.41	.96	—	—	—	—
Involvement								
Faculty Contact	2.44	.80	2.39	.80	1.11	.21	1.10	.20
Peer Contact	2.12	.72	2.11	.75	2.61	.52	2.66	.49
Participated in ethnic organizations	—	—	—	—	4%	.19	4%	.20
Achievement								
College GPA	—	—	—	—	3.85	1.16	3.96	1.10

—: measure not in data set

* $p \leq .05$; **$p \leq .01$; ***$p \leq .001$ for t-test analyses

\# $p \leq .05$; ##$p \leq .01$; ###$p \leq .001$ for chi-square analyses

Appendix C
Variable Definitions and Coding Schemes for BPS and CIRP Measures

Table C1. Variable Definitions and Coding Schemes in BPS Dataset

Variable	Measurement
Dependent Variable	
Educational Expectations 1992	Considering all practical constraints, what is the highest level of education you ever expect to complete? 1=two years or less of college or vocational education; 2=two or more years of college (including a 2-year associate's degree); 3=bachelor's degree or equivalent; 4=master's degree or equivalent; 5=M.D., D.D.S., L.L.B., or doctorate.
Pre-college characteristics	
Gender	1=male, 2=female
Age	Age of student in 1989-90
Father's Educational Attainment	1=less than high school; 2=GED; 3=high school graduate; 4=less than 1 year of vocational school; 5=1-2 years of vocational school; 6=more than 2 years of vocational education; 7=less than 2 years of college; 8=2 or more years of college; 9=Bachelor's degree; 10=Master's degree; 11=doctorate or professional degree
Mother's Educational Attainment	Same scale as father's educational attainment
Parent Income	Average of parental income in 1988-89 and 1989-90; 1=less than $6000; 2=$6000-$9999; 3=$10000-$14999; 4=$15000-$19,999; 5=$20,000-$24,999; 6=$25,000-$29,999; 7=$30,000-$34,999; 8=$35,000-$39,999; 9=$40,000-$49,999; 10=$50,000-$59,999; 11=$60,000-$74,999; 12=$75,000-$99,999; 13=$100,000-$149,999; 14=$150,000 or more
Number of Children	Number of children student has in 1989-90: 0=none; up to 6=6 or more children
Marital Status	Two dichotomous variables: Separated/Divorced coded 2=separated 1=not; Married coded 2=married; 1=not
Items Owned	Scale, combining eleven questions that asked students if their household had a daily newspaper delivered, dishwasher, reference books, more than 50 books, personal computer, vcr, two or more vehicles; and questions that asked if the students had a pocket calculator, a room of one's own, a specific place for study, and a typewriter.
Initial Expectations, Orientations	
Educational Expectations	Same scale as dependent variable.
Intellectual self-confidence	Scale, see Table 4.2
First Choice	Institution is student's first choice (2=first choice; 1=not)
Distance from home	1=5 miles or less; 2=6-10 miles; 3=11-50 miles; 4=51-100 miles; 5=101-500 miles; 6=over 500 miles.
Good Reputation	Scale, see Table 4.2
Close to home	Scale, see Table 4.2
Less expensive	Scale, see Table 4.2
Institutional Characteristics	
Control	1=private; 2=public
Level	1=two-year; 2=four-year

Tuition Cost	Cost of tuition in 1989
Size	Total undergraduate FTE
Financial Aid/Work	
Borrow/Loans	Total amount of undergraduate borrowing in 1989-90
Work Study	Total amount of work study aid received in 1989-90
Scholarship	Total amount of scholarship aid received
Hours spent working	Hours worked per week during 1990-1991 school year
Number of jobs	Number of jobs students worked in 1989-90
Involvement/Achievement	
Faculty contact	Scale, see Table 4.2
Peer contact	Scale, see Table 4.2

Table C2. Variable Definitions and Coding Schemes in CIRP Dataset

Variable	Measurement
Dependent Variable	
Educational Plans	Please indicate the highest degree you plan to complete. 1=no degree; 2=vocational certificate; 3=Associate's degree; 4=Bachelor's degree; 5=Master's degree; 6=Ph.D. or advanced professional degree
Pre-college characteristics	
Gender	1=male; 2=female
Age	Age of student as of 12/31/88 (1=16 or less; 2=17; 3=18; 4=19; 5=20; 6=21-24; 7=25-29; 8=30-39; 9=40-54; 10=55 or older)
Father's Educational Attainment	What is the highest level of formal education obtained by your parents? 1=grammar school; 2=some high school; 3=high school graduate; 4=postsecondary school other than college; 5=some college; 6=college degree; 7=some graduate school; 8=graduate degree.
Mother's Educational Attainment	Same scale as Father's Educational Attainment
Parent Income	What is your best estimate of your parents' total income last year? Consider all sources before taxes. 1=less than $6000; 2=$6000-$9999; 3=$10000-$14999; 4=$15000-$19,999; 5=$20,000-$24,999; 6=$25,000-$29,999; 7=$30,000-$34,999; 8=$35,000-$39,999; 9=$40,000-$49,999; 10=$50,000-$59,999; 11=$60,000-$74,999; 12=$75,000-$99,999; 13=$100,000-$149,999; 14=$150,000 or more
GPA	High School Grade Point Average. 8=A or A+; 7=A-; 6=B+; 5=B; 4=B-; 3=C+; 2=C; 1=D
Initial Expectations/Orientations	
Educational Plans	Same scale as dependent variable
Intellectual Self-Confidence	Scale, see Table 4.3
First Choice	Is this college your: 2=first choice; 1=not
Second Choice	Is this college your: 2=second choice; 1=not
Third Choice	Is this college your: 2=third choice; 1=not
Distance From Home	How many miles is this college from your permanent home? 1=5 or less; 2=6-10; 3=11-50; 4=51-100; 5=101-500; 6=more than 500
Social Change Orientation	Scale, See Table 4.3
Institutional Characteristics	
Control	1=public; 2=private
Level	1=2-year; 2=4-year
Single Sex	1=coed; 2=single-sex
HBCU	1=PWI; 2=HBCU

Variable	Definition / Coding
Institutional Priorities	
Commitment to Social Activism	Scale, see Table 4.3
Commitment to Diversity	Scale, see Table 4.3
Financial Aid/Work	
Borrow/Loans	How much of your first year's educational expenses (room, board, tution, and fees) do you expect to cover from each of the sources listed below? Guaranteed Student Loan, National Direct Student Loan, Other College Loan, Other Loan (Average of four items. Each item coded 1=none; 2=$1-$499; 3=$500-$999; 4=$1000-$1499; 5=$1500-$1999; 6=$2000-$3000; 7=Over $3000)
Scholarship	How much of your first year's educational expenses (room, board, tution, and fees) do you expect to cover from each of the sources listed below? Pell Grant, Supplemental Educational Opportunity Grant, State Scholarship or Grant, College Grant or Scholarship, Other private grant (Average of five items. Each item coded 1=none; 2=$1-$499; 3=$500-$999; 4=$1000-$1499; 5=$1500-$1999; 6=$2000-$3000; 7=Over $3000)
Work Study	How much of your first year's educational expenses (room, board, tution, and fees) do you expect to cover from each of the sources listed below? Work Study (Item coded 1=none; 2=$1-$499; 3=$500-$999; 4=$1000-$1499; 5=$1500-$1999; 6=$2000-$3000; 7=Over $3000)
Hours spent working	How much time did you spend during a typical week doing the following activities? Working (for pay) Coded: 1=none; 2=less than 1 hour; 2=1-2 hours per wk; 3=3-5 hours per wk; 4=6-10 hours per wk; 5=11-15 hours per wk; 6=16-20 hours per wk; 7=over 20 hours per wk.
Involvement	
Faculty Contact	Combination of the following two items: Since entering college have you assisted faculty in teaching a course; or worked on a faculty member's research project (Coded 2=yes; 1=no) And a third item: Please indicate how often you engaged in the following in the past year: Been a guest in a faculty member's home (1=not at all; 2=occasionally; 3=frequently)
Peer Contact	Indicate how often you discussed course content with students outside of class: 1=not at all; 2=occasionally; 3=frequently
Participated in ethnic organizations	Since entering college have you participated in an ethnic/racial organization: 1=no; 2=yes
Achievement	
College GPA	Undergraduate grade point average: 6=A; 5=B+, A-; 4=B; 3=B-, C+; 2=C; 1=C- or lower

Appendix D
Unstandardized Coefficients for Regression Models

Table D1. Base Regression Model of BPS and CIRP Datasets by Race/Ethnicity on Educational Expectations and Plans—Unstandardized Coefficients

Variables	BPS		CIRP	
	African American N=356	White N=357	African American N=266	White N=283
Pre-college characteristics				
Female	-.07	.13	.26	.14
Age	.00	-.03***	-.22*	-.17
Father's Educational Attainment	.03	.03	.08	.02
Mother's Educational Attainment	.05**	.04*	-.02	-.01
Parent Income	-.01	-.02	-.04	.01
Initial Expectations/Orientations				
Educational Plans/Expectations	.21***	.45***	.22*	.54***
Intellectual Self-Confidence	-.34**	.40***	.17	-.00
First Choice	-.24*	-.23*	.19	.22
Distance From Home	-.01	-.02	.19**	.07
Institutional Characteristics				
Control (private)	-.16	.25*	-.24	-.08
Level (4-year institution)	.50***	.39***	-.30	-.14
HBCU	.48**	—	-.16	1.00
Financial Aid/Work				
Borrow/Loans	.00	.00	.06	.04
Scholarship	.00	-.00	-.17***	.03
Work Study	-.00	-.00	.24**	.08
Hours spent working	-.00	-.00	.01	-.06**
Involvement				
Faculty Contact	.18**	-.06	-.08	-.10
Peer Contact	-.07	.07	.48**	.01
R^2	.34	.59	.28	.29

—: Variable did not enter regression. No White students attended HBCUs in the BPS sample.
* $p \leq .05$; **$p \leq .01$; ***$p \leq .001$

Table D2. Regression Model of BPS Dataset by Race/Ethnicity and Regression Step—Unstandardized Coefficients

	Pre-college characteristics		Pre-college Characteristics and Expectations at First Timepoint		Institutional Characteristics		Full Model	
Variables	African American N=356	White N=357	African American	White	African American	White	African American	White
Pre-college characteristics								
Female	.02	.22*	-.01	.12	-.00	.17*	.00	.15
Age	.01	-.03***	.02	-.03***	.04**	-.02***	.03*	-.02***
Father's Educational Attainment	.03	.04	.03	.03	.01	.01	.01	.01
Mother's Educational Attainment	.08***	.10***	.06**	.06**	.04*	.04*	.04	.04*
Parent Income	-.02	.00	-.02	-.02	-.01	-.03	.00	-.03*
Number of Children	-.32***	-.17**	-.26**	-.04	-.24**	-.04	-.24**	-.02
Married	-.14	.04	-.20	.07**	.04	-.11	-.02	-.16
Separated/Divorced	.14	-.33	-.03	-.17	.17	-.39	.16	-.44*
Items Owned	.01	.08**	.00	.07**	-.03	.05*	-.02	.05*
Initial Expectations/Orientations								
Educational Plans/Expectations			.32***	.54***	.19***	.46***	.19	.46***
Intellectual Self-Confidence					-.26*	.38***	-.30*	.40**
First Choice					-.28**	-.21	-.23*	-.21
Distance From Home					.00	-.05	-.02	-.04
Good Reputation					-.23*	.04	-.21*	.03
Close to Home					-.19*	-.11	-.16	-.10
Less Expensive					.07	.01	.06	.02
Institutional Characteristics								
Control (Private)					.16	.44**	.12	.47**
Level (4-year)					.38**	.30**	.39**	.32**
Per. African American Enroll.					.37*	-1.53	.39*	-1.49
Tuition Cost					.00	-.00	.00	.00
Size					.00***	.00**	.00***	.00**
Financial Aid/Work								
Borrow/Loans							.00	.00
Scholarship							.00	.00
Work Study							.00	.00
Hours spent working							.00	.00
Number of Jobs							.02	.03
Involvement								
Faculty Contact							.19**	-.04
Peer Contact							-.08	-.02
R^2	.12	.38	.21	.54	.36	.61	.38	.61

* $p \leq .05$; ** $p \leq .01$; *** $p \leq .001$

Table D3. Regression Model of CIRP Dataset by Race/Ethnicity and Regression Step—Unstandardized Coefficients

	Pre-college characteristics		Pre-college Characteristics and Expectations at First Timepoint		Institutional Characteristics		Full Model	
Variables	African American N=266	White N=283	African American	White	African American	White	African American	White
Pre-college characteristics								
Female	.26	.11	.11	.09	.05	.05	.06	.10
Age	-.18	-.08	-.22	-.05	-.26*	-.13	-.15	-.14
Father's Educational Attainment	.05	.05	.03	.02	.05	.01	.11*	.02
Mother's Educational Attainment	.06	-.03	.04	-.02	.04	-.03	-.03	-.01
Parent Income	-.00	.03	-.01	.01	-.01	.01	-.03	.01
High School GPA	-.05	.14***	-.08	.11***	-.15**	.11***	-.21***	.07
Initial Expectations/Orientations								
Educational Plans/Expectations			.31***	.48***	.31**	.48***	.20*	.54***
Intellectual Self-Confidence					.23	-.09	.21	-.10
First Choice					.37	.17	.42	.28
Second Choice					.56	.42*	.55*	.47*
Third Choice					-.34	-.03	-.19	-.02
Distance From Home					.13*	.09*	.13*	.07
Social Change Orientation					.12	.06	.03	.10
Institutional Characteristics								
Control (private)					-.23	.00	-.29	-.15
Level (four-year)					-.24	-.16	-.08	-.14
Single Sex					.79	-.04	.37	-.09
HBCU					-.42*	1.24	-.09	.77
Institutional Priorities								
Commitment to Social Activism							.21	.10
Commitment to Diversity							-.21	-.13
Financial Aid/Work								
Borrow/Loans							.02	.04
Scholarship							-.13***	.01
Work Study							.24**	.07
Hours spent working							.00	-.05**
Involvement								
Faculty Contact							-.31	-.20
Peer Contact							.47**	-.02
Participated in ethnic organizations							.30	-.40
Achievement								
College GPA							.30***	.09
R^2	.05	.09	.09	.26	.20	.30	.40	.35

* p≤.05; **p≤.01; ***p≤.001

Appendix E
Correlation Coefficients of Variables in the BPS and CIRP Regression Models

Table E1. Correlation Coefficients of Variables in BPS Regression Models

	EDGOAL92	H_GENDR	AGE	FATHEDUC	MOTHEDUC	PARINCAT	KIDS	MARCURR	SEPDIVOR	SESHAD
EDGOAL92	—	**-.02**	**-.17****	**.18****	**.26****	**.06**	**-.25****	**-.03**	**.00**	**.06**
H_GENDR	-.04	—	**.05**	**-.13***	**-.03**	**.03**	**.09**	**-.14***	**.00**	**.05**
AGE	-.47**	.11*	—	**-.21****	**-.16****	**-.18****	**.70****	**.02**	**.08**	**-.13***
FATHEDUC	.35**	.15**	-.21**	—	**.34****	**.32****	**-.24****	**.21****	**-.09**	**.17****
MOTHEDUC	.42**	-.18**	-.24**	.55**	—	**.18****	**-.14****	**.06**	**-.06**	**.18****
PARINCAT	.24**	-.19**	-.30**	.32**	.26**	—	**-.18****	**.07**	**.00**	**.38****
KIDS	-.43**	.13*	.67**	-.15**	-.23**	-.22**	—	**.03**	**.10**	**-.04**
MARCURR	.00	.08	-.07	-.11*	-.07	.03	.02	—	**-.10**	**.10**
SEPDIVOR	-.08	.04	.20**	.03	.03	-.07	.00	-.06	—	**.02**
SESHAD	.36**	-.21**	-.31**	.36**	.27**	.33**	-.35**	-.01	.07	—
EDGOAL90	.62**	-.01	-.27**	.24**	.35**	.24**	-.34**	.10	.02	.22**
CONFID	.30**	-.20**	-.08	.16**	.19**	.18**	-.22**	-.05	.09	.22**
CHOICE	-.23**	.05	.17**	-.06	-.08	-.12*	.15**	-.01	.02	-.21**
DISTANCE	.31**	-.09	-.13*	.27**	.26**	.21**	-.21**	.03	.08	.28**
GOODREP	.15**	.03	-.04	.00	.07	-.11*	.02	-.04	-.10	.04
CLOSEHM	-.35**	.13*	.36**	-.32**	-.27**	-.22**	.25**	.00	.04	-.21**
LESSEXP	-.15**	-.01	.23**	-.08	-.08	-.16**	.24**	-.06	-.14**	-.14**
CONTROL	.33**	-.10	-.18**	.17**	.26**	.09	-.17**	.00	-.05	.14**
LEVEL	.52**	-.12*	-.35**	.35**	.37**	.23**	-.29**	-.01	-.01	.36**
HBCU	.	.	.	.	.	.	.	.	.	.
BLACKPER	-.14**	.04	.11*	-.08	-.10	-.13*	-.04	.02	.08	-.01
TUITCOST	.41**	-.10	-.28**	.31**	.34**	.19**	-.25**	-.04	-.08	.26**
ENROLL88	.21**	.01	-.14**	.29**	.10	.22**	-.16**	-.07	.07	.20**
BORAMT1	.15**	-.01	-.11*	.09	.14*	.01	-.10*	.02	-.04	.08
SCHOLAMT	.21**	-.09	-.16**	.12*	.15**	-.07	-.10	-.02	-.01	.05
TOTWKST	.12*	-.01	-.10	-.01	.13*	-.13*	-.09	-.05	-.05	-.02
EMWKHR3	-.21**	-.09	.11*	-.12*	-.13*	-.10	.18**	-.06	-.17**	-.08
JOBNUM	.14**	.00	-.22**	-.03	.07	-.02	-.22**	.19**	-.10*	.07
FACCON	.28**	-.09	-.26**	.14*	.22**	.01	-.12*	-.11*	-.08	.17**
PEERCON	.48**	-.13*	-.42**	.32**	.34**	.21**	-.40**	-.04	-.09	.37**

Note: No White students in the BPS sample attended a HBCU.
Coefficients in **bold and in the top half of the diagonal** are for African American students, coefficients in lower half of the table are for White students.
* p≤.05; **p≤.01

Table E1. Correlation Coefficients of Variables in BPS Regression Models - continued

	EDGOAL90	CONFID	CHOICE	DISTANCE	GOODREP	CLOSEHM	LESSEXP	CONTROL	LEVEL	HBCU
EDGOAL92	**.37****	**.08**	**-.24****	**.24****	**-.09**	**-.33****	**.02**	**.14****	**.40****	**.28****
H_GENDR	**.02**	**-.10**	**-.02**	**.08**	**.19****	**.15****	**.24****	**.01**	**.06**	**.00**
AGE	**-.29****	**.12***	**.20****	**-.19****	**.03**	**.17****	**-.08**	**-.03**	**-.15****	**-.09**
FATHEDUC	**.15****	**.06**	**-.02**	**.07**	**-.12***	**-.21****	**.00**	**.01**	**.09**	**.05**
MOTHEDUC	**.22****	**.22****	**-.18****	**-.01**	**-.11***	**-.16****	**.05**	**.00**	**.12***	**.09**
PARINCAT	**.13***	**-.02**	**-.15****	**.05**	**-.02**	**-.12***	**-.09**	**.07**	**.02**	**.02**
KIDS	**-.27****	**.12***	**.15****	**-.21****	**-.07**	**.18****	**-.09**	**-.02**	**-.20****	**-.11***
MARCURR	**.07**	**.03**	**.10**	**-.11***	**-.05**	**.03**	**-.03**	**-.08**	**-.18****	**-.07**
SEPDIVOR	**.09**	**-.01**	**.10**	**.13***	**.08**	**-.01**	**-.05**	**-.06**	**-.04**	**-.01**
SESHAD	**.18****	**.10**	**-.10**	**.11***	**-.11***	**-.09**	**-.01**	**.04**	**.17****	**.01**
EDGOAL90	—	**.16****	**-.18****	**.25****	**.01**	**-.28****	**.01**	**.12***	**.33****	**.21****
CONFID	.28**	—	**-.16****	**.14***	**.10**	**-.17****	**-.08**	**.07**	**.30****	**.10**
CHOICE	-.15**	-.03	—	**-.11***	**-.02**	**.05**	**-.11***	**-.17****	**-.18****	**-.09**
DISTANCE	.33**	.14**	-.17**	—	**.24****	**-.47****	**.03**	**.25****	**.52****	**.18****
GOODREP	.07	.10	.05	.13*	—	**.22****	**.33****	**.17****	**.18****	**.04**
CLOSEHM	-.19**	-.13*	.18**	-.53**	-.17**	—	**.25****	**-.19****	**-.41****	**-.23****
LESSEXP	-.06	-.18**	.08	-.15**	.02	.28**	—	**-.16****	**.02**	**.01**
CONTROL	.21**	.17**	-.16**	.36**	.28**	-.33**	-.32**	—	**.31****	**.18****
LEVEL	.39**	.21**	-.20**	.48**	.24**	-.40**	-.13*	.39**	—	**.28****
HBCU	.	.	.	.	.	.	.	.	.	—
BLACKPER	-.09	.06	.13*	-.12*	-.05	.16**	-.11*	-.05	-.09	.
TUITCOST	.28**	.21**	.21**	.45**	.30**	-.46**	-.30**	.73**	.52**	.
ENROLL88	.11*	.10	.05	.08	-.10	-.09	.02	-.31**	.19**	.
BORAMT1	.11*	.05	-.03	.17**	.15**	-.13*	-.05	.25**	.18**	.
SCHOLAMT	.17**	.10	-.09	.24**	.22**	-.28**	-.10	.40**	.30**	.
TOTWKST	.12*	.06	-.06	.18**	.11*	-.15**	-.07	.28**	.19**	.
EMWKHR3	-.19**	-.13	.05	-.13*	-.11*	.29**	.09	-.09	-.18**	.
JOBNUM	.13*	.04	-.08	.05	.04	.09	.07	.08	.07	.
FACCON	.22**	.16**	-.12*	.24**	.20**	-.19**	.14**	.38**	.38**	.
PEERCON	.36**	.32**	.22**	.43**	.19**	-.48**	-.17**	.41**	.56**	.

Note: No White students in the BPS sample attended a HBCU.
Coefficients in **bold and in the top half of the diagonal** are for African American students, coefficients in lower half of the table are for White students.
* p≤.05; **p≤.01

Table E1. Correlation Coefficients of Variables in BPS Regression Models - continued

	BLACKPER	TUITCOST	ENROLL88	BORAMT1	SCHOLAMT	TOTWKST	EMWKHR3	JOBNUM	FACCON	PEERCON
EDGOAL92	.1	.23**	.23**	.16**	.20**	.04	-.11*	.09	.26**	.19**
H_GENDR	.02	.03	.02	-.01	.02	.11*	-.08	-.07	-.01	-.01
AGE	-.04	-.12*	-.15**	.03	-.04	-.04	.19**	-.05	-.04	-.07
FATHEDUC	-.07	.05	.16**	-.04	-.03	-.07	-.23**	-.04	.04	.04
MOTHEDUC	-.04	.01	.24**	-.01	.06	-.02	-.07	.10	.03	.11*
PARINCAT	-.04	.14**	.05	.02	-.18**	-.04	-.01	-.02	-.06	.02
KIDS	.00	-.13*	-.09	.01	.05	.00	.12*	-.04	-.06	-.09
MARCURR	-.06	-.14**	.03	-.01	-.05	-.14**	.15**	.03	.10	.11*
SEPDIVOR	-.04	-.07	.01	.05	-.01	.14**	.05	.09	-.06	-.09
SESHAD	.05	.13*	.05	.02	-.12*	.01	.09	.04	.03	.14*
EDGOAL90	.13*	.20**	.09	.03	.15**	.08	-.05	.15**	.14**	.16**
CONFID	.09	.10	.17**	.06	.26**	.14*	.03	-.02	.20**	.22**
CHOICE	-.01	-.24**	-.10	-.01	-.19**	-.04	.09	-.07	-.21**	-.20**
DISTANCE	.02	.40**	.06	.27**	.22**	.13*	-.20**	.07	.29**	.33**
GOODREP	.12*	.18**	-.07	.08	.07	.14**	-.07	-.15**	.03	.06
CLOSEHM	-.06	-.32**	.03	-.25**	-.22**	.01	.16**	-.07	-.25**	-.35**
LESSEXP	.05	-.10	.05	-.03	-.07	.14**	-.19**	-.10	.09	.07
CONTROL	.14**	.70**	-.23**	.21**	.41**	.05	-.06	.04	.13*	.17**
LEVEL	.20**	.46**	.20**	.22**	.28**	.16**	-.16**	.03	.21**	.30**
HBCU	.54**	.14**	-.19**	.02	.06	-.01	-.01	.00	.17**	.20**
BLACKPER	—	.03	-.33**	-.09	.00	-.02	.06	-.06	.05	.09
TUITCOST	-.12*	—	-.03	.33**	.53**	.16**	-.13*	.05	.19**	.29**
ENROLL88	.08	-.04	—	.07	.11*	.08	-.12*	.01	.02	.01
BORAMT1	-.03	.31**	-.01	—	.19**	.09	.02	.05	.18**	.24**
SCHOLAMT	-.06	.47**	-.07	.15**	—	.24**	-.17**	-.01	.28**	.25**
TOTWKST	-.02	.29**	-.10*	.21**	.41**	—	-.11*	.06	.16**	.12*
EMWKHR3	.04	-.17**	-.08	-.05	-.15**	-.03	—	.36**	-.17**	-.09
JOBNUM	-.07	.09	-.03	.12*	.03	.15**	.39**	—	-.06	.07
FACCON	-.11*	.37**	-.14**	.18**	.28**	.24**	-.06	.05	—	.48**
PEERCON	-.19**	.53**	.13*	.19**	.32**	.21**	-.09	.12*	.45**	—

Note: No White students in the BPS sample attended a HBCU.
Coefficients in **bold and in the top half of the diagonal** are for African American students, coefficients in lower half of the table are for White students.
* $p \leq .05$; ** $p \leq .01$

Table E2. Correlation Coefficients of Variables in CIRP Regression Models

	PLAN90	SEX88	AGE	FATHEDUC	MOTHEDUC	INCOME	HSGPA	PLAN88	INTELL	CHOICE1
PLAN90	—	**.10**	**-.15***	**.15***	**.15***	**.09**	**-.09**	**.24****	**.11**	**-.05**
SEX88	.06	—	**-.14***	**-.08**	**.00**	**-.06**	**.04**	**.22****	**-.26****	**-.17****
AGE	-.08	-.02	—	**-.17****	**-.19****	**-.22****	**.15***	**.00**	**.18****	**-.03**
FATHEDUC	.12*	-.11	-.02	—	**.66****	**.42****	**-.13***	**.21****	**.00**	**-.14***
MOTHEDUC	.05	.10	-.05	.48**	—	**.49****	**-.02**	**.24****	**.03**	**-.14***
INCOME	.10	-.11	-.12*	.46**	.24**	—	**-.06**	**.16****	**-.15***	**-.11**
HSGPA	.25**	.14*	-.11	.08	.19**	-.06	—	**.15***	**.26****	**.04**
PLAN88	.46**	.02	-.06	.19**	.11	.18**	.16**	—	**.24****	**-.22****
INTELL	.16**	-.18**	-.08	.17**	.05	.21**	.21**	.31**	—	**.07**
CHOICE1	.04	.05	.07	.06	.11	.02	.04	.03	.01	—
CHOICE2	.12*	-.08	-.01	.06	.02	.06	-.01	.06	.11	-.03
CHOICE3	-.07	-.11	.01	.08	.04	.13*	-.22	.07	.01	-.07
DISTHOME	.14*	-.01	-.08	.19**	.20**	.19**	.14*	.03	.18**	.05
SOCCHG	.13*	.21**	.02	.06	.14*	.11	.00	.22**	.21**	-.03
INSTCONT	.06	.09	-.05	.19**	.22**	.13*	.09	.06	.05	.05
INSTTYPE	.04	-.01	.06	.07	.08	.21**	.18**	.11	.17**	-.03
INSTSEX	.00	.16**	-.03	.02	.07	.04	-.03	.00	-.08	-.02
INSTRACE	.02	.08	.61**	-.08	-.06	-.14*	-.11	.01	-.09	-.01
COMMACT	.04	.11	.00	.04	.00	.07	.02	-.01	.18**	-.04
COMMDIV	-.05	.09	.10	-.06	.05	-.11	.06	.02	-.02	.13*
BORAMT	.08	-.03	.01	-.22**	-.15*	-.29**	.05	-.04	.01	.01
SCHOLAMT	.03	.06	.05	-.19**	-.06	-.39**	.18**	-.07	.07	-.05
AID11	.06	.08	-.03	-.08	-.07	-.29**	.23**	-.02	.06	.00
HPW9009	-.10	.11	-.10	-.12*	-.04	-.14*	-.09	.11	.07	.02
FACCON	.09	.07	.01	.11	.07	-.02	.09	.11	.18**	.08
ACTLY03	.10	.15*	-.01.	.06	.02	.13*	.09	.11	.19**	.03
COLACT18	.02	.06	-.08	.07	.24**	.01	.18**	.12*	.05	-.03
COLLGPA	.16**	.07	.03	.04	.14*	.06	.45**	-.01	.14*	.06

Coefficients in **bold and in the top half of the diagonal** are for African American students, coefficients in lower half of the table are for White students.
*p≤.05; **p≤.01

Table E2. Correlations of Variables in CIRP Regression Models - continued

	CHOICE2	CHOICE3	DISTHOME	SOCCHG	INSTCONT	INSTTYPE	INSTSEX	INSTRACE	COMMACT	COMMDIV
PLAN90	.07	-.13*	.14*	.14*	-.04	.01	.15*	-.09	-.01	-.11
SEX88	.24**	-.10	-.07	.17**	.06	-.10	.18**	-.04	.06	-.02
AGE	-.07	-.05	-.03	.10	-.13*	-.08	-.08	-.06	-.09	-.15*
FATHEDUC	-.19**	.26**	.34**	.14*	.18**	.08	.05	.12	.02	.02
MOTHEDUC	-.04	.19**	.32**	.08	.21**	.03	.05	.12*	.11	.10
INCOME	.11	.20**	.24**	.05	.20**	.08	.05	.00	.15*	.14*
HSGPA	.04	-.15*	-.00	.05	-.01	.11	.11	-.14*	-.05	-.02
PLAN88	-.12*	.11	.23**	.20**	.11	.27**	.16**	.04	.02	-.05
INTELL	.27**	-.09	.00	.18**	-.04	.15*	.10	-.09	-.01	.02
CHOICE1	-.08	-.15	-.16**	-.06	.13*	-.09	-.04	.10	-.07	.07
CHOICE2	—	-.24**	.05	.02	.06	-.02	-.07	.07	-.04	-.06
CHOICE3	.13*	—	.18**	-.13*	.22**	.12*	-.07	.18**	.15*	.13*
DISTHOME	-.00	-.04	—	.12*	.28**	.17**	.08	.35**	.34**	.15*
SOCCHG	.12*	.03	.09	—	-.04	.13*	.13*	.08	.11	.05
INSTCONT	.01	.01	.32**	.17**	—	.08	.14*	.31**	.15*	.06
INSTTYPE	-.02	.04	.27**	-.05	.01	—	.04	.22**	.00	-.03
INSTSEX	.01	.06	.06	.15*	.18**	.06	—	.00	.15*	-.02
INSTRACE	-.02	-.04	-.06	.08	-.06	.02	-.01	—	.24**	.13*
COMMACT	.10	-.02	.03	.24**	.28**	-.05	.12*	.05	—	.68**
COMMDIV	.04	.02	.03	.14*	-.09	.03	.09	.06	.31**	—
BORAMT	-.07	-.05	.16**	.03	.19**	.05	-.02	-.04	.04	.03
SCHOLAMT	.07	.00	-.05	-.04	.09	-.09	.04	.07	-.02	.05
AID11	-.05	.01	.03	-.10	.14*	-.01	.01	-.02	.04	.05
HPW9009	-.04	.05	-.20**	.05	-.12*	-.09	-.05	-.08	.02	.09
FACCON	.09	-.09	.11	.18**	.19**	-.03	.10	-.03	.17**	.04
ACTLY03	.03	.10	.06	.13*	.21**	.09	.04	.05	.16**	-.02
COLACT18	.08	.00	.05	.06	.03	.07	-.03	-.01	.04	.05
COLLGPA	.04	-.08	.05	-.00	.14*	.05	.06	.12*	.10	.03

Coefficients in **bold and in the top half of the diagonal** are for African American students, coefficients in lower half of the table are for White students.
*p≤.05; **p≤.01

Table E2. Correlations of Variables in CIRP Regression Models - continued

	BORAMT	SCHOLAMT	AID11	HPW9009	FACCON	ACTLY03	COLACT18	COLLGPA
PLAN90	.07	-.30**	.12	-.06	.01	.15*	.20**	.34**
SEX88	.02	.01	.15*	.06	-.08	-.13*	.07	.16**
AGE	-.06	.11	-.02	.17**	.14*	-.02	-.10	.00
FATHEDUC	-.08	-.03	-.16*	-.23**	-.03	.11	.02	-.06
MOTHEDUC	-.09	-.12*	-.11	-.25**	-.08	.16**	.12	.03
INCOME	-.08	-.25**	-.13*	-.18**	-.06	.16**	.10	-.08
HSGPA	-.09	.03	.11	.10	.03	.02	.24**	.36**
PLAN88	-.14*	-.06	.00	-.03	-.05	.06	.20**	.20**
INTELL	-.02	.09	.01	.01	.14*	.27**	.14*	.12*
CHOICE1	-.04	-.05	-.06	-.25**	-.02	.06	-.10	-.06
CHOICE2	.03	-.11	.01	.06	.04	-.21**	.01	.08
CHOICE3	-.01	.07	-.15*	-.22**	-.05	.07	.10	-.13*
DISTHOME	-.05	.12	.01	-.17**	-.04	-.02	-.02	.04
SOCCHG	-.10	-.15*	-.01	.17**	-.01	-.06	.02	.06
INSTCONT	.19**	.10	.02	-.21**	-.03	-.01	.05	.04
INSTTYPE	.00	.00	-.09	-.08	-.22**	-.01	.05	-.05
INSTSEX	.03	.03	.06	-.05	-.03	.07	.24**	.14*
INSTRACE	.01	.16*	-.09	-.20**	-.05	-.04	-.37**	-.12*
COMMACT	-.10	.20**	.04	-.10	.09	.19**	.04	-.14*
COMMDIV	-.15*	.16**	.06	-.05	.13*	.22**	.03	-.21**
BORAMT	—	.11	.25**	.07	.17**	.02	.10	.13*
SCHOLAMT	.22**	—	.21**	.07	.04	.09	-.07	-.14*
AID11	.29**	.30**	—	.13*	.10	-.06	.13*	.15*
HPW9009	.13*	.05	.12*	—	-.02	.25**	.02	.09
FACCON	.09	.13*	.05	.03	—	.03	.12	.15*
ACTLY03	.04	.07	.07	-.07	.15*	—	.10	.03
COLACT18	.07	-.08	.03	.01	.08	-.04	—	.18
COLLGPA	-.03	.16**	.07	-.10	.07	.10	.11	—

Coefficients in **bold and in the top half of the diagonal** are for African American students, coefficients in lower half of the table are for White students.
*p≤.05; **p≤.01

Bibliography

Agnew, R. & Jones, D.H. (1988). Adapting to deprivation: An examination of inflated educational expectations. *The Sociological Quarterly*, *29*(2), 315–337.

Alexander, K.L. & Cook, M.A. (1979). The motivational relevance of educational plans: Questioning the conventional wisdom. *Social Psychology Quarterly*, *42*(3), 202–213.

Alexander, K. & Eckland, B.K. (1975). Contextual effects in the high school attainment process. *American Sociological Review*, *40*(June), 402–416.

Allen, W.R. (1991). Introduction. In W.R. Allen, E.G. Epps, and N.Z. Haniff (Eds.) *College in Black and White: African American students in predominantly White and in historically Black public universities* (pp. 1–14). Albany, NY: State University of New York Press.

Allen, W.R. (1992). The color of success: African-American college student outcomes at predominantly White and historically Black public colleges and universities. *Harvard Educational Review*, *62*(1), 26–44.

Allen, W.R. & Haniff, N.Z. (1991). Race, gender, and academic performance in U.S. higher education. In W.R. Allen, E.G. Epps, and N.Z. Haniff (Eds.) *College in Black and White: African American students in predominantly White and in historically Black public universities* (pp. 95–109). Albany, NY: State University of New York Press.

Alwin, D. F. (1974). College effects on educational and occupational attainments. *American Sociological Review*, *39*(April), 210–223.

Anaya, G. (1992). *Cognitive development among college undergraduates.* Unpublished doctoral dissertation, University of California, Los Angeles.

Ancis, J.R. & Sedlacek, W.E. (1997). Predicting the academic achievement of female students using the SAT and noncognitive variables. *College and University*, *72*(3), 2–8.

Anderson, J.D. (1988). *The education of Blacks in the south, 1860–1935.* Chapel Hill, NC: The University of North Carolina Press.

Ashar & Skenes (1993). Can Tinto's student departure model be applied to nontraditional students? *Adult Education Quarterly*, *43*(2), 90–100.

Astin, A.W. (1977). *Four critical years.* San Francisco: Jossey-Bass Publishers.

Astin, A.W. (1990). *The Black undergraduate: Current status and trends in the characteristics of freshmen.* Los Angeles: Higher Education Research Institute.

Astin, A.W. (1993a). *Assessment for excellence.* San Francisco: Jossey-Bass Publishers.

Astin, A.W. (1993b). *What matters in college?: Four critical years revisited.* San Francisco: Jossey-Bass Publishers.

Astin, A.W., Tsui, L., & Avalos, J. (1996). *Degree attainment rates at American colleges and universities: Effects of race, gender, and institutional type.* Los Angeles: Higher Educational Research Institute, University of California.

Baker, T.L. & Vélez, W. (1996). Access to and opportunity in postsecondary education in the United States: A review. *Sociology of Education,* (Extra Issue), 82–101.

Bateman, M. & Hossler, D. (1996). Exploring the development of postsecondary education plans among African American and White students. *College and University,* 72(1), 2–9.

Bean, J.P. & Metzner, B. (1985). A conceptual model of nontraditional undergraduate student attrition. *Review of Educational Research,* 55, 485–540.

Berman, G.S. & Haug, M.R. (1975) Occupational and educational goals and expectations: The effects of race and sex. *Social Problems,* 23, 166–181.

Black graduation rates at liberal arts colleges, state universities, and Black colleges. (1996). *Autumn*(13). *The Journal of Blacks in Higher Education,* p. 69.

Blau, P.M. & Duncan, O.D. (1967). *The American occupational structure.* New York: John Wiley & Sons, Inc.

Bloom, A. (1987). *The closing of the American mind.* New York: Simon & Schuster.

Bohr, L, Pascarella, E.T., Nora, A., & Terenzini, P.T. (1995). Do Black students learn more at historically Black or predominantly White colleges? *Journal of College Student Development,* 36(1), 75–85.

Braddock, II, J.H., Royster, D.A., Winfield, L.F., & Hawkins, R. (1991). Bouncing back: Sports and academic resilience among African-American males. *Education and Urban Society,* 24(1), 113–131.

Braddock, II, J.H., & Trent, W.T. (1991). Correlates of academic performance among Black graduate and professional students. In W.R. Allen, E.G. Epps, and N.Z. Haniff (Eds.) *College in Black and White: African American students in predominantly White and in historically Black public universities* (pp. 161–175). Albany, NY: State University of New York Press.

Breneman, D.W. (1995, September 8). Public colleges face sweeping, painful changes. *The Chronicle of Higher Education,* p. B1.

Brint, S. & Karabel, J. (1989). *The diverted dream: Community colleges and the promise of educational opportunity in America, 1900–1985.* New York: Oxford University Press.

Burke, P.J. & Hoelter, J.W. (1988). Identity and sex-race differences in educational and occupational aspirations formation. *Social Science Research,* 17, 29–47.

Cabrera, A.F., Nora, A., and Castañeda, M.B. (1992). The role of finances in the persistence process: A structural model. *Research in Higher Education,* 33(5), 571–593.

Cabrera, A.F., Stampen, J.O. & Hansen, W.L. (1990). Exploring the effects of ability to pay on persistence in college. *The Review of Higher Education, 13*(3), 303–336.

Campbell, R.T. (1983). Status attainment research: End of the beginning or beginning of the end? *Sociology of Education, 56*(January), 47–62.

Carnoy, M. & Rothstein, R. (1997). Are Black diplomas worth less? *The American Prospect*, (30), 42–45.

Carter, D.J. & Wilson, R.T. (1993). *Minorities in higher education: 11th annual status report*. Washington, D.C.: American Council on Education.

Clark, B. (1960). The "cooling out" function in higher education. *American Journal of Sociology, 65*, 569–576.

Constantine, J.M. (1995). The effect of attending historically Black colleges and universities on future wages of Black students. *Industrial and Labor Relations Review, 48*(3), 531–546.

Cranston, P. & Leonard, M.M. (1990). The relationship between undergraduatesÕ experiences of campus micro-inequities and their self-esteem and aspirations. *Journal of College Student Development, 31*(September), 395–401.

Darden, J.T., Bagaka's, J.G., & Kamel, S.M. (1996). Historically Black institutions and desegregation: The dilemma revisited. *Equity & Excellence in Education, 29*(2), 56–68.

Davis, J.E. (1995). College in Black and White: Campus environment and academic achievement of African American males. *Journal of Negro Education, 63*(4), 620–633.

Dawkins, M.P. (1982). Occupational prestige expectations among Black and White college students: A multivariate analysis. *College Student Journal, 16*(3), 233–242.

Dawkins, M.P. & Braddock, II, J.H. (1982). Explaining outcomes for Black students in higher education using national longitudinal data. *The Negro Educational Review, 33*(3–4), 146–160.

Deskins, Jr., D.R. (1994). Prospects for minority doctorates in the year 2000: Employment opportunities in a changing American society. In M. Holden, Jr. (Ed.) *The challenge to racial stratification: National political science review (volume 4)* (pp. 98–148). News Brunswick: Transaction Publishers.

Dey, E.L. (1991). *Perceptions of the college environment: An analysis of organizational, interpersonal, and behavioral influences*. Unpublished doctoral dissertation. University of California, Los Angeles.

Dey, E.L. (1997). Working with low survey response rates: The efficacy of weighting adjustments. *Research in Higher Education, 38*(2), 215–227.

Dey, E.L., Astin, A.W., & Korn, W.S. 1991. *The American freshman: Twenty-five year trends*. Los Angeles: Higher Educational Research Institute, University of California.

Dougherty, K. (1987). The effects of community colleges: Aid or hindrance to socioeconomic attainment? *Sociology of Education, 60*(April), 86–103.

Drew, D.E. & Astin, A.W. (1972). Undergraduate aspirations: A test of several theories. *American Journal of Sociology, 77*(6), 1151–1164.

Eckland, B.K. (1964). Social class and college graduation: Some misconceptions corrected. *American Journal of Sociology, 70*, 60–72.

Epps, E.G. and Jackson, K.W. (1985). *Educational and occupational aspirations and early attainment of Black males and females.* Atlanta, Georgia: Southern Education Foundation.

Feagin, J.R. & Sikes, M.P. (1995). How Black students cope with racism on White campuses. *Journal of Blacks in Higher Education, 8*, 91–97.

Feagin, J.R., Vera, H, and Imani, N. (1996). *The agony of education: Black students at White colleges and universities.* New York: Routledge.

Feldman, K. & Newcomb, T. (1969). *The impact of college on students.* San Francisco: Jossey-Bass.

Fleming, J. (1984). *Blacks in college.* San Francisco: Jossey-Bass.

Foley, D.E. (1991). Reconsidering anthropological explanations of ethnic school failure. *Anthropology & Education Quarterly*, 22, 60–86.

Fordham, S. (1996). *Blacked out: Dilemmas of race, identity, and success at Capital High.* Chicago: The University of Chicago Press.

Fordham, S. & Ogbu, J.U. (1986). Black students' school success: Coping with the "burden of 'acting White'". *The Urban Review, 18*(3), 176–206.

Friesen, D. (1983). Changing plans and aspirations of high school students. *The Alberta Journal of Educational Research, 29*(4), 285–296.

Gardner, H. (1995). Cracking open the IQ box. In S. Fraser (Ed.) *The bell curve wars: Race intelligence, and the future of America.* New York: Basic Books.

Giroux, H.A. (1983). Theories of reproduction and resistance in the new sociology of education: A critical analysis. *Harvard Education Review, 53*(3), 257–293.

Grubb, W.N. & Wilson, R.H. (1989). Sources of increasing inequality in wages and salaries, 1960–80. *Monthly Labor Review, 112*(4), 3–13.

Hanson, S.L. (1994). Lost talent: Unrealized educational aspirations and expectations among U.S. youths. *Sociology of Education, 67*(July), 159–183.

Hauser, R.M. & Anderson, D.K. (1991). Post-high school plans and aspirations of Black and White high school seniors: 1976–86. *Sociology of Education, 64*(October), 263–277 .

Hearn, J.C. & Longanecker, D.L. (1985). Enrollment effects of alternative post-secondary pricing policies. *Journal of Higher Education, 56*(5), 485–508.

Hearn, J.C. (1984). The relative roles of academic, ascribed, and socioeconomic characteristics in college destinations. *Sociology of Education, 57*(January), 22–30.

Hearn, J.C. (1987). Impacts of undergraduate experiences on aspirations and plans for graduate and professional education. *Research in higher education, 27*(2), 119–141.

Hearn, J.C. (1991). Academic and nonacademic influences on the college destinations of 1980 high school graduates. *Sociology of Education, 64*(July), 158–171

Hearn, J.C. (1992). Emerging variations in postsecondary attendance patterns: An investigation of part-time, delayed, and nondegree enrollment. *Research in Higher Education, 33*, 657–687.

Hoffman, M. S. (1991). *The world almanac and book of facts.* New York, NY: Pharaos Books.

Hossler, D. (1984). *Enrollment management.* New York: College Entrance Examination Board.

Hossler, D., Braxton, J., & Coopersmith, G. (1989). Understanding student college choice. In Smart, J.C. (Ed.). *Higher Education: Handbook of Theory and Research (volume 5)*. New York: Agathon Press.

Hossler, D. & Gallagher, K.S. (1987). Studying student college choice: A three-phase model and the implications for policymakers. *College and University*, *62*(3), 207–221.

Hughes, L. (1932). *The dream keeper and other poems*. New York: Knopf.

Hughes, L. (1958). *Langston Hughes reader*. New York: Braziller.

Hurtado, S. (1990). *Campus racial climates and educational outcomes*. Unpublished doctoral dissertation, University of California, Los Angeles.

Hurtado, S., Carter, D.F. & Sharp, S. (1995). *Social interaction on campus: Differences among self-perceived ability groups*. Paper presented at the meeting of the Association for Institutional Research, Boston, MA.

Hurtado, S., Kurotsuchi, K., & Sharp, S. (1996). *College entry by age groups: Paths of traditional, delayed-entry, and nontraditional students*. Paper presented at the meeting of American Educational Research Association, New York, NY.

Hurtado, S., Inkelas, K.K., Briggs, C., & Rhee, B. (1997). Differences in college access and choice among racial/ethnic groups: Identifying continuing barriers. *Research in Higher Education*, *38*(1), 43–75.

Hurtado, S., Milem, J.F., Clayton-Pedersen, A.R., & Allen, W.R. (1999). *Improving the climate for racial/ethnic diversity in higher education institutions*. ASHE-ERIC Higher Education Report. Washington, D.C.: Association for the Study of Higher Education.

Hurtado, S. & Navia, C. (1997). Reconciling college access and the affirmative action debate. In M. Garcia (Ed.) *Affirmative Action's Testament of Hope: Strategies for a New Era*. Albany, NY: SUNY Press (In Press).

Institute for the Study of Social Change. (1991). *The diversity project: Final report*. Berkeley: University of California.

Isaac, P.D., Malaney, G.D., & Karras, J.E. (1992). Parental educational level, gender differences, and seniors' aspirations for advanced study. *Research in Higher Education*, *33*(5), 595–606.

Jackson, K.W. & Swan, L.A. (1991). Institutional and individual factors affecting Black undergraduate student performance: Campus race and student gender. In W.R. Allen, E.G. Epps, and N.Z. Haniff (Eds.) *College in Black and White: African American students in predominantly White and in historically Black public universities* (pp. 127–141). Albany, NY: State University of New York Press.

Kamens, D.H. (1979). Student status aspirations: A research note on the effects of college. *Youth & Society*, *11*(1). 83–91.

Kao, G. & Tienda, M. (1998). Educational aspirations of minority youth. *American Journal of Education*, *106*(5), 349–384.

Karabel, J. & Astin, A.W. (1975). Social class, academic quality, and college ÒqualityÓ. *Social Forces*, *53*(3), 381–398.

Kempner, K. & Kinnick, M. (1990). Catching the window of opportunity: Being on time for higher education. *Journal of Higher Education*, *61*(5), 535–547.

Kerckhoff, A.C. (1976). The status attainment process: Socialization or allocation? *Social Forces*, *55*(2), 368–381.

Kerckhoff, A.C. (1984). The current state of social mobility research. *The Sociological Quarterly*, *25*(Spring), 139–153.

Kerckhoff, A.C. & Campbell, R.T. (1977). Race and social status differences in the explanation of educational ambition. *Social Forces*, *55*(3), 701–714.

Knight, W.H. & Wing, A. (1995). Weep not, little ones: An essay to our children about affirmative action. In J.H. Franklin & G. R. McNeil (Eds.) *African Americans and the living Constitution*. Washington: Smithsonian Institution Press.

Knotterus, J.D. (1987). Status attainment research and its image of society. *American Sociological Review*, *52*(February), 113–121.

Komaromy, M., Grumbach, K., Drake, M., Vranizan, K, Lurie, N, Keane, D., & Bindman, A.B. (1996, May 16). The role of Black and Hispanic physicians in providing health care for underserved populations. *New England Journal of Medicine*, *334*(20), 1305–1310.

Labovitz, E.M. (1975). Race, SES, contexts and fulfillment of college aspirations. *The Sociological Quarterly*, *16*, 241–249.

Lee, V. E., Mackie-Lewis, C., & Marks, H.M. (1993). Persistence to the baccalaureate degree for students who transfer from community college. *American Journal of Education*, *102*(November), 80–114.

Levine, A. & Nidiffer, J. (1996). *Beating the odds: How the poor get to college*. San Francisco: Jossey-Bass.

Loo, C.M & Rolison, G. (1986). Alienation of ethnic minority students at a predominantly White university. *Journal of Higher Education*, *57*(1), 58–77.

Marini, M.M. (1984). The order of events in the transition to adulthood. *Sociology of Education*, *57*(April), 63–84.

Maxey, J., Lee, J.S., & McLure, G.T. (1995). Are Black students less likely to enroll at their first-choice college? *Journal of Blacks in Higher Education*, 7, 100–101.

McClelland, K. (1990). Cumulative disadvantage among the highly ambitious. *Sociology of Education*, *63*(April), 102–121.

McDonough, P.M. 1997. *Choosing colleges: How social class and schools structure opportunity*. Albany, NY: State University of New York Press.

McJamerson, E.M. (1992). Undergraduate academic major & minority student persistence: Individual choices, national consequences. *Equity and Excellence*, 25(2–4), 35–48.

Morrow, R.A., & Torres, C.A. (1995). *Social theory and education: A critique of theories of social and cultural reproducation*. Albany, NY: State University of New York Press.

Mow, S.L. & Nettles, M.T. (1990). Minority student access to, and persistence and performance in, college: A review of the trends and research literature. *Higher Education: Handbook of Theory and Research*, 7, 35–105.

National Center for Education Statistics. (1994). *Beginning Postsecondary Students Longitudinal Study First Follow-up (BPS:90/92) Final Public Technical Report*. Washington, DC: National Center for Education Statistics.

Nettles, M.T., Thoeny, A.R., & Gosman, E.J. (1986). Comparative and predictive analyses of Black and White students' college achievement and experiences. *Journal of Higher Education*, 57(3), 289–317.

Ogbu, J.U. (1988). Class stratification, racial stratification, and school. In L. Weis (Ed.), *Class, race, and gender in American education*. Albany, NY: State University of New York Press.

Ogbu, J.U. (1990). Literacy and schooling in subordinate cultures: The case of Black Americans. In K. Lomotey (Ed.) *Going to school: The African-American experience* (pp.113–131). Albany, NY: State University of New York Press.

Ogbu, J.U. (1983). Minority status and schooling in plural societies. *Comparative Education Review*, *27*(2), 168–190.

Otto, L.B. (1976). Social integration and the status attainment process. *American Journal of Sociology*. *81*(6), 1360–1383.

Overall graduate rates of African-American college students are on the rise. (1996) *Autumn*(13). *The Journal of Blacks in Higher Education*, p. 68.

Pantages, T., & Creedon, C. (1978). Studies of college attrition: 1950–1975. *Review of Educational Research*, *48*, 49–101.

Pascarella, E.T. (1984). College environmental influences on studentsÕ educational aspirations. *Journal of Higher Education*, *55*(6), 751–771.

Pascarella, E.T. (1985). Students' affective development within the college environment. *Journal of Higher Education*, *56*(6), 640–663.

Pascarella, E.T., Duby, P.B., and Iverson, B.K. (1983). A test and reconceptualization of a theoretical model of college withdrawal in a commuter institution setting. *Sociology of Education*, *56*(April), 88–100.

Pascarella, E.T., Smart, J.C., & Smylie, M.A. (1992). College tuition costs and early career socioeconomic achievement: Do you get what you pay for? *Higher Education*, *24*(3), 275–291.

Pascarella, E.T. & Terenzini, P.T. (1991). *How college affects students*. San Francisco: Jossey-Bass.

Paulsen, M.B. (1990). *College choice: Understanding student enrollment behavior*. ASHE-ERIC Higher Education Report No. 6. Washington, D.C.: The George Washington University, School of Education and Human Development.

Pedhazur, E.J. (1997). *Multiple regression in behavioral research*. (3rd ed.). Orlando, FL: Harcourt, Brace & Company.

Peeks, E. (1971). *The long struggle for Black power*. New York: Charles Scribner's Sons.

Peng, S.S. & Fetters, W.B. (1978). Variables involved in withdrawal during the first two years of college: Preliminary findings from the National Longitudinal Study of the high school class of 1972. *American Educational Research Journal*, *15*(3), pp. 361–372.

Phillips, C.P. & Asbury, C.A. (1993). Parental divorce/separation and the motivational characteristics and educational aspirations of African American university students. *Journal of Negro Education*, *62*(2), 204–210.

Porter, J.N. (1974) Race, socialization and mobility in educational and early occupational attainment. *American Sociological Review*, *39*(June), 303–16.

Portes, A. & Wilson, K.L. (1976). Black-White differences in educational attainment. *American Sociological Review*, *41*(June), 414–431.

Quilter, S.M. (1995). Academic self-concept and the first-year college student: A snapshot. *Journal of the Freshman Year Experience*, *7*(1), 39–52.

Riehl, R.J. (1994). The academic preparation, aspirations, and first-year performance of first-generation students. *College and University*, *70*(1), 14–19.

Rippa, S.A. (1997). *Education in a free society: An American history*. (8th ed.). New York: Longman.

Schmidt, J.A. & Hunt, P.F. (1994). Relationship between precollege attributes and subsequent development in college students. *Journal of College Student Development*, *35*(November), 481–485.

Seneca, J.J. & Taussig, M.K. (1987). The effects of tuition and financial aid on the enrollment decision at a state university. *Research in Higher Education*, *26*(4), 337–362.

Sewell, W.H., Haller, A.O., & Ohlendorf, G.W. (1970). The educational and early occupational status attainment process: Replication and revision. *American Sociological Review*, *35*, 1014–1027.

Sewell, W.H., Haller, A.O., & Portes, A. (1969). The educational and early occupational attainment process. *American Sociological Review*, *34*(February), 82–92.

Sewell, W.H. & Hauser, R.M. (1980). The Wisconsin longitudinal study of social and psychological factors in aspirations and achievements. *Research in Sociology of Education and Socialization*, *1*, 59–99.

Sewell, W.H. & Shah, V.P. (1967). Socioeconomic status, intelligence, and the attainment of higher education. *Sociology of education*, *40*(1), 1–23.

Shepard, J. (1991). *1990 National Postsecondary Student Aid Study: Methodology Report (Technical Report)*. Washington, DC: National Center for Education Statistics.

Shuit, D. P. (1996, May 16). Study Warns of Less Health Care for Minorities. *Los Angeles Times*, p. A3.

Smedley, B.D., Myers, H.F., & Harrell, S.P. (1993). Minority-status stresses and the college adjustment of ethnic minority freshmen. *Journal of Higher Education*, *64*(4), 434–452.

Smith, A.W. (1988). In double jeopardy: Collegiate academic outcomes of Black females vs. Black males. *National Journal of Sociology*, *2*, 3–33.

Smith, D. G. (1989). *The challenge of diversity: Involvement or alienation in the academy?*. ASHE-ERIC Higher Education Report No. 5. Washington, D. C.: Association for the Study of Higher Education, 1989.

Smith, D.G. (1990). Women's colleges and coed colleges: Is there a difference for women? *Journal of Higher Education*, *61*(2), 181–195.

Solorzano, D.G. (1992). An exploratory analysis of the effects of race, class, and gender on student and parent mobility aspirations. *Journal of Negro Education*, *61*(1), 30–43.

Somers, P.A. & St. John, E.P. (1993). Assessing the impact of financial aid offers on enrollment decisions. *Journal of Student Financial Aid*, *23*(3), 7–12.

Spady, W.G. (1970). Lament for the letterman: Effects of peer status and extracurricular activities on goals and achievement. *American Journal of Sociology*, *75*(January), 680–702.

St. John, E.P. (1991). What really influences minority attendance?: Sequential analyses of the High School and Beyond sophomore cohort. *Reseach in Higher Education*, *32*(2), 141–158.

St. John, E.P. & Noell, J. (1989). The effects of student financial aid on access to higher education: An analysis of progress with special consideration of minority enrollment. *Research in Higher Education*, *30*(6), 563–581.

St. John, E.P, Oescher, J. & Andrieu, S. (1992). The influence of prices on within-year persistence by traditional college-age students in four-year colleges. *Journal of Student Financial Aid*. *22*(1), 27–38.

Stage, F. K. & Hossler, D. (1989). Differences in family influences on college attendance plans for male and female ninth graders. *Research in Higher Education*, *30*(3), 301–315.

Stage, F.K. & Rushin, P.W. (1993). A combined model of student predisposition to college and persistence in college. *Journal of College Student Personnel*, *34*, 276–281.

Thomas, G.E. (1991). In W.R. Allen, E.G. Epps, and N.Z. Haniff (Eds.) *College in Black and White: African American students in predominantly White and in historically Black public universities* (pp. 61–74). Albany, NY: State University of New York Press.

Thomas, G.E., Alexander, K.L. & Eckland, B.K. (1979). Access to higher education: The importance of race, sex, social class, and academic credentials. *School Review*, *87*(2), 133–156.

Trent, W.T. (1991). Focus on equity: race and gender differences in degree attainment, 1975–76; 1980–81. In W.R. Allen, E.G. Epps, and N.Z. Haniff (Eds.) *College in Black and White: African American students in predominantly White and in historically Black public universities* (pp. 41–59). Albany, NY: State University of New York Press.

Turner, R.H. (1960). Sponsored and contest mobility and the school system. *American Sociological Review*, *25*, 855–867.

U.S. Department of Education. (1996). *The condition of education 1996* (NCES 96–304). Washington, D.C.: U.S. Government Printing Office.

Vélez, W. (1985). Finishing college: The effects of college type. *Sociology of Education*, *58*(July), 191–200.

Vital signs: Statistics that measure the state of racial inequality. (1996) *Autumn*(13). *The Journal of Blacks in Higher Education*, p. 67.

Washington, M. (1996). The minority student in college: A historical analysis. In C. Turner, M. Garcia, A. Nora, and L.I. Rend—n (Eds.), *Racial and ethnic diversity in higher education* (pp. 69–83). Needham Heights, MA: Simon & Schuster Custom Publishing.

Weidman, J.C. (1989). Undergraduate socialization: A conceptual approach. In J.Smart (Ed.), *Higher education: Handbook of theory and research* (vol. 5). New York: Agathon.

Weiler, W.C. (1993). Post-baccalaureate educational choices of minority students. *The Review of Higher Education*, *16*(4), 439–460.

Wilson-Sadberry, K.R., Winfield, L.F., & Royster, D.A. (1991). Resilience and persistence of African-American males in postsecondary enrollment. *Education and Urban Society*, *24*(1), 87–102.

Wright, R. (1941). 12 million Black voices: A folk history of the Negro in the United States. New York: Viking.

Author Index

Subject Index